BUFFALO SHOUT, SALMON CRY

"There is no cheap grace available in these pages, but there is great encouragement to move ourselves toward the deepest, most demanding places of hope in our mutual search for a truly just and compassionate life together with all creation. Every participant in these "conversations" urges us to take all the great, imperative risks of spiritual and intellectual growth, insisting on our deepest truths as our guide."
—**Vincent Harding,** veteran activist and scholar, Illif School of Theology

"*Buffalo Shout, Salmon Cry* offers precisely the sort of dialogue essential to the establishment at long last of respectful relations between peoples in this hemisphere. Such conversations are necessary to forging a sustainable relationship between humans and the rest of creation. Steve Heinrichs is to be commended for having assembled this book."
—**Ward Churchill**, author of *Struggle for the Land*

"Mind blowing. Once you read the book, you will never look at the world, or your place within it, the same way again. The voices within these covers offer sobering and challenging truths. I am uncomfortably humbled."
—**Christine J. Sabas**, attorney and advocate with Christian Peacemaker Teams

NOTE ON THE COVER ART:

It wasn't long ago that millions of buffalo wandered the prairies in large herds. For thousands of years, our ancestors lived off these resources, receiving food, clothing, medicines, and shelter. In respect, they took only what they needed to care for their families, and gave prayerful thanks to the buffalo for giving up their lives. Tragically, over a short period of time, this great nation of animals was hunted almost to extinction by foreign governments and big business. Today the buffalo only exist in small, protected herds, in parks or on farms.

Today the salmon of the West Coast are in danger of being killed off by foreign fish farms, corporations, and governments focused on jobs in the present and profits for the immediate future. Will the salmon nation go the way of the buffalo? Or will we learn a better way of relating to our natural relations? Can we live in respect with the rest of creation? Can we steward the earth, but even more importantly, let the earth, and the One who made it, steward us?

My artwork depicts a resurgent buffalo carrying within her the life and bones of the salmon. In a spirit of solidarity, they resist extinction and erasure.

—Jonathan Erickson (Nak'azdli, Carrier-Sekani)

BUFFALO SHOUT, SALMÓN CRY

CONVERSATIONS ON CREATION, LAND JUSTICE, AND LIFE TOGETHER

EDITED BY STEVE HEINRICHS

HERALD PRESS
P R E S S

Harrisonburg, Virginia

Herald Press
PO Box 866, Harrisonburg, Virginia 22803
www.HeraldPress.com

Library and Archives Canada Cataloguing in Publication
Buffalo shout, salmon cry : conversations on creation, land
justice, and life together / edited by Steve Heinrichs.

Includes bibliographical references and index.
ISBN 978-0-8361-9689-4

    1. Indians of North America—Religion. 2. Indians of North
America—Colonization. 3. Indians of North America—Social
conditions. 4. Indian cosmology. 5. Liberation theology.
6. Christianity and culture. 7. Christianity and other religions.
I. Heinrichs, Steve, 1976–

E98.R3B83 2013   299.7   C2013-901608-2

BUFFALO SHOUT, SALMON CRY
Copyright © 2013 by Herald Press, Kitchener, Ont. N2G 3R1
    Published simultaneously in the United States of America by Herald
    Press, Harrisonburg, Va. 22802. 800-245-7894.
All rights reserved.
Library of Congress Control Number: 2013934430
Canadian Entry Number: C2013-901608-2
International Standard Book Number: 978-0-8361-9689-4
Printed in the United States of America
Interior and cover design by Merrill Miller
Cover drawing by Jonathan Erickson (Nak'azdli, Carrier-Sekani)

20 19 18   11 10 9 8 7 6

for indigenous cousins
    fractured by church
    yet keeping on like few others
        living icons of enemy love
        re-membering a trickster more than crucified

for the church
    segregated from host
    a body struggling to guest its way,
        naming red skins there, forgetting white camouflage here
        we offer hope, and calculate too

    behold that body, broken, blessed, bloodied
        there it is
        more than hope, healing too
        touch, see, and go

for other creaturely cousins
    all around but more distant than plastic
        dying and knocked off
        forced out of womb by an idolatrous lust
            back to the soil of a menstrual mother

    what can we give?
        not much
    but here's a fool's gift for you
        and with any luck, some animalized lives

    —SH

CONTENTS

Part 2—Unsettling Theology

Part 3—Voices of Challenge and Protest

Acknowledgements

I'm deeply grateful to Mennonite Church Canada for making this book possible. It isn't an easy text; it is full of challenges, as well as a number of "unsettling" voices (some of which rub against our cherished faith traditions). Many denominations wouldn't have risked it. But because of your desire to pursue authentic relationships between settler and Indigenous peoples, you've courageously stuck your neck out, privileging the ones who should be privileged in these matters. I am so thankful, and proud. This is a significant step for us as we seek a better way, something like that "cousin" bond envisioned by treaty elders long ago.

The same goes for Herald Press. I celebrate your willingness to take on this project, for believing in it, and for patiently working with an editor who has lots of passion, but precious little experience.

To those who offered up their editorial hands and insights, I lift my hands to you. To Ched Myers of Bartimaeus Cooperative Ministries, for your encouragement and support, your honest, critical feedback, and your deft work on a number of these chapters. To Brander "Standing Bear" McDonald (Mennonite Church British Columbia Indigenous Relations), for your insights and questions that kept me accountable, for your overall "indigenuity," not to mention twisted humor. To Elsie Rempel (Mennonite Church Canada Christian Formation), for your thoughtful reading of the text and instructive suggestions. To Dad, for being a wise sounding board, for your prayers, and for your sensitive feedback. To Byron Rempel-Burkholder of MennoMedia, for massaging the manuscript and ushering the work to its completion. And to the small circle that originally gathered to pray and ponder the possibilities of this project. Thank you, Edith and Neill von Gunten, Norman Meade, and Kyle Penner.

To all the authors who gave energy and emotion and intellect to create this conversation, my sincere appreciation. For those within the church, thanks for helping address matters that don't get the attention they justly deserve. For those outside the church, I admire your courage to enter the fray. It's not easy putting one's mind and heart into the lion's den. Thank you so much! We need you. Keep on engaging us.

To those who shared their pocketbooks to help make this happen—especially Henry Neufeld, Egon and Erna Enns, and my parents, Betty and John Heinrichs—thank you! And of course, my sincere gratitude to the broader Mennonite church; without your ongoing support of the Indigenous Relations program, this wouldn't have been possible. I am blessed to be a part of this peculiar people.

Finally, thanks to my life partner, Ann, and our three wonderful kids—Abby, Aiden, and Isabelle. Putting this text together was hard. The contents weighed heavily on me, and on you, too. Thanks for loving me, hugging me, and putting up with me while I struggled through this, with joy, tears, and some grumpiness. In many ways, this text is the fruit and hope of our family: learning what it means to live out our hybrid—Stó:lō, Nuu-chah-nulth, white Baptist, and Mennonite—identities. I hope it will make you proud one day. With love,

—*Steve Heinrichs*
Director, Indigenous Relations
Mennonite Church Canada

Introduction

AN INDIGENOUS INTRUSION TROUBLES THE HOUSE:
A CALL TO DECOLONIZATION

By Steve Heinrichs

Rather than debating the dichotomy of victim/oppressor,
we have focused on cultivating an ethic of responsibility
based on understanding ourselves as beneficiaries—intended
or not—of an illegal appropriation of Indigenous Peoples'
resources and jurisdiction. . . . Whether we define ourselves
as migrants or settlers, it is undeniable that we are on lands
unjustly seized and are complicit in a culture that sees
"Indians" rather than settlement as the problem.

—*Harsha Walia*[1]

It's eleven o'clock on a Sunday morning in Winnipeg, and I'm
sitting in church. We're in the midst of a chorus when, out of
nowhere, three figures come busting through the back—a Cree
woman, an enormous buffalo, and Salmon boy[2]—bursting heavy

---

1. "Moving Beyond a Politics of Solidarity toward a Practice of Decolonization,"
in *Organize!: Building from the Local for Global Justice*, eds. Aziz Choudry, Jill
Hanley, and Eric Shragge (Oakland: PM Press, 2012), 246–47.
2. Salmon boy is a common teaching figure in many Indigenous traditions on
the West Coast. A young boy who disrespects the salmon people is saved from
drowning by that very people. The salmon welcome the boy into their community and teach him respect for the more-than-human creation. The boy, who
has "taken on the flesh" of a salmon to learn obedience to these lessons, eventually returns to his former community and blesses them as a powerful shaman.

13

upon our sea of whiteness. Snorting steamy breath, the buffalo runs straight for the front, slams into the pulpit, and cracks it in half. The boy throws himself into the pews and onto a few unsuspecting faithful; he's wailing, "Beothuk! Eskimo Curlew! Sixties scoop!" while holding in clutched hands two bottles—poisoned waters in one, blood of martyred relatives in the other.

And then the woman speaks, standing on a chair. She's no more than thirty, wearing a "1492 Homeland Security" T-shirt and a skirt with traditional beads. A manifesto buried too long in her heart, words nervously erupt, splitting the sky:

"Listen *kiciwamanawak*, my cousins![3] We can't bear it any longer!"

Brown eyes swoop the crowd of blue and green stares to see if anyone's there.

"Don't you feel the catastrophe that's coming, that's here, that's been for far too long? Shattered peoples all around; shattered lands right below. *Manitou Ahbee*, this place where Spirit sits, is weeping a death cry because of this civilization's culture-fracking ways. She won't tolerate it any longer, and neither will her allies. The time's come; it's long past! Resist the colonial ways, rip up the concrete and remember the Indigenous truths—yeah, even yours!—or in seven generations of weeks, it'll all be gone!"

Longing for a response, the young Cree hears nothing but Buffalo's weighty breathing. The congregation is shocked silent. Shocked not because we're dumbfounded by this Balaam-beast-revelation. Shocked because these strangers have stormed our space—but we're the good guys, the justice oriented—and called us to what? Repentance? Shouldn't this act be happening elsewhere?

Within seconds an ambulance is on the scene with a cadre of attendants, psychiatric workers, and tranquilizers—cops, too, for good measure. The boy tries to make a dash—"Let's get out of here!"—but is tasered after a few feet. In minutes, all three guests are subdued and dragged away.

---

3. I am indebted to Harold Johnson (Cree) for the use of *kiciwamanawak*, a term of relational respect that the treaty elders used for white settlers who entered into (or inherited) those sacred covenants. See *Two Families: Treaties and Government* (Saskatoon: Purich Publishing, 2011), 13–14.

Then something unthinkable takes place. One by one, beginning with the children, then the elderly, and eventually us middle-agers, we drop to our knees.

Start praying.

Form a circle.

And cry.

A minimal discussion ensues, and with full agreement a delegation is sent to the city jail to seek the release of the three, to post bail, and to ask these messengers to come back, to teach us, even to lead us. They're right. Something is wrong. Our hands, yes, even our pink palms, are stained with violence. And we've got to do something about it.

The urgency, the call

It's an improbable, disturbing story. But it's nothing new. It's merely a riff on a subversive parable found in the sacred Scriptures, a tale of a frustrated Israelite prophet making a trek some 2,700 years ago to Nineveh, capital of Assyria. Jonah lobbed a message of radical reorientation into the midst of a brutal imperial system and a million hardened hearts. And miraculously, the whole city—animals included—forms a circle, chants Amen, and does life differently.

The usual reading of that parable asserts that the prophet was a missionary sent to save unenlightened pagans—"Straighten up! Believe in the only God, or it's over!" Translated into our current context, we envision white missionaries running off to Afghanistan, to China, or to every Native reserve in America to convert peoples who just don't know the truth. But as Miguel De La Torre has pointed out, that totally misses the point.[4] Nineveh was the center of a colonial superpower, and Jonah came from the oppressed margins. Nineveh is Bay Street, Wall Street, and yes, even the white—not seemingly powerful—churches of Winnipeg, Seattle, and rural America. Jonah is not a white Mennonite settler like me, but stands among and with the colonized. He's a word-swinging Lakota warrior (think Vine Deloria Jr.), a Stó:lō poet of colonial deconstruction (think Lee Maracle), a shouting buffalo,

---

4. Miguel A. De La Torre, *Liberating Jonah: Forming an Ethics of Reconciliation* (New York: Orbis, 2007).

a weeping salmon, coming out from the shadows of the rez and urban occupied territories to confront the privileged powerful. This Jonah speaks unsettling truths, not to save the empire, but to stop its rapacious ways in defense of all relations, including us settlers.

This is what the book in your hands is about. It's a Jonah text, perhaps as scandalous, implausible, and necessary as that old anti-imperial myth. A bunch of Jonahs and several settler-ally friends have come together to speak a word to, against, and for the dominant settler-colonial[5] culture in North America. Some employ sharp rhetoric akin to that of the disgruntled prophet; others speak in more hopeful terms. They certainly don't agree on everything. But they all do sound (with maybe one or two exceptions) a common warning: the controlling culture is violently sick, devastating peoples and lands. The need is urgent: repent, resist, do something.

I know. It sounds alarmist. But contemplate a few of the ways in which settler civilization is wreaking havoc on Indigenous life-forms and the planet at large and maybe you'll deem the apocalyptic language appropriate:

- If we were to weigh all the fish in today's oceans and compare it to what there was in 1850, we'd discover that less than 10 percent are left.[6]

- The current rate of species extinction is an astonishing 100 to 1,000 times greater than the average extinction rates during the evolutionary time scale of the earth. This means that our culture will destroy one-third to one-half

---

5. Richard Horvath defines settler colonialism as consisting of the following: "1. Domination over territories and behaviors of other groups by the migration of permanent settlers; 2. Exploitation of the dominated territory's natural and/ or human resources for extraction and profit; 3. An enforced culture-change process involving destruction of indigenous life-ways." As quoted in Raymond Evans, "Crime Without a Name: Colonialism and the Case for 'Indigenocide,'" in *Empire, Colony, Genocide: Conquest, Occupation, and Subaltern Resistance*, ed. A. Dirk Moses (Oxford: Berghahn Books, 2010), 142.
6. Charlie Kohlhase, "*Stand Up and Scream: Earth at Risk*," YouTube, 9:29, posted by Desiree Rose, 9 November 2010, http://www.youtube.com/watch?v=h52yCZoknRY (accessed 5 November 2012).

of the planet's species in the next generation. It is "the slaughter of the innocents."[7]

- Climate scientists agree that we cannot up global temperature by more than two degrees, or we are cooked (we've already upped it by a degree). We cannot add 565 more gigatons of CO_2 or we will exceed two degrees, and the reality is that there are 2,795 gigatons of carbon contained in the fossil-fuel reserves that the big corporations are invested in and plan to burn. If global emissions continue to go up by 3 percent each year—the current rate—we have only sixteen years before we exceed that 565 and muck the planet.[8]

- In 2003 the U.S. Environmental Protection Agency reported that there were 602 hazardous waste sites on or impacting Indigenous communities, and fifty-five of those sites were deemed "seriously contaminated" and placed on the National Priorities List for long-term remedial action.[9]

- In 2011 the United Nations Human Development Index —measuring health, knowledge, and standard of living— ranked Canadian settler society sixth out of 177 nations. Indigenous peoples in the same country were ranked some fifty-seven places lower.[10]

- Globally, there are between six and seven thousand languages, and by the end of this century 50 to 90 percent

7. Thomas Berry, *The Dream of the Earth* (San Francisco: Sierra Club Books, 1990), 204.

8. Bill McKibben, "Global Warming's Terrifying New Math," *Rolling Stone*, 19 July 2012, http://www.rollingstone.com/politics/news/global-warmings-terrifying-new-math-20120719 (accessed 1 August 2012).

9. Joy Porter, *Land and Spirit in Native America* (Santa Barbara: ABC-CLIO, 2012), 95.

10. Gale Courey Toensing, "U.N.: Canada Continues Discrimination Against Indigenous Peoples," *Indian Country Today*, 14 March 2012, in http://indiancountrytodaymedianetwork.com/article/u.n.%3A-canada-continues-discrimination-against-indigenous-peoples-102906 (accessed 10 November 2012).

will be gone.[11] Half of those languages are located in just
2.3 percent of the Earth's surface, areas that are home
to a majority of the world's vascular plants and over 40
percent of terrestrial vertebrate species. Many Western
scientists now believe what Indigenous peoples have been
saying for years—that it's not only diverse ecosystems
that nurture diverse human cultures and languages, but
also the converse.[12]

There's a real emergency in our world on a scale that humanity
has never seen before. It's bigger than the biggest of wars. The planet
is in the process of being killed (geo-cide), and Indigenous cultures
and creatures are taking the heaviest deathblows. And here's the
key: it's not the Indigenous that are responsible for sabotaging the
only ark we have. It is, by and large, colonial settler civilization. As
philosopher Derrick Jensen writes:

> Traditional communities do not often voluntarily give up
> or sell the resources on which their communities are based
> until their communities have been destroyed. They also do
> not willingly allow their landbases to be damaged so that
> other resources—gold, oil, and so on—can be extracted. It
> follows that those who want the resources will do what they
> can to destroy traditional communities. This can be accom-
> plished more or less physically, such as through the murder
> of the peoples and the land on which they depend, or more
> or less spiritually or psychologically, through the destruction
> of sacred sites, through aggressive and/or forceful proselytiza-
> tion, by forcefully addicting them to the aggressor's products,
> by kidnapping their children (most often legally), and through
> many other means all-too-familiar to those who attend to the
> relations between the civilized and noncivilized.[13]

11. Prior to European contact, there were fourteen language families in what is
now Oregon. That's more than what all of Europe had. Today there are only five
left, with a handful of speakers.
12. L. J. Gorenflo, Suzanne Romaine, Russell A. Mittermeier, and Kristen
Walker-Painemilla, "Co-occurrence of linguistic and biological diversity in biodiversity hotspots and high biodiversity wilderness areas," *PNAS* 7 May 2012,
http://www.pnas.org/content/early/2012/05/03/1117511109.full.pdf (accessed
November 2012).
13. Jensen, *Endgame: Volume 1, The Problem of Civilization* (New York: Seven
Stories Press, 2006), 51.

For generations, Indigenous peoples in Canada and the United States have been told by government, church, and business that there's an "Indian problem," and that we settlers can fix it through education, salvation, or economic development. But the disturbing truth is that the problems in Indian country have not been created by Indians. The problems, as Luther Standing Bear said, are "due to the white man's cast of mind."[14] There's a "settler problem," an ongoing colonialism that is ravaging Indigenous peoples and the planet.[15] And, as black liberation theologian James Cone passionately notes—with less nuance then we desire—it's all inextricably tied to whiteness, white power, and white peoples:

> No threat has been more deadly and persistent for black and indigenous peoples than the rule of white supremacy in the world. The logic that led to [genocide,] slavery and segregation in the Americas, colonization and Apartheid in Africa, and the rule of white supremacy throughout the world is the same one that leads to the exploitation of animals and the ravaging of nature. It is a mechanistic and instrumental logic that defines everything and everybody in terms of their contribution to the development and defense of white world supremacy. . . . For over five hundred years, through the wedding of science and technology, white people have been exploiting nature and killing people of color in every nook and cranny of the planet in the name of God and democracy.[16]

This is not about demonizing white people, or inducing guilt; there are many morally outstanding white people (just as there were, no doubt, Ninevites). It's about confessing and resisting a system that perpetually privileges "white skin tones and European genetic lines" as it devours "whole peoples in its hungry economy and phobic gaze."[17] It's about taking responsibility as "heirs of oppression."[18]

---

14. As quoted in Taiaiake Alfred, *Peace, Power and Righteousness: An Indigenous Manifesto* (New York: Oxford, 1999), 84.

15. See note 5, above.

16. James Cone, "Whose Earth Is It Anyway?" in *Earth Habitat: Eco-Justice and the Church's Response*, eds. Dieter Hessel and Larry Rasmussen (Minneapolis: Fortress, 2001), 24.

17. James Perkinson, "Upstart Messiahs, Renegade Samaritans, and Temple Exorcisms," in *Christology and Whiteness: What Would Jesus Do?*, ed. George Yancey (New York: Routledge, 2012), 138–39.

18. See Angelo J. Corlett, *Heirs of Oppression: Racism and Reparations* (Lanham, MD: Rowman and Littlefield, 2010).

Global warming is largely a white settler-colonial problem.[19] Yes, we can cast an eye to the Fort McKay First Nation, who are caught up in tar sands exploitation, or we can point to China and its coal industry (the largest in the world), or to the Philippines and its catastrophic levels of deforestation (over 90 percent gone).[20] But better, more historically and economically honest, to start with that massive log in our culture's eye. The United States and Canada consume, for instance, more than 25 percent of the world's oil—more than any other two countries combined—yet have less than 5 percent of the world's population.[21] And let's not mention the trillions that white North America has invested in those resource-extraction corporations doing the destruction in faraway places (which remove Indigenous peoples from their lands, or force them to collaborate).[22] Even my socially responsible pension plan, I recently learned, is tied up in all this.

Or consider a different set of facts: a staggering 68 percent of the kids in Alberta's child and family services are Indigenous, though

---

19. Thomas Berry, the respected Catholic philosopher and geologian, argues that the ecological crisis is not simply a Western, white problem, but a specifically Christian problem. "The present disruption of all the basic life systems of Earth has come about within a culture that emerged from a biblical-Christian matrix. It did not arise out of the Buddhist world or the Hindu or Chinese or Japanese worlds or the Islamic world. It emerged from within our Western Christian-derived civilization. If these other civilizations were not ideal in their presence to the natural world, if they intruded extensively into the functioning of the planet, their intrusion, in its nature and in its magnitude, nowhere approaches the disturbance brought about by our modern Western disruption of the planetary process. Although our Western industrial civilization was itself a deviation from Christian ideals, it came originally from within a Christian context. In its historical expression it could not have arisen out of any other tradition." As quoted in *The Christian Future and the Fate of the Earth* eds. Mary Evelyn Tucker and John Grim (New York: Orbis, 2011), 35.

20. Bill McKibben, *Eaarth: Making a Life on a Tough New Planet* (New York: Random House, 2011), 47.

21. "BP energy statistics: the world in oil consumption, reserves and energy production," *The Guardian*, June 2010, http://www.guardian.co.uk/news/datablog/2010/jun/09/bp-energy-statistics-consumption-reserves-energy (accessed 20 November 2012).

22. See Todd Gordon, "Violence and Eco-Disaster: Canadian Corporations in the Third World," in *Imperialist Canada* (Winnipeg: Arbeiter Ring, 2010): 205–75.

Indigenous peoples only comprise 3 percent of that province's population.[23] That's not a Native issue, not owing to their culture being "backwards," or because "those people" (as it was commonly argued, and sometimes still is) "suffer an inferior biology." It has to do with settler-colonialism.

Or what of the stark reality that the wild salmon population on the West Coast is facing a collapse similar to that of the East Coast cod?[24] It'll be like the plains without buffalo. Does this have anything to do with Native rights and Native overfishing? Not really. It has a whole lot to do with a capitalist-consuming culture that historically removed host cultures from their sustainable fisheries and lands, a culture that continues to put corporate rights and profits above the well-being of host cultures, forcing its foreign logics (think fish farms) against local wisdoms because "we know better."

There's a settler problem, and we desperately need to do something to undo it, because "the time is near" and, for far too many, it's already long gone. We've got to turn, like those Ninevites. We've got to invert the infamous agenda of our settler states—"to kill the Indian, and save the man"[25]—and do as Ward Churchill boldly advocates: "kill the colonizer in settler society."[26]

---

23. "Number of aboriginal kids in provincial care raises concerns," *CBC News Online* (6 November 2012) http://www.cbc.ca/news/canada/calgary/story/2012/11/06/calgary-aboriginal-children-care.html (accessed 5 December 2012).

24. See the three-volume B.C. government report, "The Uncertain Future of Fraser River Sockeye," *Cohen Commission Report* (October 2012) http://www.cohencommission.ca/en/FinalReport/ (accessed 10 December 2012). Also Richard Atleo, *Principles of Tsawalk: An Indigenous Approach to Global Crisis* (Vancouver: UBC Press, 2011), 17–18.

25. The motto of Richard Henry Pratt, the founder of the first Native American non-reservation boarding school in the United States (1879: Carlisle, Pennsylvania), whose "civilizing" work was supported by the U.S. Congress. Duncan Campbell Scott, a senior official in the Canadian Department of Indian Affairs expressed similar sentiments in 1920: "I want to get rid of the Indian problem. . . . Our objective is to continue until there is not a single Indian in Canada that has not been absorbed into the body politic and there is no Indian Question and no Indian Department." As quoted in Bonita Lawrence, *"Real" Indians and Others: Mixed-Blood Urban Native Peoples and Indigenous Nationhood* (Lincoln: University of Nebraska, 2004), 31.

26. Ward Churchill, *Kill the Indian, Save the Man* (San Francisco: City Lights Books, 2004), xxx, 82.

My hope for this book is that a few souls within the dominant system might be unsettled by its contents and stirred to join those who have been working at this problem for years, in a tradition that goes back centuries. It's an earnest ambition. And I recognize the foolishness of it. Like Jonah, there's part of me (and perhaps you, too) that doubts whether these words will make a real difference. But we need to try, even if we despair of the possibility of change. Life literally depends on it. Remember the above litany of woes, and don't let them go. The problems are pressing and overwhelming—so much so that we might feel like putting that Ninevite sackcloth on our heads to shut our eyes and ears to the deathly injustice that surrounds us. Yet that response won't do anything but ensure greater loss. We must

> fall on our knees
> pray for strength
> and rise to struggle
> > together, in an alliance of settler and Indigenous peoples.

And perhaps, in doing so, something miraculous will happen.

The genesis of the book and its contents

In the fall of 2011, I attended the Atlantic Truth and Reconciliation Commission on Indian Residential Schools in Halifax, one of a series of public events to help Canadian settler society grapple with the legacy of cultural genocide against Indigenous communities through government and church-run "assimilation" institutions. On day two, I found myself sitting in a small circle, listening to a Mi'kmaq elder share his ideas for a more equitable future. At one point, he passionately spoke with a mix of hope and anger, "What we really need in this country is two-eyed seeing! Indigenous and Western knowledges teaching together. We haven't had that. But that's the pathway to reconciliation." He went on to explain how it was largely the imposition of Western miseducation that got us all—both Native and non-Native—into this mess, and that it would be a common education that took Indigenous worldviews seriously that would get us out.

I was moved by his words and by the feeling with which he communicated. But I didn't wholly agree. I don't think education will get us out of this situation, for education will not move the powerful to redistribute wealth, stop plundering Indigenous lands, undo white privilege and cease burning fossil fuels. But it does help. It can animate lives and impact larger systems. And that prospect got me thinking.

I had recently begun a job with Mennonite Church Canada as director of Indigenous Relations, and sitting on my desk was a project that a small circle of us (Mennonite and Métis) were working on: a curriculum for adult groups that would explore Indigenous and non-Indigenous Christian understandings of Creator and creation. It was still in its initial stages, and contained some interesting pieces, but it didn't reflect the two-eyed vision that this Mi'kmaq elder was talking about. Contributions from Indigenous and settler authors were not in dialogue. Settler contributions were thoughtful reflections on biblical texts, exploring themes of creation care and God's presence in nature.

Yet they were not wrestling with Indigenous epistemologies, traditions, or, of fundamental importance, the connections between settler-Christian theologies/history/praxis and the ongoing colonial injustice impacting Native lands and life-forms. The same was true of the Indigenous reflections. They weren't in conversation with the church and settler society. They were bits of traditional wisdom—prayers and descriptions of ceremonies—and that made us apprehensive; well-meaning white Christians might read this stuff and either appropriate it uncritically (and dangerously—i.e., we take their land, now we take their spiritual resources) or dismiss it as romanticism because we had failed to create space for critical Indigenous explanation of these traditions in relation to and in contrast with Christianity. We needed something more dialogical that could push us toward "two-eyed" seeing. And so the circle decided to switch gears, encouraging me to take the project in a new direction.

Instead of a short curriculum, we'd do a full-length book, inviting authors to engage the topics of Creator and creation, not abstractly, but in the context of colonialism's twin legacies: the ongoing dispossession of Native peoples and the ecological crisis. Instead of welcoming just "the good Indians"[27] into the discussion—those whose

---

27. Not my words, but those of an Indigenous author who questioned whom the church was truly willing to engage in this conversation.

theologies and ideologies are compatible with our own (i.e., explicitly Christian)—we would invite a number of other, less comfortable voices from beyond the walls of the church, voices that could push our settler church (the primary audience) to think much differently and perhaps more critically about our worldview(s) and praxis. Finally, it was important that at least half of the authors be Indigenous, and, in order to facilitate a deeper discussion, that each settler chapter be paired with an Indigenous author who would reflect on that piece through poetry or prose (with the same, in turn, for the Indigenous chapters). I wasn't—and still am not—aware of any text out there that would have this kind of intentional interaction.

So I went to work, contacting authors and activists I knew, professors and prophets I had read, to see if they'd be interested in participating. With some, I simply floated the theme of the book and its "unsettling" posture, and left what they would write about to them. With others, I suggested particular foci—matters I thought needed tackling and for which I knew they had passion.

Of course, not everyone responded. But of those who did, there were two reactions. Many loved the idea and were surprised that a church would have the chutzpah to do something of this nature. Others were unsure, on a couple of fronts.

First, the notion of "two-eyed" seeing did not appeal. To some, the goal of this text shouldn't be to bring Indigenous and Western knowledges together, but to keep them separate and respectful of one another, or, in some cases, to privilege Indigenous knowledges (Western ways being replete with oppressions that need undoing). A few said they'd like to write, yet had their doubts as to whether the church would be willing to give space to their thoughts, critical and deconstructive as they need be to represent their convictions faithfully. I assured them that there was room for their viewpoints (particularly since these views are representative of significant segments in the Indigenous world), that our church could handle it, and that, in fact, we needed it. Furthermore, I shared how I thought the church had a responsibility to create room for such challenging perspectives, given the history of Christian complicity in the deculturation of Indigenous peoples, which regrettably continues today. The response? With genuine excitement, and some hesitation, the authors said, "Okay, let's do it!"

And this book is the result: more than thirty contributors in total—half of them Indigenous, from nations all around North America, half of them settlers from both the United States and Canada, coming from a diverse array of worldviews and spiritualities. They include traditional Indigenous practitioners, Christians (Anabaptist, anarchist, evangelical, and liberal), hybrid Christian traditionalists, post-Christians, agnostics, and animists. Together, they produced eighteen chapters and eighteen sets of reflective pieces that should stir conversation, a little controversy, and, I hope, a desire for better relations and the *action* that can bring this about.

The book is comprised of four parts, with the first setting out the colonial context in which our conversation takes place. Anthony Hall (chapter 1) starts at the very beginning with the primal myths of creation and their principles of reciprocity and alliance. He then details the history of Turtle Island, taking us through the precontact period, through imperial conquest, down to the Royal Proclamation of 1763, and finally *back to* today's struggles for Indigenous land justice ("back to," because the model of Crown-Aboriginal treaty-making in Canada—over against the patterns of conquest and expansionism embodied primarily by the United States—offers a potential return to those genesis principles).

Leanne Simpson (chapter 2) invites us to consider the colonial reality in her backyard: the traditional territory of the Michi Saagiig Nishnaabeg in what is today known as southern Ontario. As she narrates the historical and experiential impacts of settler-colonialism on her peoples, Simpson calls upon those of us who are "living on top of someone's home . . . to work out the implications of that truth."

Disturbingly, the colonial reality known by a disproportionate number of Indigenous women and men is the prison. Frances Kaye (chapter 3) takes us there, so that we can understand the traumas of colonization—how the loss of children and land has led to mass incarceration. But she also shows us the *survivance*[28] of Indigenous peoples; for here, among the barbed wire and armed security, one finds Indigenous movements of resurgence and reconnection to culture and Creator.

---

28. A neologism coined by Gerald Vizenor (Anishinaabe) combining "survival" and "resistance."

Neil Funk-Unrau (chapter 4) ponders the stark power imbalances and social divides between Indigenous and settler societies. He asks, "What are the prospects of reconciliation?" Using Canada's Truth and Reconciliation Commission as a case study, Funk-Unrau tests the promise and perils of reconciliation and invites us to set aside this easily abused word and the inspirational visions that accompany it. Better to commit ourselves, he counsels, to the first steps—really listening to what Indigenous peoples are saying.

In part 2, five authors take on the task of theologically re-visioning the Christian tradition, attempting to indigenize and/or decolonize the ways we think about God, creation, land, and even civilization. Randy Woodley (chapter 5) brings together Keetoowah traditions, the ancient Genesis words, and nature's voice in order to broaden Christ's "kingdom" vision toward a "community of creation." The result is a theological construct that challenges anthropocentric interpretations of the biblical message, elevating harmony with creation as a Christian imperative.

Like Woodley, Ched Myers (chapter 6) also engages the Genesis tradition, yet in a dissimilar fashion. Myers seeks to reinterpret this contested identity-myth as "anti-civilization" good news. Walking us through the first eleven chapters, he reveals a prophetic Word that deconstructs Western narratives of progress and asks the church to join Indigenous peoples in the fight against "the social pathologies and ecocidal consequences" of empire.

But whose side are we really on? Dave Diewert (chapter 7) asserts that settler Christians have cause for concern as they read the biblical text. Exploring the exodus tradition, Diewert discerns not only an anti-imperial Word, but argues that non-Indigenous peoples have much more in common with the "master" Egyptians than with the Hebrew slaves. As such, the liberating Word of this scriptural memory is revolution: "recognize, resist, and dismantle the structures of oppressive power, not just reform their most harmful policies."

Moving us to a consideration of creation's eschatology, Laura Donaldson (chapter 8) confronts Paul's words in Romans 8 regarding creation's "bondage to decay." Through traditional and contemporary Indigenous teachings, Donaldson asserts that decay ought to be understood as a gift, that the earth doesn't require a final liberation, for it has already obtained its glory. If only we could see it.

Lawrence Hart (chapter 9) finishes by asking what role Christian liturgy can play in reconnecting us to the lands in which we live. Reflecting on Cheyenne ceremonies and knowledges that tie his community so deeply to the earth, Hart laments how most Christian worship is fundamentally "placeless." The task for settlers, and for many decultured Indigenous Christians, is to learn the traditions of the land in which we live, risk (but seek to avoid) appropriation, and reimagine worship in spirit, truth, and place.

The most difficult part of the book for many readers will be the third section, in which we give space for voices of challenge and dissent. You may not agree with everything that's said—I don't. You might find some of this material uncomfortable—I do! But if you adopt an open posture, one of curiosity and loving intellectual suspense, you'll be surprised by the truths that you'll find. As I've worked through this material, I've found it helpful to keep Jesus' startling example in mind. The Galilean Prophet not only learned from religious outsiders who challenged his ethnocentrism (see Matthew 15:21-28), he even lifted up these "heretics" (so defined by his church) as models of the just action about which his faith community had talked so much, yet failed to practice (see Luke 10:25-37). In other words, engaging the kinds of voices that follow is something that Jesus did and something we might want to imitate.

Tink Tinker (chapter 10) begins part 3 by disavowing "belief" in "Creator" and "creation," maintaining that these are Euro-colonial constructs that have had a devastating impact on all things Indigenous. Though treated as universal givens, these concepts are invasive, loaded with hierarchic and anthropocentric baggage that distorts the beauty, coherence, and difference of Indigenous cultures. In Tinker's reckoning, there can be no harmonious wedding of euro-Christianity and American Indian worldviews: "the deep structure realities of the two worlds . . . are inherently opposite to one another."

Tomson Highway (chapter 11) takes us on a journey to his Eden—the northern lands of Manitoba and Nunavut—and explains how the languages of that place birthed an Indigenous vision of God distinct from that of the Christian God. Echoing feminist Mary Daly—"if God is male, then male is God"—Highway asserts that the time's come to queer the Creator by making "her" Cree. In doing so, he suggests, we settlers might realize that we've never been kicked out of the garden.

Setting forth a challenge from a much different direction, Will Braun (chapter 12) argues that much of the theoretical discussion between Indigenous and settler peoples is too simplistic and ultimately unhelpful because it fails to take into consideration the disturbing facts on the ground—that many Indigenous communities have joined settler society in the bulldozer. Braun recognizes that "Indigenous people would not be participants in the complicated mess had the colonizers not shown up"—but the reality is still there, so how do we deal with it? Instead of figuring out who has the better worldview, Braun urges us to set aside the "good Indian, bad settler" binary so that, together, in all the grey diversity that exists, we can address the woes of the industrial culture of which we are all a part.

Reminiscent of Lynn White Jr.'s famous eco-critique of Christianity back in the 1960s, Waziyatawin (chapter 13) contends that Christianity has an insufferable weight to bear for the ongoing ecocide and genocide in North America.[29] Euro-Christian ideology, fueled by the Genesis dominion mandate and the Great Commission, is committed not only to human supremacy but specifically to white Christian supremacy, which has led to an overwhelming erasure of Indigenous life-forms and lands. Contrasting Christianity with her Indigenous worldview, Waziyatawin asserts that the former has little, if anything, to offer the Indigenous, and wonders whether Christianity itself can be redeemed.

Peter Cole (chapter 14) draws the section to a close by taking us on a trip to the underworld with his friends raven and coyote. Sounds like fun, but the temperature is hot down there, and the conversation even hotter. Raven and coyote visit with Jesus, Satan, and other notables, exploring how the Christian tradition, in its lust for epistemological certainty, has reaped settler colonialism and dominated Indigenous "others." Interestingly, Cole's two-spirited Jesus is an ally to the Indigenous, encouraging his red relatives to hold fast to the original instructions.

---

29. Lynn White Jr., "The Historical Roots of Our Ecologic Crisis," *Science* 155 (1967), 1203–7.

The concluding section offers up four "Where from here?" responses. Derek Suderman (chapter 15) considers what it means to follow a Christ who proclaims Jubilee justice in his backyard—the contested Haldimand Tract of southern Ontario. Suderman discerns in Scripture a call to question received (settler) traditions, to engage Six Nations voices, and to do that which is so often talked about but rarely done—actually nurture living relationships with host peoples.

Steve Berry (chapter 16) then grabs our hand and invites us to see discipleship as a journey of rooting one's story in place. Describing key moments of consciousness raising and conversion in his life, we find Berry purposefully learning the Indigenous histories of the lands in which he has settled, and cultivating friendships with those who help him rethink his theology to make it more attuned to creation's harmony. The outcome is a living commitment to struggle against the earth's destruction.

Where should we go from here? Dan Wildcat (chapter 17) maintains that we all need to go outside, get out of our insulated ignorance, and open ourselves to the possibility that other-than-human life-forms and Indigenous knowledges—practical wisdoms that emerged through millennia of interaction with specific bioregions—may teach us a better way of living together. Settler Christians have shared, often with force, their understandings for centuries. The time's come, says Wildcat, to listen to those who have been here much longer, to heed the voices of the land, and to celebrate with gratitude the beauty that surrounds.

Jennifer Harvey (chapter 18) wraps things up by speaking a corrective word to settler Christian communities advocating environmental justice: "We can't do this apart from reparations." Harvey gives seven reasons why the *dangerous* good of "creation care" must entail struggles for Indigenous sovereignty and land rights, offering two small but hopeful examples in which settler Christians have done this. It's tough work, but it is possible to pierce the broken legacy of Indigenous-settler relations.

Thank you, friend, for picking up this book, and for your willingness to engage in this conversation. My prayers are with you and your communities as you make your way:

Be strengthened as you receive truths as good as old
Be challenged as you contemplate new ways of being
Be unsettled as you ponder loss beyond imagining
Be angered as you lament situations that none asked for
Be broken as you discern what you can't do . . . and what you can

And as you
    join hands with that fierce, but life-giving circle
    join all things in a courageous search for interdependence
    join all peoples in a cruciform way of healing resistance

May you be graced with hope, beyond fear, to risk-taking love
    indigenous and settler
    together
    in a good way

—*Steve Heinrichs*
Winnipeg, January 2013

PART 1

NAMING THE COLONIAL CONTEXT

When earth is property, where is covenant?

How can we understand each other across cultural differences?
Some say the earth is the Lord's, but it is destined to be private
    property.
Some say the earth is "our mother," and yet we take from the earth
    without offering thanksgiving.

The earth is sacred and land is our life, but we continue to exploit
    and destroy.
Will we find ways to respectfully discuss the relationship between
    individual and community rights? Can we maintain covenant
    treaty relationships for "as long as the sun shines, the grass
    grows, and the rivers flow"?

In a generation of exploitation of resources and accelerated
    materialism we are polluting the earth. We have been invited to
    plan for seven generations. What will the inheritance be for
    those who are yet to come?

—Stan McKay (Cree)

1

CREATION, ORIGINAL PEOPLES, AND THE COLONIZATION OF A HEMISPHERE

By Anthony J. Hall

With perception came time's illusions; with the presence of Mind came consciousness and language. In the beginning there was the Word, as articulation preceded the coming into existence of beings and objects. The representation of things, both animate and inanimate, ushered in their embodiment in time and space.

Then came history. The Mother of Humans fell through a hole in the sky world, fell through the roots of giant celestial tree. Cushioned by birds flying below, she descended onto the shell of a huge sea turtle. Turtle was happy to take on the load. Even then, in those long-ago times, Turtle came from an ancient line of great evolutionary distinction. Eons of Turtle Elders had passed on ancestral wisdom gained in moving readily between sky and water.

And so there they were: Turtle, Birds, and Mother. But they were not alone. Fish and furry creatures shared the ocean with them.

Turtle Island

It was Muskrat that saw the distress of Mother Human and Elder Turtle. He dove down to the sea floor and brought up mud. The sea was deep, and Muskrat died while bringing up the dirt. As he floated to the surface with soil in his claws, Mother Human extracted the mud and rubbed this tiny, precious source of ooze from the ocean's

floor onto the shell covering Turtle's back. With constant stimula-
tion Earth erupted from the sea.

Turtle Island gave humans a place to build habitations, sacred
pyramids, irrigation works, and elaborate networks of canals. It was
a magnificent place. Some parts of the land were carefully cleared
through the human direction of fire. The original peoples of Turtle
Island perfected this fire technology to draw out great biodiversity
among our plant and animal relatives. The women of many agricultural districts in Indian Country were especially adept at cultivating
hybrids and the synergetic three sisters—Corn, Beans, and Squash.
Strawberries, tomatoes, and potatoes were also added to the cor-
nucopia drawn from Plant World's bounty. And of course, there
was tobacco, the sacred medicine. Tobacco spread from nation to
nation on Turtle Island. Tobacco was put in many sacred pipes as
a medium to be burned and smoked for the enhancement of ritual,
ceremony, and contemplative interaction amongst the two-leggeds.

Many other herbs, fruits, and vegetables came to being through
Earth Mother. She spread seeds far and wide, and in order to stimu-
late new life, she poured her essence into Mother Earth. The blood
of Earth Mother became the pure, sweet water whose cycles of
transformation replenish life's essences according to the cycles of
the Moon and other celestial bodies.

Trickster

Trickster stands at the beginning of a new stage in the creation. Trickster
joins us in our human journey right up to the present. Trickster
appears and reappears in various guises. He has many names. He can
be Napi, Nanabush, Coyote, Raven, Kokopelli, and Wisakedjak. In the
history of creation, Trickster is a key figure, responsible for sculpting
whole landscapes, breathing life into new beings, giving instructions
and apportioning titles. Trickster draws connections. Trickster is mis-
chievous. Sometimes he tries to get sex. Sometime he acts the buffoon
to elicit laughter, injecting meaningful fun into public education. But
always, Trickster is a teacher, a mentor, a companion.

Because of Trickster, people start to know the four directions,
the sacred rituals, the ways to renew physical, emotional, and
spiritual health. Trickster tells stories, and lives through the stories
told about him. We all inhabit the stories we express, concoct, and

embrace. Trickster's stories teach us how to come to terms with our many imperfections as human beings.

The rise of empire and the coming of Jesus stories

Whereas Trickster stories suggest ways for us to work through the paradoxes of imperfect human nature, Jesus stories emphasize ways to transcend evil through salvation, grace, and the strength of human will.

When Christians stumbled upon Turtle Island in 1492, most of those proclaiming the power of the Book demanded Trickster be put aside. And with the taking of more and more Indian land, the spiritual, intellectual, and cultural spaces for telling and enacting Trickster stories were diminished. We must note that the vitality of this narrative tradition defied extermination. The wisdom Trickster brings us could not be killed, even by the most genocidal extremes of the centuries-long holocaust that followed. The playfulness and instructive power of Trickster and his stories live on in a discourse of discovery available to any of us. By becoming acquainted with Trickster and the know-how he offers for living more effectively on this earth, we can all move closer to those motifs of global citizenship that are Turtle Island's gift to the world.[1]

But back then, in 1492, the newcomers saw no place for Trickster, and they did their best to remove him from his rightful place, as well as his Indigenous sisters and brothers. Imperial claims of alien ownership and control were thrust on the original people, and theories of superiority were developed to justify the nations and the church's conquest. First, through the Roman Catholics, the Spanish empire, and that infamous papal bull (Inter caetera), in which Pope Alexander VI granted Spain "divine" rights to possess the "new world"; then, through competing claims of Protestant empire emanating primarily from England, the Netherlands, and some parts of Germany.

After 1492

After 1492, Jesus stories become mixed with sagas of conquest and colonization throughout the Americas. The cross was raised

---

1. Who knows? Maybe the time since 1492 will turn out to be just the opening act in a Trickster saga culminating in an era when universal peace will prevail in a global harmony of interactive trade, negotiation, reciprocity, and love.

many times to signify the remaking of the old-world civilizations of Indigenous peoples into new worlds for Christian immigrants and their descendants. And it's not over; the Manifest Destiny acted out in the early baptismal christening of "America" continues to this day. America is still a work in progress, a polity that has drawn much of its own self-image from a zeal to overcome one manufactured enemy after the next. From red savages to red communists to Islamic terrorists, the demonized enemies of American expansionism have been made to serve and justify the incursions of imperial governance.

Protestant missionaries

The protest against the monopoly powers of Roman Catholicism helped drive the movement of immigrants from Europe to North America. And it was here, in the making and spread of the United States, that the Protestant Reformation found one of its most fertile fields for expansion. Max Weber, the German sociologist, was certainly onto something when he identified the importance of the Protestant work ethic of New England's farmers, artisans, and traders as a major dynamo of capitalism.

Not all the Protestant settlers, however, accepted an individualized, atomized treatment of property. Some pictured a more collectivist orientation of Christian communities to shared property. Some posited that those traveling along the Jesus path could only be accepted as genuine if they opted, in freedom, without coercion, to take the plunge of baptism when fully adult and fully aware of the import of their choices.

Many of the Protestant missionaries sought forms of conversion that placed great pressure on Indigenous peoples to model themselves on the cultural norms of the colonizers. They favored assimilationist strategies. Yet some of the missionaries sought to lead America's Aboriginal inhabitants to Christianity in ways that still left room for Trickster stories and traditional medicine.

Some of these evangelists so identified with the plight of the victimized peoples that they became great advocates for more just treatment of the diverse array of peoples that came to be known as Indians. They became champions of the ideal that the incursions of colonization should be mediated. They believed that Indigenous peoples should be afforded some protections for their persons, their lands, and their cultural inheritances from their ancestors. One such evangelist was Reverend Jeremiah Evarts.

Jeremiah Evarts, ca. 1830

Jeremiah Evarts

Evarts became a major voice of protest in the late 1820s, championing Aboriginal and treaty rights wherever he went. Specifically, Evarts railed against the plan to uproot the Cherokee people from their ancestral lands in the Georgia region and relocate them, along with all the other Indigenous peoples east of the Mississippi, to new homes west of the famous river.

The Cherokee were well known for being "successful." They made good commercial use of their lands, and by the 1820s they had their own written constitution, their own schools, and their own newspaper published in their own written language. Many of the Cherokee were Christian. And some of these Christian Cherokees, like their white neighbors, incorporated black slaves into the political economy of their farms.

The Cherokee lands, of course, were coveted by their non-Indian neighbors in Georgia. In the ongoing creation of the Americas, an inescapable, consistently repeated narrative is settler hunger for Indian land—the unrelenting drive of newcomers to own privatized pieces of Aboriginal Earth.

Reverend Evarts studied all the old British and American treaties guaranteeing the security of Cherokee land tenure and the preeminence of federal jurisdiction over state jurisdiction when it came to the protection of Aboriginal rights. He developed a well-documented defense of the Cherokee right to hold ground and the United States' responsibility to defend those Indigenous lands from the inroads of Georgia's pioneer farmers and real estate speculators.

In advancing his arguments, Reverend Evarts evoked the name of William Penn, the Quaker founder of Pennsylvania, who had famously gone to the Delaware Indians in 1683 in order to secure Aboriginal consent for the consolidation of his little colony of Friends (even though King Charles had officially "granted" him this land). In taking this step, Penn renewed a precedent set by Roger Williams a half century earlier, when the maverick broke with the Puritan founders of Massachusetts by seeking consent from Narragansett Indians for the establishment of Rhode Island. Little by little, the principle developed that a grant from the English king was not enough to invest the Anglo-American colonies with full legitimacy. Only Indigenous peoples could grant the permission necessary for the development of colonies on their Aboriginal lands and waters.

In his widely disseminated "William Penn" essays (1829), Evarts explained the implications for the future reputation of the United States if Cherokee removal was allowed to go forward. As the Christian activist saw it, any uprooting of the Cherokee would amount to "tearing out sheets from every volume of our national statute-book and scattering them to the winds." Evarts worried that if the United States pressed ahead with Indian removal in spite of the treaty promises formalized by George Washington and the U.S. Senate, then "an indelible stigma will be fixed upon us [that] will ultimately be understood by the whole civilized world." Evarts added, "No subject, not even war, slavery, nor the nature of free institutions will be more thoroughly canvassed."[2]

Shamefully, Cherokee removal was pressed ahead, even in spite of a ruling of the U.S. Supreme Court specifically outlawing this initiative. In the eyes of Evarts, the United States would henceforth stand naked, forever revealed as an immoral country mired in the infamy of illegally violating treaties transacted with great solemnity in the republic's early dealings.

The Royal Proclamation of 1763

The transformation of the Americas from a vast Indian country into a promised land for newcomers is the essence of American

---

2. Anthony J. Hall, *Earth into Property: Colonization, Decolonization, and Capitalism* (Montreal: McGill-Queen's University Press, 2010), 296.

Manifest Destiny. The stakes have been huge, and continue to be so in determining who will be the winners or losers in the transfer of land and resources from Indian ownership and control to settler possession and jurisdiction. Sometimes this process was pushed forward by genocidal wars, or, as during the California gold rush, by unchecked and unpunished episodes of vigilante violence. Sometimes the process involved consent rather than coercion. In these instances, efforts were made to give the gloss of legality, the appearance of legitimacy, to the transfer to newcomers and their descendants of privatized title to portions of Indian country.

A key document in all these land matters is the Royal Proclamation of 1763. It was (and is) integral to a legal and moral tradition concerning the transfer of lands and resources to non-Indian individuals and corporations based on mutual consent, rather than the legal fiction of "discovery," which has so dominated land relations between Natives and newcomers.

The Royal Proclamation was the chosen instrument whereby the British imperial government of King George III incorporated Canada into Britain's thirteen Anglo-American colonies after the Seven Years' War. It was an effort to incorporate the peoples of French-Aboriginal Canada into British North America on the basis of law and consent, rather than coercion. A vital part of this proclamation—with tremendous significance for today's Turtle Island—is its recognition of an enormous Indian reserve. This reserve extended throughout the eastern half of the Mississippi Valley and north of the Great Lakes up to the beginning of the arctic watershed. These were "Lands reserved to the Indians for their hunting grounds." Here are two excerpts from the proclamation that acknowledge (some form of) Indigenous title to these unceded territories:

> And whereas it is just and reasonable, and essential to our Interest, and the Security of our Colonies, that the several Nations or Tribes of Indians with whom We are connected, and who live under our Protection, should not be molested or disturbed in the Possession of such Parts of Our Dominions and Territories as, not having been ceded to or purchased by Us, are reserved to them, or any of them, as their Hunting Grounds.

> And We do further strictly enjoin and require all Persons whatever who have either willfully or inadvertently seated themselves upon any Lands within the Countries above described or upon any other Lands which, not having been ceded to or purchased by Us, are still reserved to the said Indians as aforesaid, forthwith to remove themselves from such Settlements.

In detailing these "Lands reserved to the Indians," the British monarch and his advisors lodged a very consequential phrase into the origins of British imperial Canada, and established the basis of many constitutional controversies to come. The divergent interpretations of the Royal Proclamation—*the* document forming Canada's constitutional foundation—would be tested, for instance, in the 1880s, when the government of Ontario took the government of Canada to court in the notorious case *St. Catherine's Milling v. The Queen* (the province argued that Natives had rights only to those small "Indian reserve lands" that they currently occupied, not to their traditional territories). The constitutional contentions would be tested again in arguments leading up to the Supreme Court of Canada's ambivalent ruling in 1973 concerning the assertions of the Nisga'a people of the Nass River Valley in British Columbia (three Supreme Court judges acknowledged that the Nisga'a held title to the Nass Valley "from time immemorial," and that such title remained unextinguished).

On the need to obtain Indian consent for Euro-American expansion

The drafters of the Royal Proclamation envisaged a gradual and orderly process for the westward expansion of Euro-American settlers into the vast Indian reserve created by the British imperial government. To ensure the orderly conduct of westward expansion, the Crown stipulated, "If at any Time any of the Said Indians should be inclined to dispose of the said Lands, the same shall be Purchased only for Us, in our Name, at some public Meeting or Assembly of the said Indians."

A key to unlocking the importance of this provision in the Royal Proclamation lies in its reference to the *inclination* of Indians to change the terms of their legal relationship to their ancestral lands. The need to obtain Indian consent for the westward expansion of

Euro-American settlement gave Indigenous peoples the prospect of exercising some considerable bargaining power in charting the future of British North America. A balancing corrective was thereby injected into the process of colonial expansion, which had been overwhelmingly one sided.

In this fashion the imperatives of reconciliation might have been made to prevail over the pitfalls of violent conflict between Native and newcomer. Like the instruments for the abolition of slavery that would follow the Royal Proclamation throughout the century after 1763, the requirement to secure Indian consent favored the rule of law over the rule of force, and the rule of self-determination over the rule of arbitrary command. This innovation, therefore, represented a step away from the inequitable and unconscionable division of humanity into rights-bearing citizens and those considered too inferior for a democratic say in making their own history according to their own estimation of rights, interests, and priorities.

The Indian provisions of the Royal Proclamation introduced a whole new dynamic into the constitutional makeup of British North America. However limited and imperfect, the king's recognition that Indigenous peoples have the inherent human right to a say in determining their own destinies established a fundamental principle of international law that has yet to be fully embraced and applied even throughout Canada, let alone in larger theaters of global geopolitics.

To this very day, the need to obtain Indian consent is being expressed in the contemporary negotiation of Crown-Aboriginal treaties in Canada. This process is most elaborate and intense in British Columbia, Canada's westernmost province. The current treaty-making negotiations in that territory are based on the cumulative efforts of activists who over generations politicized the failure of Crown officials to recognize Indian title in exploiting the abundant resources of that land. It was the legal team of the Nisga'a Nation who in 1973 succeeded in getting an answer from the Supreme Court of Canada on the Indian title question. The judges' ambivalent ruling on the Nisga'a case—the Court split three to three on whether the claim to land was still valid—opened the way to further rounds of Crown-Aboriginal treaty negotiations.

Allies of the Crown or merciless Indian savages

The Indian provisions of the Royal Proclamation were immediately unpopular with many Anglo-American colonists. Local settlers, together with many land speculators on both sides of the Atlantic, were unwilling to accept enhanced imperial and Aboriginal roles in determining the lucrative course and pace of westward expansion. It was this rejection of the principles of Indian consent that was instrumental in the development of a secessionist movement within British North America that would give rise to the creation of the United States as a federal republic. In other words, the revolution wasn't merely about imperial taxes on American colonies. The government was saying to settler society, "We can't simply appropriate this land." And settler society didn't like it. They revolted.

So whereas the Royal Proclamation had favored negotiations with Indigenous peoples as allies of the imperial Crown, the founders of the United States announced the arrival of their new polity onto the global stage by criminalizing those best placed to block westward expansion. The American Declaration of Independence issued on July 4, 1776, included the following provision, which might be seen as the true origins of what is today described as the Global War on Terror. The drafters condemned King George and his Royal Proclamation for inflicting on "the inhabitants of our frontiers, *the merciless Indian savages, whose known rule of warfare, is undistinguished destruction of all ages, sexes, and conditions."* With these few words, the founders of the future military superpower put in place a dark rationale for the removal and elimination of the very populations living on those lands and resources which the United States was created to encompass, appropriate, privatize, and incorporate into the marketplace of capitalist accumulation.

Between 1776 and 1871 the U.S. government replicated its own version of the Royal Proclamation, making the federal government responsible for the waging of war on, and the making of treaties with, the Indigenous peoples on the western frontiers of U.S. expansion. About four hundred of these agreements, which required ratification from Congress, were transacted. The treaties with the Cherokee were prominent among these instruments, and were deployed very consciously by President George Washington and other federal officials as a means of demonstrating the new republic's sovereign personality in the international arena.

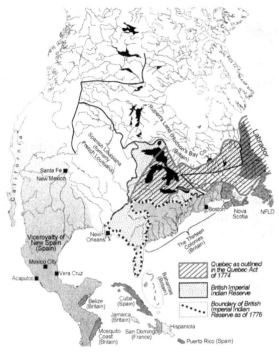

European claims on the eve of the American Revolution

Very often these treaties were made only after Indian groups had been vanquished through the actions of the U.S. Armed Forces. Much like the treatment by Israel and the United States of Palestinians in Gaza and the so-called "occupied territories", no treaties with subject Indian groups would be made as long as they retained members who were armed and motivated by the spirit of resistance. By taking charge, militarily and diplomatically, of the process of U.S. transcontinental expansion, federal authorities based in Washington, D.C., began to express the imperial personality that has marked the global orientation of the U.S. government, the U.S. Armed Forces, and U.S. corporations to this day.

In 1871 the U.S. Congress enacted legislation prohibiting the making of any further treaties with the Indigenous peoples encompassed within the continental extent of the United States. The other side of this complete and utter abandonment of the nascent principles of international law, as rooted in the Royal Proclamation, was a growing emphasis on conquest as a primary vehicle of national expansion and of formal and informal empire building. Sometimes the United

States built up its imperial power formally, as in the acquisition of the Philippine Islands through the conquest of Spain. More often the United States has deployed informal imperial tactics through strategies such as covert regime changes or the funding, organizing, and arming of proxy armies, like the Mujahedeen in Afghanistan in the 1980s.

Crown-Aboriginal treaties

In Canada the year 1871 marks the beginning of the negotiation of a new round of Crown-Aboriginal agreements described as the "numbered treaties." These treaties were negotiated to cover portions of the Hudson's Bay Company territory—territory that the newly created Dominion of Canada had purchased in a flawed transaction. This transaction, however, was rendered more acceptable to Indigenous peoples through the creation of Manitoba and the negotiation of eleven numbered treaties.

The extension of protocols for the negotiation of Crown-Aboriginal treaties into this region (once described as Rupert's Land and the North-Western Territory) marks an important milestone in the evolving application of the Indian provisions of the Royal Proclamation. Not only have these provisions become essential to Canada's systems of land tenure from coast to coast to coast (they are referred to in section 25 of the Constitution Act, 1982), but they also have far-reaching global implications. The Royal Proclamation's prohibition on the conquest of Indigenous peoples as a means of national or imperial aggrandizement can be seen as the root source in the development of an important principle of international law. Nowhere in the world should the conquest of Indigenous peoples be treated as the underlying basis for legitimate assertions of jurisdiction and law, but especially the law of property relations.

Treaties 1 to 11 were negotiated between 1871 and 1929. In that latter year, bush planes were able for the first time to fly into Big Trout Lake, where Oji-Cree people put their marks on an adhesion to Treaty 9. Forty-four years later, the Supreme Court of Canada's ruling on the Nisga'a case (1973) helped set in motion a new cycle of Crown-Aboriginal treaties. This cycle began in northern Quebec in 1975 with the negotiation of the James Bay Agreement aimed at transforming Cree hunting territory into the dammed waterworks of Hydro Québec.

Indian title continues to be an especially controversial issue in British Columbia, where the vast majority of land is unceded Indigenous territory. British Columbia is the site of about fifty ongoing negotiations of Crown-Aboriginal treaties. The legitimacy of this process, however, is contested. Some believe it affords far too much prominence to the dubious band council system emanating from the federal Indian Act. Some believe the province should not be involved, for treaties can only take place between nations. And in the meantime, various groups, such as the self-declared Shuswap Defenders—who courageously sought to reoccupy sacred spiritual grounds in spite of settler-state resistance in the 1995 Battle of Gustafsen Lake—seek some form of justice.

Even with all its flaws and inadequacies, the ongoing negotiation of Crown-Aboriginal treaties in Canada projects an example to the world worthy of international attention. It sets an example of the resolution of differences through application of the rule of law rather than the rule of force. The continuation of this process of compromise and accommodation draws on deep principles brought forward with the patriation of the Constitution of Canada from Great Britain. And thus we find in the Constitution Act, 1982, a provision, section 35, which recognizes and affirms the existence of Aboriginal and treaty rights.

As long as the sun shines and the water flows

Crown-Aboriginal treaties should be understood more as a *process* of continuing negotiations rather than as a *thing* collecting dust in the archives. In other words, Crown-Aboriginal treaties are better imagined as functioning more like verbs than nouns . . . better understood as an ongoing activity of invention, reinvention, and transformative interpretation than as a fixed or static outcome. Crown-Aboriginal treaties must be set in the context of the words spoken orally as the agreements were transacted, rather than as exercises in draftsmanship by lawyers without knowledge of Aboriginal languages. In a very real sense, it's more about the spirit than the letter of those sacred treaties.

As the world changes, the interpretation and application of treaty principles has to keep pace. The need to continually revisit the principles of alliance and reciprocity embodied in the creation of

Crown-Aboriginal treaties sends us back again and again to the deeper meanings embedded in the creation stories underlying the Indigenous and imported heritages of this hemisphere. This process of reinventing relations between peoples brings us face to face with many of the most fundamental issues that arose when the old-world civilization of Turtle Island was christened as the new-world civilization of the Americas following Columbus's transformative voyage of 1492.

Rev. Jeremiah Evarts was prophetic in anticipating the violence and lawlessness that would flow from uprooting the Cherokee and many other Indian nations contrary to federal treaties—contrary even to a specific ruling by U.S. Supreme Court Justice John Marshall. The implementation of the Indian removal policy of 1830, one of the most ambitious schemes of apartheid and so-called ethnic cleansing ever conceived and attempted, boded poorly for the future of the United States as a responsible, law-abiding member of the international community.

We have yet to see if Reverend Evarts's well-documented case— that the Indian removal policies of the United States ran contrary to domestic law and especially to international treaty law—will eventually attract the kind of considered and widespread condemnation that the Protestant missionary had anticipated. Certainly Canada's retention, sometimes grudging, of the Royal Proclamation's constitutional heritage needs to be seen in light of the factors resulting in the creation of the United States, a state whose very origins in violence would see it become the most heavily militarized country in the world.

By honoring our treaties with Indigenous peoples and by negotiating new ones, we embrace and celebrate the permanence of Indian nations as host peoples and contributing members in a society of equals. Such celebration requires that we recognize the importance of human difference as an essential aspect of human rights, as a universal harbinger of the human condition. To be equal is not to be the same. We need ways of recognizing difference in the spirit of enlightened adherence to the natural laws for renewing biocultural diversity.

By respecting Crown-Aboriginal treaties, we help honor the Crown, together with the sanctity of those sacred pipes so frequently smoked in the process of investing these agreements with Indian legitimacy. We reach back to the history of the world's creation, and of Canada's creation, even as we point the way to a better, more harmonious world for our posterity seven generations hence.

Together we share

Great Spirit (Kisay—Manitou)
With humility and thanksgiving we come acknowledging that we
    live on land that the elders called the Creator's resting place
    (Manitoba—Manitou-apa).
We seek to understand the fullness of life (Pimadizewin).
Each life is a gift for the community to share (mamawi).

Together we share stories,
feast and dream of the mystery of all our relations
    (ka-ki-nu-in-wa-ma-gun-uk),
all plant life, the ones that crawl, swim, and fly, the four legged and
    the two legged.

The water is sacred (ka-na-tun-ni-pi).
The earth is sacred (ka-na-tun-us-ki).
We acknowledge that we are part of the earth, Our Mother
    (ni-ka-we-nan).
We ask only for what we need and with the guidance of the
    spirit helper,
of what we have, we will share.

—Stan McKay (Cree)

Unsettled

As a child, I lay down—did you play this game too?
body melting to ground,
ear to earth,
listening for sounds
of footsteps
secret stories
asking sticks stones soil "do you remember?"
wondering
knowing
another story whispers

I learned to love the land
through raspberry thorns, potato eyes, corn ears,
acres dotted with swamps and sugar maple trees
land nurturing growth
connecting seed to harvest to God

My people were the quiet in the land:
Do not conform to this world.
Be transformed by the renewing of your minds.
Be in the world, but not of it.

Each year, my grandparents grew bountiful produce:
"I love every square inch of this land," Grandpa said.
"I was born here, and I want to die here too."

Permanence.
Land.
Home.

Through perennial plants dug up and shared my grandparents live on,
each spring a reminder that they will never die.
As long as there is land to hold them.
Their land, now paved with asphalt—

a parking lot offering new produce:
drive-thru Tim Horton's coffee.
My heart, forever cracked, like pavement over gardens.

I crouch down,
ear near concrete,
straining to hear
another story whispers
through unforgiving asphalt ceiling
I'm unsettled.

And those whispers multiply to a loud shout
impossible to keep out
unsettled.

—*Rebecca Seiling*

2

LIBERATED PEOPLES,
LIBERATED LANDS[1]

By Leanne Simpson
(Michi Saagiig Nishnaabeg)

'd like to take you back about two hundred years ago to my homeland in what is now known as central Ontario. I want to do this because the landscape has been degraded to such a degree—through highways, farmlands, and megacities—that it is difficult to envision the place that my ancestors called home.

My elder, Doug Williams, tells me that Lake Ontario had its own resident population of salmon that migrated all the way up to Stoney Lake to spawn. There was also a large population of eels that journeyed each year from the Atlantic Ocean.[2] An ancient old-growth forest of white pine stretched from Curve Lake down to the shore of Lake Ontario; the forest had virtually no understory except for a bed of pine needles. There were tall grass prairies and black oak savannahs where Peterborough stands today and along the south shore of Rice Lake or Pimadashkodeyong.[3] Pimadash means "going across," and it refers to fire moving across the prairie beside the lake. This lake was teeming with *manomiin* (wild rice), and the land was dotted with sugar bushes.

---

1. This title was inspired by Waziyatawin, *What Does Justice Look Like? The Struggle for Liberation in Dakota Homeland* (St. Paul, MN: Living Justice Press, 2008).
2. Doug Williams, Elder, Curve Lake First Nation, 10 July 2011.
3. Doug Williams, Elder, Curve Lake First Nation, 18 January 2012.

It sounds idyllic because it was idyllic. The knowledge systems, the education systems, the economic systems, and the political systems of Indigenous peoples were designed to promote more life. They were, and still are, designed to generate life—not just human life, but the life of all living things.

Over the past two hundred years, without our permission and without our consent, we have been systematically removed and dispossessed from most of our territory.[4] We have watched as our homeland has been cleared, subdivided, and sold to settlers from Toronto. We have watched our waterfronts disappear behind monster cottages. We no longer have salmon in our territory. We no longer have eels. We no longer have old-growth white pine forests, and our rice beds were nearly destroyed. Most of our sugar bushes are under private, non-Native ownership.

Our most sacred places have been made into provincial parks for tourists, with concrete buildings over our teaching rocks. Our burial grounds have homes and cottages built on top of them. The veins of our Mother (the rivers) have lift locks blocking them. The shores of every one of our lakes and rivers have a cottage or a home on them, making it nearly impossible for us to launch a canoe. Our rice beds have been devastated by raised water levels from the Trent Severn waterway, boat traffic, and sewage from cottages. And to top it off, we original peoples—the Anishinaabeg, Haudenosaunee, Cree, Wendat, and Métis—have all of Ontario's exploitative resource industries within our territories, not to mention all of Ontario's urban population.

The land, our Mother, has largely been taken from us. And so have our children. Our young were stolen from us and sent to residential schools, day schools, and child welfare, and are now placed

---

4. It is important in this context to understand that Indigenous nations had strong treaty-making traditions prior to colonial times. Nishnaabeg, like other Indigenous peoples, for the most part made treaties not in order to cede land, but rather to establish ongoing international diplomatic relationships with other nations. It was expected that each nation would respect the self-determination and sovereignty of the other while working together on issues at hand. Our vision of treaties affirmed and protected our way of life, and promoted the idea of separate jurisdictions over a shared territory. For more on this, see Leanne Simpson, *Dancing on Our Turtle's Back: Nishnaabeg Re-Creation, Resurgence and a New Emergence* (Winnipeg: Arbeiter Ring Publishing, 2011).

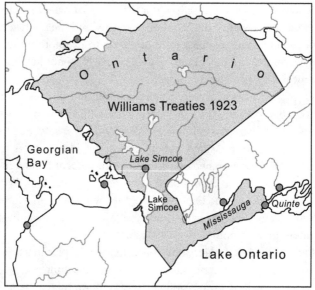

Map of 1923 Williams Treaties

within an education system that, on the whole, refuses to acknowledge our culture, our knowledge, our histories, and our Indigenous experience.

And then, of course, there is the Indian Act, which until 1951 made our ceremonies illegal, made it illegal for us to hire a lawyer, made it illegal for us to leave the reserve without the permission of the Indian agent, and made it illegal for us to organize. The act still controls virtually every aspect of life, from birth to grave. It is a continuous system of control over Indigenous peoples.

I believe my ancestors signed several treaties with the Crown in order to affirm our sovereignty, nationhood, self-determination, and jurisdiction over lands; to ensure that I would be able to live in my homeland according to Mississauga laws; to ensure that I could participate in Mississauga governance; to ensure that my children could grow up immersed in the beauty of Kina Gchi Nishnaabeg-ogaming.[5]

This understanding has not been reflected, recognized, or respected within the 1923 Williams Treaties, because the Crown

---

5. Simpson, *Dancing on Our Turtle's Back*, 14.

dishonorably and unjustly took away our hunting and treaty rights—a direct attack on our ability to feed and sustain ourselves in our own territory.[6] As a result, our grandparents grew up eating squirrel and groundhog, since their parents would have been criminalized if they were caught hunting deer or fish. I am here today because of their resistance . . . resistance as survival.

As a mother, it is very important for me to do everything I can to connect my children to their land and to their culture. But it is also very difficult. Last spring, we were harassed by municipal workers for picking wild leeks on our land, leaving my five-year-old girl terrified and in tears. We have been laughed at for taking rocks from the bush for our sweats, and are constantly questioned by settler Canadians for picking cedar, our medicines, and even berries. In the fall, when it is time to harvest rice, we are faced with the dilemma of gaining access to the rice beds, because all of the shoreline is owned by private landowners.

None of this had to happen. None of this was inevitable. Colonialism was and is a choice that Canadians make every day. It is a choice to maintain and to uphold a system that is based on the hyperexploitation of the land and of Indigenous peoples. It is a choice to maintain a system that overwhelmingly promotes greed over creation.

Throughout Canada's colonial history there has always been a small group of settlers that has refused to uphold this system, that have chosen not to follow the inherited mandate of their forefathers. In Paulette Regan's words, they have chosen to "unsettle the settler within."[7] We need many more unsettled settlers.

I consider the exploitation of our lands as the most pressing issue facing Indigenous peoples in the twenty-first century. Indigenous peoples are intimately connected to our traditional territories,

---

6. The negotiation, signing, interpretation, and subsequent court cases regarding this treaty have been fraught with injustice. For a detailed account, see Peggy Blair, *Lament for a First Nation: The Williams Treaties of Southern Ontario* (Vancouver: UBC Press, 2008). As a Michi Saagiik Nishnaabeg person, I do not believe that my ancestors intended to give up their rights to hunt and fish; they thought this treaty was reaffirming previous treaties with the Crown.
7. Paulette Regan, *Unsettling the Settler Within: Indian Residential Schools, Truth Telling, and Reconciliation in Canada* (Vancouver: UBC Press, 2010).

whether we live in those territories or in urban areas. Everything that is important to us comes from the land—including our system of governance; our ceremonies, songs, and dances; our healthcare and education systems; our philosophies, life-ways, and worldview; and our languages. Our lands hold our stories, our histories, and our values. Our relationship to the land heals us and gives us the will to live, even under the most dire conditions. Our resurgence and recovery depends upon our ability to connect with our lands. We Indigenous peoples—whether living in rural or urban areas—are particularly apt at this, despite all the pressures and barriers placed on these connections by colonialism. Michi Saagiik Nishnaabeg people know the life-giving power of the land intimately, for despite severe environmental destruction, which began in our territory in the early 1800s, and despite being made the victims of dramatic settler encroachment, we have maintained our relationship with our territory.

Canadians enjoy the highest standard of living in the Americas. Their economy is built upon and relies on resources that were stolen, and continue to be plundered from Indigenous territories to fuel 100 percent of the natural resource sector. The affluence and standard of living that most Canadians enjoy is a direct result of the exploitation of Indigenous Peoples and our territories. Be it deforestation, mining, or the tar sands, it is the direct result of the hyperexploitation of the natural world. While Canada enjoys its affluence, many Indigenous communities are coping with a poverty imposed on us by the colonial system. Of course, large-scale, multinational economic development (i.e., more resource exploitation of Indigenous territories) is routinely the solution touted by governments, and communities are forced into a false dichotomy: *land versus jobs*. Rarely is there space to discuss small, local, community-based, and community-controlled economic initiatives that strengthen and promote local economies.

In 1987 the United Nations released *Our Common Future*, also known as the Brundtland Report, which introduced environmental issues onto the world's political agenda and highlighted traditional ecological knowledge as a source of understanding that had the potential to liberate humanity from impending environmental disaster.[8] This was nearly thirty years ago! Much of the hope generated by Agenda 21 and the Rio Summit has evaporated, as has interest in the knowledge of Indigenous peoples.

Over a decade ago I was teaching a class with Nishnaabeg elder Robin Green and a scientist at the Centre for Indigenous Environmental Resources in Winnipeg, Manitoba, and our class was discussing what is meant by the term *sustainable development.* The scientist was explaining that it means meeting the needs and wants of humans without compromising the needs and wants of future generations—in other words, allowing development to the maximum threshold, up to that point where it starts to impinge on future generations. I asked Robin if there was a similar concept in Nishnaabeg thought. He thought for a moment and then answered, "No, there isn't." He told me and the class that sustainable development thinking is backwards. What makes sense from a Nishnaabeg perspective is that humans should be taking as little as possible and giving up as much as possible to promote sustainability and promote *mino bimaadiziwin*[9] in the coming generations. We should be as gentle as possible with our Mother. We should be taking the bare minimum to ensure our survival. He talked about how we need to manage ourselves so that life can promote more life.[10] How much are you willing to give up to promote sustainability?

We need to make different decisions. Colonialism is a calculated system that obfuscates truths. Colonialism attempts to cloud issues around exploitation by invoking imposed bureaucracy and government policy. Colonialism is designed to neutralize dissent. It is designed to disconnect us from what we know in our hearts. Colonialism and the capitalist system tell us that we need a lot of stuff to be happy, that our worth as humans is measured by how much money we make and how many goods we have. Yet Indigenous knowledge tells us the exact opposite; it teaches us to live healthy, fulfilling lives that are not based on exploitation and consumption, but on relationships of reciprocity—relationships with the land, our elders, our families, and each other.

---

8. See the "Report of the World Commission on Environment and Development: Our Common Future," (March 1987) http://www.un-documents.net/wced-ocf .htm (accessed 31 December 2012).
9. *Mino bimaadiziwin* means "the good life."
10. Simpson, *Dancing on Our Turtle's Back*, 141.

The most dangerous thinking—so often advocated by settler society—is that economic development is going to solve our systemic problems. While poverty is an extremely serious issue in our communities, this poverty was designed as part of the colonial system and is a result of the colonial exploitation of Indigenous peoples. We've got to address this system.

Every day individual Canadians are given opportunities to make different decisions and to live differently. We can consume less. We can choose alternative energy over oil. We can choose justice over contempt. And we can educate ourselves, and others, differently. We can impact and subvert the system.

The Canadian education system teaches Canadian children very little about Indigenous peoples. What is taught often focuses on past ways of living, some arts and crafts, and maybe some "legends." Indigenous truth-telling—about historic dispossession and cultural genocide and contemporary Indigenous realities—is virtually absent from the curriculum.[11] And thus we are creating generations of Canadians largely blind to the colonial system, who will uphold it because they are unaware of past and present injustices and the need for decolonization.[12] I still see far too many university students taking their first Indigenous studies courses, feeling shocked and betrayed as they learn about a history they've never imagined from a system they are expected to uphold. This needs to change.

I hope that Canadians take it upon themselves to learn a more faithful history of this place and to teach their children to recognize these injustices and to understand how they contribute to the colonial legacy. I hope that Canadians learn to acknowledge whose land they are living on, and to recognize how their presence on our lands interrupts our ways of being in this world. I hope they take up the responsibility to prevent further intrusion into Indigenous lives, and, if called upon, I hope they will lend their support to various expressions of Indigenous nationhood. Ultimately, choosing to resist the colonial system means making some costly choices in

---

11. Some Canadian provinces, like Saskatchewan and Manitoba, have recently incorporated materials on "treaty" into the public school curriculum. Good steps, but we are not where we need to be.

12. See Waziyatawin, *What Does Justice Look Like?*, 173–74, for a similar, Dakota perspective coming from the United States.

mind, spirit, and body—individually and collectively—as we begin to recognize that Canadians are living on top of someone else's home, and as we try to work out the implications of that truth.

My vision for the future is to continue to cultivate a presence that nurtures the relationship between Indigenous peoples and our homelands, one in which Indigenous peoples and Canadians can live liberated and just lives, free of oppression, and in utter awe of the magnificence of creation and the natural world.

Unsettled (continued)

Whose lands are these? Yours? God's? Settler? Indigenous?
Every division a fragile line . . .
if this is your home, where is mine?

Ashamed of skin and story,
every identity a sorry embarrassment
I carry guilt, anger, a muted voice,
claiming: this is not my story.
This was not my choice.

But these were my people.
My ancestors: settlers.

I'm unsettled.
Listening
to creation's moans and groans
to the violence in silence
sifting
through broken pieces
molding, shaping, holding a new story
of home
of land shared
of peoples who dared
to reconcile

We are connected.
We all fall down, ring around roses,
pockets full of poppies, bleeding hearts, forget-me-nots,
arms outstretched
bodies to earth
listening
sharing our stories of loved-lands, lost and found

hearing
knowing
living
another story

Create in me a clean heart, O God.
Unsettle my soul and renew a right spirit within me.
Unquiet me to shout this story's whispers
so that I won't settle for less than your kingdom come
on earth as it is in heaven.

—Rebecca Seiling

3: Opening

. . . in my own land[1]

I am a ghost in my own land
you look through me
as looking into frozen water
I exist in your imagination
as a strong warrior
as a silent elder
as a thing to be admired and respected
but I persist in your mind
as a drunk
as a thief
as an enemy to be feared or despised
I am a ghost in my own land

you fear me
because you do not know me
only when I look like you
can you tolerate me

but
do not presume that the warrior is dead
do not assume that wisdom is buried and gone
I am not a ghost
I live and breathe and love this land
where Creator placed us long ago
the land recognizes me
I am good
I am clean
I have a strong voice
I have good words to share
I am not a ghost in my own land

—Cheryl Bear (Nadleh Whut'en)

---

1. The inspiration for this poem came from a conversation with Virgil Dawson
(Kwagiulth and Yinka Dene).

3

WHERE CREATION WAS BEGUN:
NASCA AND INDIGENOUS REGENERATION

By Frances Kaye

As the Dakota teacher Ohiyesa (Charles Eastman) tells it, "At the beginning of things, He-Who-Was-First-Created found himself living alone. The earth was here before him, clothed in green grass and thick forests, and peopled with the animal tribes." One day, the Lonely One returned home with a sore foot and drew out from it a long splinter. He threw it away "through the smoke hole of the lodge" and listened as it rattled to the ground, where it immediately turned into a crying baby, Boy Man, "the father of the human race here upon earth."[1] Boy Man had many adventures. He was killed by monsters and resuscitated by his brother in the first sweat lodge of the people. He went to war with the animals and broke forever the peace and fellowship that had first existed in the world.

Francis La Flesche, an ethnographer from a prominent Omaha family, tells a different version of the story in his account of his own school days one hundred fifty years ago at a Presbyterian mission. Here the splinter becomes a baby girl. When one of the more assimilated boys pooh-poohs the story, the others answer that it is no more far-fetched than the Sunday-school tale he prefers—a girl made from a rib and seduced by a talking snake.[2]

---

1. Charles Eastman and Elaine Goodale Eastman, *Wigwam Evenings: Sioux Folk Tales Retold* (Lincoln: University of Nebraska Press, 1990), 125–26.
2. Francis La Flesche, *The Middle Five: Indian Schoolboys of the Omaha Tribe* (Lincoln: University of Nebraska Press, 1978), 58–63.

But perhaps it is the case that the Lakota Oyate and the Pte Oyate—the Lakota Nation and the Buffalo Nation—lived mixed together like mist in Wind Cave in the Black Hills, and only separated and acquired shape when they emerged into this world in the center of the sacred hills. Or perhaps, like the Kiowa people, a nation came into this earth through a hollow log. Or perhaps there was a woman who fell from the sky. And as she fell, ducks caught her and placed her safely on the back of a turtle. And perhaps a muskrat or water beetle dove down and down, to come up with a tiny bit of mud. And from that mud, on the turtle's back, grew a whole world for that woman, a world that is our continent of Turtle Island. And perhaps Raven, the trickster, brought the light.

Always, whatever the sacred narrative of creation in Native North American traditions, what is created is *this* world, *our* particular place, which somehow becomes distinct from the worlds that preceded it. Just so, the fellowship of the Native American Cultural and Spiritual Awareness group (NASCA) is also creating a new world, a new sacred space for the men who have been tossed away, the men who have fallen from the sky, the men who are emerging from the mists of their own dark background, the Native men incarcerated in Tecumseh State Correctional Institution.

TSCI is located on a hill two miles north of Tecumseh, Nebraska, a town oddly named for the Shawnee leader Tecumseh, who lived most of his life 1,200 miles away in Ohio, and who died in Ontario in 1813. Tecumseh's name lives on in irony: William Tecumseh Sherman was the U.S. general to whom is attributed the statement "The only good Indian is a dead Indian." William's parents must have believed it was a strong fighter's name, though Tecumseh was an even better diplomat than general. The white founders of Tecumseh, Nebraska, must have believed in the potency of the name; Tecumseh was to have been a fierce town, not a rural backwater, revived by becoming the site of Nebraska's newest and most secure prison, providing the white town with jobs guarding black and brown men from the state's urban areas and from the reservation neighborhoods in the northeast and northwest.

Here in the Tecumseh SCI, a few people wait in the reception area to visit loved ones. Volunteers slowly gather. All, except for me, are there for the Bible study group. Most prison volunteers are Christians, and I admire these men and women, content in the virtue that they model simply by their presence, without preaching or exhorting, sharing their presence joyfully with all who care to use this alternative to the mind-numbing, grey boredom of prison. I am welcome to join their prayer circle before we enter the prison proper, but they respect my choice to abstain.

We clear the metal detectors—so touchy I have to take off my wedding ring. Finally we proceed down the long tunnel bored into the side of the hill, emerging as if from a hollow log into the turn-key area and finally the high sky of the yard. Hawks fly overhead, but volunteers must be herded like geese in a sheep-dog trial, in tight patterns, by guards faithful to the fiction that everyone who is incarcerated is already and always dangerous. Our real protection is afforded by the men who prize the freedom of mind and spirit that the volunteers facilitate, and who let this be known as a priority to the men who do not.

The desks are pushed along the walls of the big education build-ing, and Mystery Hawk, lead singer, centers the room around the drum. *Oyate Wanji*—one nation. For in here, we are one nation of people (even though I am not Native) trying to live in the way of the pipe and the drum. *Oyate Wanji*—a tribute to the American Indian Movement (AIM) of the 1960s and 1970s, which arose out of the streets and prisons of Minneapolis. AIM took over the Bureau of Indian Affairs building in Washington in 1972, the same year the NASCA brothers launched a federal lawsuit demanding their right to the sweat lodge and the drum, the pipe and the recognition of spiritual and cultural freedom. The Tecumseh prison had not been built then, but some of our elders are veterans of that successful struggle, which resulted in a 1974 judgment recognizing those rights. One of the men, *Hehaka*, is our rememberer, the one who knows exactly what happened and who made it happen. That con-sent decree, won by the men of NASCA, opened all U.S. prisons to the sweat lodge and proved that the power is not lost, has never been lost, and can prevail even in the *maza tipi*—the iron lodge—and the whitestream society's justice system. The Lonely One and Boy Man live in the sweat lodge they created, live within these walls and the walls of all U.S. prisons that incarcerate Native men.

The drum plays until we are all in, as many of us as can come, as will come, this night. And then Danny gives us a short prayer. (The young guard who has been assigned to watch us has to be asked a couple of times to stand up in respect for our ceremony.) Danny asks *Tunkasila*, Grandfather, to watch over our families, our children, and our elders, and gives thanks that we are all able to be together in the circle.

When the Kiowas entered the world through the hollow log, there was a pregnant woman who got stuck. So, the Kiowas are a small nation. NASCA, too, is a small nation, Native populations having been reduced by something like 90 percent since 1492. But Native men, proportionately, are a larger nation inside the prisons than outside. African American and Native men tend to be incarcerated at five to six times the average rate for the state, nearly ten times the average rate for whites. This disproportion holds true in Canada, as well, especially on the prairies. Part of the disproportion is the result of selective enforcement. Study after study has shown that black and Native individuals are more likely than the average citizen to be stopped by police, more likely to be charged if stopped, more likely to be arrested if charged, more likely to be jailed if arrested, more likely to be convicted and imprisoned. In addition, centuries of cultural genocide have inflicted all manner of damages on Indigenous communities. Disease, famine, dispossession, and relocation are all demoralizing, but the most potent destroyer has been the stealing of children, first for the boarding and residential schools that were supposed to "kill the Indian and save the man," and more recently for out-of-home placements in foster care, group homes, and adoptive families.

Child stealing was done in good faith by "friends of the Indian"— by people like General Colby, who picked up a tiny baby girl, a survivor of the 1890 massacre at Wounded Knee, and brought her home as a kind of souvenir to his wife, Clara.

What in the world could he have been thinking? He thought he was establishing dominance and continuing the killing by more "civilized" means; he thought he was giving this child a chance to escape the burden of growing up to be an "Indian"; he thought he was giving his independent wife something to take her mind off his failings. He probably did not ever think that he was impoverishing this child by taking her from a loving extended family—her mother had perished at the hands of his soldiers—and he almost certainly did not bother to think that she would be treated with disrespect by men in his own family, and that she would come to be known as Lost Bird. And he did not need to think that the stealing of children is a form of genocide, one that would effectively quiet all Indian claims to land in the United States. For if there are no Indians—if they are all assimilated and have no Native identity that white men are obliged to respect—there

General Colby with Zintkala Nuni (Little Lost Bird), found on Wounded Knee Battlefield, South Dakota, ca. 1890

can be no Indian land. And if there is no Indian land, generals need not look like bullies, killing women and children, fleeing through the snow. And that way of thinking was not a conspiracy, just an article of faith. How far more harmonious it seemed to make Native children into "make-believe white men," as the followers of Francis La Flesche's father, Joseph—Iron Eyes—called themselves in their attempt to hold onto their land and not be deported four hundred miles away to Oklahoma as their Ponca kinsmen had been.

Oh yes—many of the nineteenth- and twentieth-century American statesmen and generals and educators did an exceptional job of convincing themselves that they were taking children and not land, that they were saving children and not stealing them. But they were wrong. The Omahas were not exiled to Oklahoma, but their land was allotted, and it did not take long for most of it to be lost to taxes, or unscrupulous white neighbors, or both. Most of what remains is leased out to predominantly non-Native farmers, leaving only fractionated lease checks for the children. And if the children cease to be recognized as Omahas, then even the fiction of the leases may disappear. Yes, stealing the children was about stealing the land.

The loss of the land and the loss of the children shreds family relationships and warps a person's sense of self-worth. As Laguna Pueblo novelist Leslie Marmon Silko has her protagonist realize:

> He wanted to scream to Indians like [his friends with whom he has been drinking] that the white things they admired and desired so much—the bright city lights and loud music, the soft sweet food and the cars—all these things had been stolen, torn out of Indian land. . . . The people had been taught to despise themselves because they were left with barren land and dry rivers. But they were wrong. It was the white people who had nothing; it was the white people who were suffering as thieves do. . . .[3]

Still, it is the Indians who are taught to despise themselves. Many of the brothers in NASCA grew up all or in part in boarding schools or group homes, or with foster or adoptive families. Anxiety, learned helplessness, mistrust (especially of authority figures), and an exaggerated *carpe diem* frame of mind are all logical outcomes of such an upbringing and good indicators of problems in adulthood. It is hard to have healthy self-confidence and self-esteem if you grew up with the unspoken knowledge that while *you* might be worth "rescuing"—and even that is debatable if you are placed in an abusive home—your family and culture are so defective that you need to be rescued from *them*. Even many of the men who grew up in their own families found their lives disrupted by the intergenerational trauma inherited from parents who, institutionalized as children, had no positive role models for being mom or dad. And many of the guys see their own families disrupted by their own incarceration, often propelling their own children into foster care, or into gangs or other self-destructive behaviors, picking up the same anxiety, learned helplessness, mistrust, and snatch-and-grab ideas that landed their dads in prison. Silko is describing troubled Native World War II veterans, but her words have relevance for the men in NASCA and for other Native people who struggle.

> The white people would shake their heads, more proud than sad that it took a white man to survive in their world and that these Indians couldn't seem to make it. At home the people would blame liquor, the Army, and the war, but the blame on the whites would never match the vehemence the people would keep in their own bellies, reserving the greatest bitterness and blame for themselves, for one of themselves they could not save.[4]

---

3. Leslie Marmon Silko, *Ceremony* (New York: Viking, 1977), 204.
4. Ibid., 253.

Is NASCA, this small nation, then, a depressing place to visit? Not at all. For here, at Tecumseh, creation is begun again at every meeting of NASCA, at every sweat ceremony, at every friendly interchange between brothers, at every small, private decision to do good in the course of a day, a year, a sentence. The splinter is withdrawn from the foot and rattles down, a younger brother. The woman falls again from the sky. The Lakota Oyate and the Pte Oyate enter the world and take their places. The Kiowas emerge again from the log. And Raven brings the light. Some of the healing is human decency, offered forth in a place whose rules seem devised to stamp out all empathy and good will. The brothers take care of each other, joking, giving encouragement, teasing about the group's sports teams, sharing their writings in the circle. Jesus, a man with Mexican, Native, and white family, is particularly adept at generosity: art lessons for newcomers, information about a federal program offering tax breaks to employers who hire recently released ex-felons, connections that allow the community to view the prison with sympathy, or simple letters of encouragement to another brother's son who is getting himself in trouble.

At every meeting this informal healing takes place, but at the center of the group's re-creation, the group's healing, are the traditional ways of the sweat lodge, the pipe, the drum, the medicine wheel. While a few of the men, usually the elders, have grown up around these ways and are conversant with them, many of the brothers have grown up in urban areas, sometimes in non-Native households, and have only come to learn Indigenous life-ways in prison. Because of the need created by the high rate of Native incarceration, many healers, including those who have themselves done time, serve as prison counselors. James Waldram, a medical anthropologist, wrote *The Way of the Pipe*, exploring how Indigenous men found restoration in Prairie prisons. After discussing the traumas of colonization and how it leads to behaviors that can result in incarceration, he provides four case studies of inmates who healed themselves through the teachings of the spiritual leaders. Thus, "Jeff" says,

> The Creator came into my life as a spiritual awakening in the [sweat] lodge. And you know this kind of disturbed me because I knew that this is for real and the path that I was on wasn't what I wanted. That's probably why I was in there in the first place. I took lives because I disrespected my own life and

all living life. . . . And I couldn't handle living violence anymore,
prison life, the screwed up way. . . .[5]

Jeff participated more and more fully in Cree spirituality, and,
learning from the elders and the ceremonies, he was able to turn
away from violence, to sacrifice through fasting, to enfold the conventional prison psychological treatment into his spiritual context,
and to achieve a successful parole. The way of the pipe leads not to
material success but to a rededication to the life of the people and
the land, to a lifting of the intergenerational trauma of colonization,
to an acceptance of one's basic human dignity, and, eventually, to
change in a good way.

Tonight at the meeting we have our usual business. The men
are finalizing everyone's duties for the upcoming powwow. The
activities coordinator and the early morning lieutenant have to
be informed that some routines will differ from that of an ordi-
nary Saturday. I ask permission to write this essay, explaining that
a "small honorarium" will come to us for it. Myst wonders if that
could be seed money for an external fund to pay for outside dancers
and speakers at powwows and symposia, so that they would not
have to wait ninety days for a government check. We will have to
find out if this is permissible.

Talk turns to the fall symposium, to be held in six months. The
men have chosen a book of Sioux tales compiled by Ohiyesa, the
Dakota physician Charles Eastman, and his New England-born
wife, Elaine Goodale (both of whom witnessed the Wounded Knee
massacre). Working with a couple of drama students from the university, they are planning to transform the tales into plays to be presented at the symposium: slam drama—a new way to embody and
pass on the old ways, both to the men and to our outside guests.

Mitakuye oyasin (usually translated as "all my relations" or "we
are all related") ends many prayers in Dakota or Lakota, and it is
quite literal. Not only does it attest to the basic brotherhood of the
NASCA men, it also includes the guests, other volunteers, my students, me, and even the activities coordinator and the sometimes
suspicious guards. The powwows are open to NASCA members

---

5. James B. Waldram, *The Way of the Pipe: Aboriginal Spirituality and Symbolic Healing in Canadian Prisons* (Peterborough, ON: Broadview Press, 1997), 187.

and to all (except family and friends, who are only allowed into the prison on visiting days) who are willing to come, and who can pass the state-required security check. Women, especially, are welcome, to balance the circle with the complementary powers of the universe represented by masculine and feminine. And so, I will come and try to dance in the small steps appropriate for a woman elder, even though I am not Native. And the fringes of my shawl will tremble like the leaves on the sacred Sundance tree, the *waga can.*

Cover of a NASCA fall program, 2011

Tonight it is time for us to leave. Myst and the other singers put away the drum and the drumsticks. The rest of us move the tables and chairs back into their classroom positions, take down the posters of Tatanka Iyotaka (Sitting Bull) and Mahpiya Luta (Red Cloud), and put the books and the coffee urn back in their proper places. For these moments, the grey fog that is the prison has solidified into these men who, like the Raven and other Trickster figures, are both creator and destroyer, hero and fool. The men are one nation, at least for this time, and when you look at them you see that this is where creation was begun. The men walk with me as far as the Religion Building, where I wait for the Bible study group so we can be escorted out together. Perhaps Raven brought the light to them, too, and perhaps a splinter became a child, but the stories they tell will be different from ours, and perhaps one day it would be good for them all to hear ours.

Come back, good as old

Lying face-up in the park, too frozen to uncurl my toes
    and move
Wanting something to numb the pain, to take me, my love,
    my people
Away and back   way back

How did we get to this place?
Place of despair and—please, no overstatement—seven unending
generations of colonial, settler—let us fix you good—trauma.
Waking up to cold waters on the face—no cedar brush here—abuse
in our stomach and chants in our soul of what could have been
Where are we? Who are we?
We don't remember our names; and most of the time I don't want to.
It hurts.

Can we find a safe place? Where?
Did we fall far from the sky, from earth, from grace
or was it really us that fell? Did someone, something, some . . .
    you know . . . push us . . . keep pushing us?
We need a safe place, but who are we?
Given names that gift, names with power and responsibility
I can't even remember my name . . . he doesn't either.
We need a helper, an elder, sister in spirit, someone.

Don't look at us
With eyes full of fear and pity; it's not weakness, it's not biological,
    trust me
You too would sniff a dreamy bag, drink the warmth down,
find some body, a few bodies to get lost and found in

Tortured memories drive us out of ground
    Relocated to storm clouds and city culverts

What about you? Do you know where you are? Do you know how
     you got here?
What's your name?
     No, not that name
     your real name

How do we get to that place of healing and find the medicines?
Where are you Sizee Klee?
     Creator?
     Jesus?
     Whatever.
Who are you?
Do you know our names?
How can you?
     Look at us . . .
We've got artists and poets, yeah, yeah
carvers, lawyers and plenty of MBAs, ay ay
Fancy dance, jingle dance, ghost dance and more.
     O the peoples are rising
But don't you see the empty cupboard, coke 'n crap poverty?
Beautiful red divines littered on the highway, chewed up in maple(s)?
The babes pickled with alcohol?
Little ones ponied with guns, missing their
daddies
and mommies,
uncles and aunties and whole communities
They've been clearcut, cut off, demoralized, shot down,
they've fallen asleep in Pigeon Park, are filling that tank, that pen,
     that morgue . . .
Do you know those names?

UN Report—Canada is once again ranked amongst the top eight
nations in standard of living. Small footnote. This excludes First
Nations, ranked seventy-eighth.

Remember Charlie? That man from Babine, from Thompson,
     from Siksika.

71

Honest inside-out, a man of his word, faithful to that One, hated
wrong with passion. And he lost everything.
wife
children
pit-house, smokehouse, longhouse,
three thousand salmon, five hundred moose,
a grandfather buffalo, a cousin named horse.
Moved to the city, and now he hears, sometimes, all the time,
"What did you do to mess up so badly?"

Sometimes he thinks he sees you
    Thunderbird splitting the sky
    Thunderbird swooping down to give a kiss
    Thunderbird calling
        Gayla gyakun Niki Gikumi
        Come to me
        Not beyond hope
            with you, for you

Not sure.
Look at them doves.
They got it all . . . and together, mostly at least.
Three-quarters of the circle (and more) occupied
    almost every medicine resourced-extracted-exploded
Blessed . . . blessed . . . blessed . . . and not . . . blessed.
    Ravens never were.
When will it end?

So tired   I just want to sleep.
But the sandwich lady from the nearby church wakes me up,
Puts an umbrella over me, hot chocolate in my mouth
She uncurls her toes with ease
Wants to talk to   to   to me.
Good lady
    yet she doesn't know where she is, doesn't know her name.
I want her to go away
I want it all to go away

to die
even a trickster death
then come back to me,
good as old.

—Cheryl Bear (Nadleh Whut'en)
with Steve Heinrichs

Tels'tmat (hearing news)

Silence was uttered, "A voice for those," they said, "with no chords
    of their own";
Quiet pierced them; it was so long since their speech had been made.
Life had come, though substance was gone; all creation remorsed
    it seemed.
The Word oft heard so seldom seemed real; was Truth, after all,
    meant for others?
Perhaps one day they'd comprehend—in part, if not the whole;

Knowing the way, so clear to some, for others had been a path
    not understood.
Yet the land had taught and life had changed; in the end the
    Spirit wind was heard.
Wind had called, voices were heard; upper dwelling stricken with fire!
Hearing this at last they asked, perceiving now what had not
    been learned.

That day so clear that they'd believed, their ears decisively attuned.
As sight was sought, the loss came clear.
Was it faith, or grace, gift and generosity, or the loss of verbosity?

Now eyes were opened, and ears had adapted; hearts no longer
    held in fear;
They had found what others heard; now through tears the two
    connected.

All knew then it was not voice that lacked these many long years;
It was ears that could hear.

                    —*Terry Leblanc (Mi'kmaq)*

4

SMALL STEPS TOWARD RECONCILIATION:
HOW DO WE GET THERE FROM HERE?

By Neil Funk-Unrau

> The dominant group in any nation state often resorts to
> nostalgia, to mental or cultural ellipses, and to general
> forgetfulness in search of meanings and definitions to serve
> its own ideological needs of the moment.
> —*Amritjit Singh, Joseph T. Skerrett Jr.,*
> *and Robert E. Hogan*[1]

Two very different peoples received special dispensation from the Canadian government in the early 1870s and were granted "reserves" of land in the open spaces of what was to become the Province of Manitoba. One group was pushed out of the path of oncoming settlers and onto small, relatively isolated patches of land, out of sight and out of mind. The other was welcomed with open arms and encouraged to find a place where they could sink roots and grow and prosper. Two different stories, two separate histories, mingled at their edges but remained very distinct at their cores; one increasingly marginalized in a rapidly changing society while the other grew and prospered.

I grew up on the northern edges of the "West Reserve" of southern Manitoba, the second area of land granted to the Mennonite

---

1. As quoted in Susan Dion, *Braiding Our Histories: Learning from Aboriginal People's Experiences and Perspectives* (Vancouver: UBC Press, 2009), 3.

newcomers. The West Reserve (west of the Red River) was given to the Mennonites as an additional land grant when the original Mennonite settlers realized how much more fertile this plot was than the original "East Reserve" grant. I grew to adulthood blissfully unaware of the parallel history of the people who were not given more fertile land when their own reserves proved to be inadequate for sustenance.

Only many decades later am I confronted with the dilemma expressed so well by the Mennonite poet, Di Brandt, who grew up in the same West Reserve:

> It is impossible for me to write the land. This land that I love, this wide, wide prairie, this horizon, this sky, this great blue overhead, big enough to contain every dream, every longing. . . . How I loved you, how I love you, how you keep me alive. This stolen land, Metis land, Cree land, buffalo land. When did I first understand this, the dark underside of property, colonization, ownership, the shady dealings that brought us [Mennonites] here, to this earthly paradise?[2]

Today, we hear the call to reconcile across the wide gulf between these parallel histories. But is authentic dialogue and reconciliation even possible across this Indigenous-settler divide? Can the settlers ever pierce the veils of nostalgia and forgetfulness to truly understand the perspective of those without our privileges? Can Indigenous peoples, with the strength of their knowledges, laws, and traditions, move past the societal, communal, and individual barriers they face to engage deeply with those who have all the advantages (certainly all the economic advantages)? And, if this is even possible, how can we get across the gap from here? This article represents my attempt to struggle with these questions and my belief in the importance of continuing this difficult journey, despite all obstacles.

Uncovering harsh truths

What does it mean to cross power imbalances and social divides to move toward reconciliation? One part of the answer lies in the

---

2. Di Brandt, *So this is the world & here I am in it* (Edmonton: NeWest Press, 2007), 1–2.

capacity and willingness to hear and understand uncomfortable and unsettling truths. In the last two decades, Mennonite and other faith communities across Canada have begun to explore this concept and this practice. Slowly and tentatively, a dialogue is beginning. Slowly but surely, those who spent too much time and energy talking are learning to listen, while those who have been silenced too long are beginning to speak.

We are beginning to learn, to listen, and to hear the uncomfortable stories of past relations as we become more aware of the harm committed through the government- and church-run Indigenous residential schools. One of the most destructive expressions of the dominance of settler society over Indigenous society was the coercive imposition of an educational system designed to isolate Indigenous youth from their families, communities, and lifestyles in order to change them into exemplary Christian-Canadian citizens.[3] By isolating the children from their families, communities, and cultures, the authorities of the day were also able to more easily isolate the next generations from the lands and resources cherished by their ancestors.

This imposed educational system—with devastating parallels in the United States and Australia—began with the development of church-run residential and day schools as early as the mid-1600s. After 1880, the Canadian government took control of Aboriginal schooling and began a concentrated effort to get Aboriginal children into government-sponsored residential facilities. At the height of the residential school system, the Canadian government funded approximately eighty institutions, all run through the day-to-day administration of church agencies (primarily Catholic, Anglican, Methodist, and Presbyterian, although a few Mennonite-run schools were also involved). Most of these schools continued to operate until the 1950s or later, with the last ones closing in the 1990s.[4]

---

3. For a more comprehensive summary of the history of Indigenous residential schools, see J. R. Miller, *Shingwauk's Vision: A History of Native Residential Schools* (Toronto: University of Toronto Press, 1996), and J. S. Milloy, *"A National Crime": The Canadian Government and the Residential School System, 1879 to 1986* (Winnipeg: University of Manitoba Press, 1999).

4. It should be noted that hundreds of thousands of Indigenous children were also forced to attend Indian day schools. Though children could go home to

Father (Quewich) with his three children at the Qu'appelle Residential School, Saskatchewan, ca.1900

The impact of the Indigenous residential school system extends far beyond the lives of the individual survivors. Many of these survivors returned home years later, completely alienated from their home communities and from the outside world, unprepared to thrive in either setting. Some communities lost entire generations to these schools—generations unable to pass on the ideals, the parenting skills, and the survival skills of their ancestors. The loss of these generations has had a profound impact through the decades, an impact that has been passed on from residential school survivors to their children, their grandchildren, and to their wider community networks. It exhibits itself through increased alcoholism, drug

---

their families each school day, they suffered similar forms of cultural genocide and physical/sexual/spiritual abuse in the classroom as the children in residential schools.

dependency, violence, suicide, and various patterns of abuse and family dysfunction.

One significant response to this devastating history, based upon the conviction that reconciliation is only possible through the courage to speak and to hear the truth about the pain and suffering, has been the creation of a Truth and Reconciliation Commission.[5] Since 2010, commissioners have crossed the country, gathering statements from residential school survivors and staff at large national events and smaller community gatherings, collecting documentation and doing research into this history, and presenting these truths through public conferences, presentations, and publications. For those who choose to tell their stories, this act of speaking out can become a first step toward healing. For those who hear these stories, many for the first time, the act of hearing can become the first step toward reconciliation.

However, hearing and understanding new truths can only take us part of the way. The stories of the individual survivors and their communities must be seen as part of a larger story of colonialism and dispossession, a story that began before the schools were established and still continues today in more subtle forms. This struggle to connect individual and communal hardships with the evils of a system of oppression was also evident in the work of what may be the most famous of all truth and reconciliation commissions, the commission that facilitated the transformation of South Africa from an apartheid state into a more democratic and open society. In the midst of the many stories and testimonies of the abuses of apartheid, commissioners struggled with the dilemma of how to take that step from truth about individual injustices to societal reconciliation.

A widely read cartoon of that time portrays the commissioners and their staff at the edge of a deep chasm, beside a signpost labeled "TRUTH," clustered around a road map. On the other side of the chasm is another signpost, labeled "RECONCILIATION." The unanswered question in the caption of the cartoon remains with us still: "How do we get there from here?"

---

5. One common misperception is that the TRC is a government commission. It is not. The commission is an independent body financed from the legal settlement negotiated by survivors, mainline churches, and the government.

Acknowledgement and responsibility

We cannot simply hear the harsh truths and then walk away from them untouched. Once received, the stories of past dispossessions and impositions must be acknowledged and accepted as part of the settlers' story, as well as the story of the colonized. One public and at times ritualized way of doing this is through some sort of public expression of remorse and apology, a process that has become a widely accepted way of responding to historic wrongs and attempting to renegotiate unjust social relations.

Such a public apology can represent a potential turning point in the relationship between Indigenous and settler societies, but the long-term impact of this attempted renegotiation of relations is dependent on the extent to which the apology succeeds in fulfilling certain tasks. First, an apology acknowledges a particular situation as morally and politically wrong and unjust. Second, the event is named in terms that clearly indicate the apologizer's remorse and acceptance of responsibility for the damage done. Third, while naming the wrongdoing and taking responsibility for it, the apologizer offers assurance that the wrongdoing will not be repeated by expressing a commitment to changed behavior. Fourth, the apology may or may not offer some form of reparation or compensation.

In this context, a public apology provides the opportunity to retell and acknowledge the story of past dispossessions to show that we as settlers can begin to understand the impact of historic losses. Through the public expression of remorse and acceptance of responsibility for the wrongdoing, the apology can affirm a mutually acceptable moral norm to show that this was wrong and must not be allowed to happen again. Then, the offering of some form of mutually acceptable amends through a process of restitution and reparation could also serve as a negotiated symbolic affirmation of the new understanding.

As general public awareness about the damage done by the residential school system and by the legacy of European colonialism grew, various faith communities and other public institutions responded with such statements of remorse and apology. Perhaps the best-known example of a Canadian faith-based apology for the church's role in the legacy of colonialism is the apology offered by the United Church of Canada (UCC) in 1986, but this was only one of a number of similar responses.[6] In 1992, the Mennonite Central Committee acknowledged the five hundred years since the arrival of Christopher Columbus with a statement asking "First Peoples" for forgiveness for centuries of conquest and domination.

As the silence about residential school abuses was broken and survivors began to demand compensation and justice, other churches and non-faith public institutions added their words of remorse and apology for these specific institutions. Among others, the Missionary Oblates of Mary Immaculate, a Catholic order, presented their apology in 1992; the Primate of the Anglican Church of Canada followed suit in 1993; and the Presbyterian Church of Canada issued their own statement of remorse in 1994. The Moderator of the UCC also presented another "Statement of Repentance" in 1997, drawing attention to their own specific role in the life and work of residential schools.[7]

All of these statements stand as more or less successful attempts. The words used and the ways in which these words were delivered to acknowledge the wrongs committed indicate remorse for the damage done and commit to building a new relationship with Indigenous society. But how much meaning can we really attach to these good words? While this form of public declaration can create the space for mutual vulnerability and reconciliation, it can also be distorted and misused, especially if their intent is to present a favorable self-image, and nothing more. In the words of one residential school survivor speaking on a reconciliation panel in the fall of 2011, "An apology can be a very good thing—for the apologizer. It really does nothing for me!"

The Canadian government's apology to Indigenous residential school survivors, presented by Prime Minister Stephen Harper on June 11, 2008, provides a classic example of a statement that says

---

6. The story of the development and delivery of this statement is told in Stan McKay and Janet Silman, "A First Nations Movement in a Canadian Church," in *The Reconciliation of Peoples: Challenge to the Churches*, eds. Gregory Baum and Harold Wells, (New York: Orbis, 1997), 172–83.
7. For a more complete discussion of the series of Canadian church apologies to Indigenous peoples, see Neil Funk-Unrau, "The Re-Negotiation of Social Relations Through Public Apologies to Canadian Aboriginal Peoples," *Research in Social Movements, Conflict and Change* 29 (2008): 1–19.

all the right things on the surface but ultimately falls short due to the lack of concrete action designed to effect reconciliation with Indigenous communities. Harper's willingness to acknowledge and recite the harms done through the residential school system represented an important step—the clearest federal affirmation of a painful history as the victims of that history have come to understand it.

However, the statement fell short of fully acknowledging the colonial history behind the residential school legacy by locating the oppression of Canadian Indigenous peoples as an event in the past, separate from the ongoing context of colonial violence and dispossession. Harper's statement attempted to articulate a clear, distinct break between the assimilationist policies of the past and the responses of the enlightened government of our time, thereby covering up the underlying, hidden connection between the past and the present.[8] One year later, at the Pittsburgh G20, Harper took a further step backward when he pronounced that Canada, unlike the world's other great powers, had "no history of colonialism."[9]

The portrayal of contemporary Indigenous people in the apology is also limited by its portrayal of their culture as historically lost and disconnected. Nothing is said about Indigenous claims to land and resources, or to some form of Indigenous nationhood within (or alongside) the Canadian nation-state. Nothing is said about the continued situation of social and economic disparity, which was partially caused and exacerbated by the residential school system, but still exists despite the repudiation of this system. In the end, the statement paints a more benevolent picture of a Canadian state remorseful over its role in the loss of Indigenous culture, but also of a state that asserts control over a subordinate Indigenous population and over Indigenous lands, refusing to negotiate any more equal sharing of natural and economic resources and political power.

---

8. An excellent critique of the federal apology is found in Matthew Dorrell, "From Reconciliation to Reconciling: Reading What 'We Now Recognize' in the Government of Canada's 2008 Residential Schools Apology," *English Studies in Canada* 35:1 (2009): 27–45.

9. The refusal to acknowledge the impact of colonialism within the apology statement is also noted in Pauline Wakeham, "Reconciling 'Terror': Managing Indigenous Resistance in the Age of Apology," *American Indian Quarterly* 36:1 (2012): 1–33.

Reconciliation—how do we get there from here?

Every journey begins with a first few steps, but it only becomes a significant journey if those steps move in the right direction. This "right direction" may be difficult to determine when confronted with the term, widely used in public discourse today, *reconciliation.* "Reconciliation" has been popularized and romanticized as the "happily ever after" ending of every dispute, and the almost painless answer to every interpersonal or social conflict. In the end, we are still confronted with the seemingly unbridgeable gap between the ideal and the real, between the heartfelt words and the meaningful action. So, how do we really get there from here?

Reconciliation is not the deliberate effort to forget the past, to let it all go and move on. Reconciliation is not simply a demand for an apology or an offer of forgiveness, as if a few well-chosen words can now negate a history of injustice. Reconciliation is a once-and-for-all settlement of accounts, as if each iota of pain and suffering can be added up and totaled to balance the ledger of loss and compensation.

It is much easier to visualize what reconciliation is not than what it is, but we can begin to visualize the first few steps in the right direction. These first few steps must include the courage to hear the stories and the painful histories that undergird current settler-Indigenous relations. These first few steps can include statements of remorse and acknowledgement, statements that create a space for new relations to arise. But this is still only the beginning of a new journey, and no one can know where and how we will continue to move forward as we seek to bring together our parallel histories to create a new and more enriching combined story.

So what would this combined story of reconciliation look like? Indigenous and Mennonite-Christian traditions all include rich images of living in peace and harmony with respect for all peoples and all things. I hesitate to lay out a detailed vision, however, because ultimately such a vision must be a mutual one, which arises out of a mutual commitment to deep dialogue and the renunciation of colonial barriers and privileges that we now take for granted. Before we can lose ourselves in some inspirational vision of two different peoples living together as sisters and brothers, each sharing from their unique gifts and abundance and each receiving with gratitude the gifts shared with them, we will need to commit ourselves to those first few steps.

As a small child, I loved the open spaces of the southern Manitoba Red River floodplain—the room to run and the clear, fresh air. As a more mature adult whose vision is blocked by city skylines and lungs filled with the smells of the city, I walk more slowly now. But I treasure the small steps that brought me closer to those who cherished this land before the settlers came. For me, these small steps included the opportunity to visit and briefly live within a few of the semi-isolated Indigenous communities of northern Manitoba. More recently, these steps led me to an inner-city university setting with ample opportunity to meet and get to know the Indigenous students and academics who congregate there. May these small steps continue to push me forward into closer and deeper dialogue as we acknowledge the painful past, take responsibility for our part in it, and together seek to discern the unknown shape of reconciliation in this, our time and place.

Awtiget (a clear path)

It started some years, a while ago,
A journey, one hundred or fifty, uncertain to know;
What track, none knew, uncertain steps they took to right
  some wrong,
Few felt a crook it had taken so long.

Who is secure when the Guide is sought? He who makes clear all
  error and fault.
Was injustice the cause now so long forgot, as time's tide swirled
  and swallowed it up?
We remorsed this burden now carried by each; no other could
  take it—it was ours.
Seeking the Spirit we inquired which path, which way to advance?

Had he made the path we had taken to here? Perhaps.
Surely though, we had discovered at last, that our interest
  was together,
both public and proud,
Whether Menno newcomer, traditional brown, or those from
  the Metissage.

The trail we must take lies both ahead and behind,
and uncertainty doubtless will hang like a veil,
Yet hope compels us to journey ahead, for onward to generations,
  we must travel.

As at last it is certain—it's all we could know—together the road,
together we prevail.

—*Terry Leblanc (Mi'kmaq)*

PART 2

UNSETTLING
THEOLOGY

Talking Waters[1]

Confidential: Gentlemen of the Senate[2]
Regarding Exploration of the West 1803

First: Encourage the Indian to abandon hunting
and apply them to the raising of stock
to agriculture and domestic manufacture
and thereby prove to themselves that less land and labor
will maintain them better than in their former mode
    of living

The extensive forests necessary in the hunting life
will then become useless and they will see advantage
in exchanging them for the means of improving their farms
increasing their domestic comforts

Saint Louis Missouri
not home but
in the foreshortened measurements of history
halfway there

Between dreams
I pay out my glances
through the arch

I see whitecaps

It is really the wind on the rivers
but I think the Pacific
has come to greet me

---

1. This poem comes from my upcoming book, *Saarinen's Arch.*
2. President Thomas Jefferson, "Confidential message to Congress concerning relations with the Indians, 18 January 1803," http://www.ourdocuments.gov/doc.php?flash=true&doc=17&page=transcript (accessed 1 January 2013).

Gulls cormorants pelicans
soar and drop
through the glory hole of the gateway
calling calling

I smell smoke
salmon on a spit
wrapped in red kelp

Never did we bow beneath her living archways

Never fell contrite before the setting sun

Only hammered God's six and one
into a wheel rim
bearing wagons west
iron married with oak

In the church
a priest swoops his hands
in the baptismal font
brings up water
sour briny

Three drops from his holy fingertips
gather thunderheads on the child

> *The gift of one's body*
> *the highest form of sacrifice*

No one cries out at this Christ-making

Drums do not pound out the ceremony

No low dust huddles around the feet of women

Perhaps
though it is entirely uncertain
I see a ripple of belief
cross the bodies of believers
who brood over this child

> *Is this the place where crying begins?*[3]
> *Is this the place?*

Now sung to and seduced from his brothers
a young fir is stripped before dawn
by the eldest woman

The sun pole suspended

> *Cedar tree*
> *Cedar tree*
>
> *we have it in the center*
> *we have it in the center*
>
> *when we dance*
> *when we dance*
>
> *we have it in the center*
> *we have it in the center*
>
> *Cedar tree*
> *Cedar tree*[4]

---

3. *A-nea thibiwa hana, A-nea thibiwa hana—Thi aya ne, Thi aya ne* (The place where crying begins, The place where crying begins—the death mound, the death mound) is a Lakota song sung in the sweat lodge. The sweat lodge is a place associated with tears. James Mooney, *The Ghost Dance Religion and the Sioux Outbreak of 1890* (Chicago: University of Chicago Press, 1965), 231.

4. Similar to the Ghost dance, the sun dance is celebrated around a tree set up in the center of a circle. The cedar tree is sacred in many Indigenous traditions. Mooney, *The Ghost Dance Religion*, 228.

Bark mutilated, cross-notched
a crotch for eagle
spirit hole for Thunderbird

> *Lumen Christi*[5]
> *Deo gratias*

This one is mine dove descendent
My beloved on whom my favor rests

> *Guato adaga nyaongum*
> *Guato adaga nyaongum*[6]

> *I scream because I am a bird*
> *I scream because I am a bird*

> *Talyi imahago*
> *Talyi imahago*

> *The boy will rise up*
> *The boy will rise up*

—*Rose Marie Berger*

---

5. Responsorial from the Roman Catholic Easter Vigil, Latin: "The Light of Christ. Thanks be to God."
6. According to Mooney, "This song was composed by Pa-guadal, 'Red Buffalo,' at a Ghost dance held on Walnut creek in the summer of 1893, under the direction of the prophet Pa-ingya, for the purpose of resurrecting Red Buffalo's son, who had recently died." *The Ghost Dance Religion*, 314–15.

5

EARLY DIALOGUE IN THE COMMUNITY OF CREATION

By Randy Woodley (Keetoowah)

The body of meaningful theological dialogue between North American Indigenous peoples and settler-Christians is paltry, and mostly covered with deep scars. Indigenous peoples have been the recipients of the superabundance of Christian thought for over half a millennium, but most of the discourse has been directed *at* us, not *with* us. In spite of these colonial and paternalistic realities, we—both Indigenous and settler peoples—share something unique and primal. We all belong to a great *community of creation*, and we are participating in it together here on Turtle Island. Each of us, including every non-human creature in this land, has a vested interest in seeing this creation community living and working well together.

The kingdom of God as the community of creation

Jesus, in his ancient context of imperial occupation, was also concerned with creation's harmony, and used the phrase *kingdom of God* to communicate this idea. The metaphor was rightly understood by Jesus' audience in contradistinction to the kingdom of Caesar. God's kingdom stood over against the death-dealing ways of the Roman Empire; God's kingdom was a Spirit-filled community living out the Creator's *shalom* purposes on earth. Of course, throughout Christian history this kingdom metaphor has been used to inspire action of diverse and even contradictory kinds, from the early monastic communities to the medieval Crusades, and from the Reformation to modern millennial movements. Fortunately, kingdom discourse has recently taken on a softer, less militant tone, and is referenced by newer Christian movements to describe a faith that is holistic, broad in scope and cooperative in spirit. I believe this fresh path in Christianity is a good starting point for dialogue with Indigenous peoples, for we have wisdom, stories, ceremonies, and theologies that might help us understand in deeper ways what Jesus meant by God's kingdom.

In our globalized and globally warming world, there is an urgent need for the Western church to recognize integrated constructs that encompass reciprocal relationships and the well-being of all things. The rapacious industrial-imperial situation that we live under necessitates a theology that can combat the death-dealing impacts of this "Roman Empire." Perhaps engaging the biblical witness from an Indigenous perspective can help Western Christians do this, enabling us to revision Jesus' kingdom construct into what I call the "community of creation."

Jesus used kingdom language in his context because it made sense to the people and powers to whom he spoke. His kingdom goal was stated simply: "On earth as it is in heaven." In other words, heaven's economy is to be made manifest in creation. And what is heaven's economy? It is *shalom*, a Hebrew term often translated as "peace." But peace doesn't capture the depth of this word. *Shalom* is who the Creator is—the one God, a trinity of persons (from a Christian perspective) dwelling in harmony, mutuality, and deference toward one another and the creation. *Shalom* embodies wholeness, completeness, and love. It is strikingly similar to many Indigenous constructs of "harmony," which emphasize the interconnectedness and interdependency of all things, the need for balance, and the primacy of community.[1] And if that is what Jesus' kingdom was about—radical *shalom* and harmony—it is helpful to translate this metaphor into something like *community of creation*, a phrase infused with Indigenous meaning, which more readily emphasizes

---

1. See my "The Harmony Way: Integrating Indigenous Values within Native North American Theology and Mission" (PhD diss., Asbury Theological Seminary, 2010).

that all living things are participating in this new peace that the Creator is bringing about through Christ. God's *shalom* community includes more than just humans.

This vision of a cooperative community living in *shalom* is referenced throughout the Scriptures, from Genesis to Revelation. Here's one example from the prophet Isaiah:

> In that day the wolf and the lamb will live together; the leopard will lie down with the baby goat. The calf and the yearling will be safe with the lion, and a little child will lead them all. The cow will graze near the bear. The cub and the calf will lie down together. The lion will eat hay like a cow. The baby will play safely near the hole of a cobra. Yes, a little child will put its hand in a nest of deadly snakes without harm. Nothing will hurt or destroy in all my holy mountain, for as the waters fill the sea, so the earth will be filled with people who know the Lord. (Isaiah 11:1-9)

Isaiah gives us a picture of lizards, animals, and humans who "know the Lord" all dwelling together. Traditionally, Western Christian theologies are anthropocentric, placing human beings at the apex of the created order. Isaiah points beyond such, welcoming nonhuman life-forms into his vision.

Recontextualizing kingdom language as "community of creation" can help move Western Christians to understand Scripture through the lens of Indigenous teachings, which can be a key to healing our world. For example, the classic New Testament phrase "For God so loved the world" is most often interpreted as addressing human beings. But a more faithful reading of this text, which a "community of creation" lens facilitates, is that God loves everything, that God sent the Son to heal and redeem the entire creation, human and nonhuman.

Both Indigenous constructs about harmony and Scripture's teaching on *shalom* articulate the Creator's preferred ways of realizing peace and balance. Both set forth practical steps for life as the Creator designed it. They both also require specific action when these life-ways are broken, for restoration and wholeness are the goal. Most importantly, they both originate in gratitude, always remembering that life in all its forms is a gift from the Creator.

One reality, three expressions

As a follower of Jesus from a Keetoowah Indian heritage, my "canon" consists of Scripture, creation, and the "Native American Old Testament."[2] I take all three seriously, and each informs my faith. My own experiences are also crucial as I navigate these traditions. Each tradition has an authoritative message for me from the Creator concerning the way I live my life on earth as I follow the Waymaker. For Westerners, it may be helpful to think of these as "books":

- The Book of Tribal Traditions (the Keetoowah Old Testament)
- The Book of Scripture (the Bible)
- The Book of Creation (nature)

I will try to demonstrate from these authoritative traditions what I mean by the community of creation.

The Book of Tribal Traditions

A story from the Keetoowah:

> In the old days, all the animals, birds, fish, and plants could talk, and everyone lived together in peace and friendship under the delight of the Creator. But after a while, the people began to spread over the whole earth. The animals, birds, fish, and plants found themselves cramped for room. This was bad enough, but then humans began to slaughter the animals needlessly, becoming wasteful. The humans no longer thanked the Creator for supplying food, nor did they thank the animals for feeding their families by giving their lives. Every traditional Cherokee knows that it is considered polite to show gratitude to the Creator, and to the animal when it furnishes its own flesh so people may eat and sustain their lives for another day.

---

2. As Steve Charleston puts it: "The place I stand is the original covenant God gave to Native America. I believe with all my heart that God's revelation to Native People is second to none. God spoke to generations of Native People over centuries of our spiritual development. We need to pay attention to that voice, to be respectful of the covenant." As quoted in "The Old Testament of Native America," in *Native and Christian: Indigenous Voices on Religious Identity in the United States and Canada*, ed. James Treat (New York: Routledge, 1996), 69.

In order to protect themselves from the evil that had come upon them from the no-longer-grateful Cherokee, the animals resolved to hold a council to discuss their common survival. The council was first led by the bears. The Great White Bear asked, "How do the people kill us?"

"With bows and arrows," someone replied.

"Then we must make bows and arrows," declared the leader. But soon the bears found they could not shoot straight with their claws, and they needed their claws to dig for grubs and such. After much debate, the animals decided to bring diseases upon the Cherokee people. The Cherokees began getting sick and were dying from these diseases. After many Cherokees had died, they pleaded with the animals, "Please, we will become grateful, and kill only that which we will eat." But the animals would not take back the diseases they had created to kill the Cherokee.

At the same time, the plants were watching all of these things. They watched as the Cherokee children and old people got sick. Then the strong warriors and even the women began to die. The plants decided to hold a council, and in that council they agreed to provide medicine for the Cherokees. Each night, as the Cherokees would sleep, the plants would come to them in their dreams and show them how to use the plants to heal the diseases that the animals had brought upon them.

The Cherokees recovered and agreed from now on to kill only what they absolutely needed. They also agreed to say a prayer of thanks to any animal that they killed, and to any plant that would be harvested for food or medicine. The Creator was happy with the Cherokees once again, because harmony was restored among all that he had created.

This Keetoowah account of "The Origins of Disease and Medicine" begins with all creation, including human beings, living in harmony with one another and the Creator. They were all equal and everything was very good. The problem arises when the humans overcrowd the rest of creation, disrupt the harmony, begin to overconsume, and become ungrateful. Ingratitude naturally follows greed. The humans believed they could have more resources than anyone else, causing there to be a great imbalance to the world. Christians would describe this greed as sin. Native Americans generally refer to it as broken harmony.

We humans too easily consider ourselves superior to the rest of creation, competing for space with the animals instead of caring for them (and letting them care for us) and sharing the land. Our ingratitude is displayed by refusing to show respect to the nonhumans we kill, by forgetting to give thanks, and by being wasteful in how we use animals. The key assumption of the Keetoowah tale is that, when humans have broken harmony with creation, they have broken harmony with the Creator.

The Book of Scripture

With this Indigenous origin story in mind, let us recall the narrative of Genesis 1 and 2. God creates everything, and calls it not just good, but "really good" (Hebrew *tov ma-ov*). Every creature and living system is excellent, in right order, and as it should be: embodying *shalom*. The Genesis account of creation purposefully shows the Creator taking time to fashion this harmonious cosmos.

God begins work with the celestial water, space, and sky, and then creates the terrestrial waters and the earth, including the plants, trees, and fruits. Next, God watches the seeds from those plants bear in kind. After that the Creator sets the celestial and the terrestrial in rhythm and balance as night and day; as summer, fall, winter, and spring; and as months and years. The waters are then filled with fish and the skies with birds, which all increase. Finally, after bringing animals into being, the Creator speaks human beings, both male and female, into existence.

One gets the sense from this Genesis account that the Creator enjoyed making the world. The work of creation was neither impetuous nor hurried, but deliberate and thoughtful, stretched out over time in order for the Creator to receive maximum pleasure. God's creation-work is leisurely and sedate, unlike most Western capitalist modes of industrial creation. It is also remarkably diverse, unlike the homogeneity of today's mass production systems. Each part of creation is differentiated, unique and fruitful, multiplying after its own kind. And yet, each part is incomplete without the whole;

everything exists in interdependent relationships. The celestials regulate the balance of the terrestrials. The night compels all creation to rest as it brings refreshing coolness. The day provides new life and opportunities like warmth for plants, animals, and humans. The moon regulates the water. The sun regulates the seasons. The seasons regulate annual activities. Everything is in harmony, in balance with each other and with the Creator. It is a picture of a creation in community, a picture in which the audience is being asked to see both the beauty and symmetry of many parts in relation to the whole.

The Genesis and Keetoowah stories agree that there is an interconnectedness of everything God has made. Each part of the created whole comes from the unique mind of the Creator. Each works in relationship with the other, connected through their common origin and location in the universe, with the well-being of all at the center. In both stories, this community of creation seems very good—so good that in Genesis 1 there is a pause after the sixth day in order to celebrate the way things are. In Australia, the Aboriginal Rainbow Elders say the Creator sang on the seventh day, meaning there was a community gathering where celebration was the only priority. This seventh-day creation party acknowledged that everything was living harmoniously: this was God's wonderful and intricate *shalom*, the Harmony Way.

But there are two creation accounts in Genesis (as there are other Keetoowah origin stories). The second story in Genesis 2 illustrates how *shalom* is broken:

> The LORD God placed the human being in the Garden of Eden to tend and watch over it. But the LORD God warned the human being, "You may freely eat the fruit of every tree in the garden—except the tree of the knowledge of good and evil. If you eat its fruit, you are sure to die." Then the LORD God said, "It is not good for the human being to be alone. I will make a helper who is just right." So the LORD God formed from the ground all the wild animals and all the birds of the sky. God brought them to the human being to see what he would call them, and the human being chose a name for each one, giving names to all the livestock, all the birds of the sky, and all the wild animals. But still there was no helper just right for the man. (vv. 15-20)

Note in this text the unstated but clear sense of equality and kinship among all creation. All creatures are made of earth (including organic elements, minerals, water, salts, and trace elements). Humans also share spirit with other creatures, for God breathed life into us all. The result is that both humans and animals are "walking earth," in which our physical self is also spiritual and vice versa. This concept challenges Western dualistic traditions that posit "salvation of the soul" apart from our physical being. The implications of this unity are startling. What we do to the earth, and to other creatures with whom we share the earth, we do to ourselves. Likewise, when we take seriously the healing of the earth, it affects the whole community of creation. God never intended human beings to consider ourselves—theologically or experientially—separate from creation, but rather as part of its community.

The biblical text is also clear that human beings have a special role as "stewards" of creation, or what I call "creation keepers." (In Native communities, a "keeper" of a particular ceremony or tradition is someone who has been properly trained for that task, who has been entrusted with it by the community, and who maintains that responsibility through knowledge, experience, and practice.) We see this, for example, in God's command that humans name the animals. But perhaps this charge is different from what many Western traditions have envisioned; it is not an invitation to *control* animals or the earth, but to care deeply for them in a covenant relationship. The Creator is saying: "Get to know the animals, learn from them, allow them to teach you their ways; make your covenants with them, and take care of them." I like how Job 12:7-10 is rendered in *The Amplified Bible*:

> For ask now the animals, and they will teach you [that God does not deal with His creatures according to their character]; ask the birds of the air, and they will tell you; Or speak to the earth [with its other forms of life], and it will teach you; and the fish of the sea will declare [this truth] to you. Who [is so blind as] not to recognize in all these [that good and evil are promiscuously scattered throughout nature and human life] that it is God's hand which does it [and God's way]? In His hand is the life of every living thing and the breath of all mankind.

Given this charge, the sin of greed portrayed in the Keetoowah story is all the more significant.

The other charge that Genesis gives to humans is to re-create the abundance of nature in the soil through cultivation (something many Indigenous origin stories also speak about). This is an invitation to imitate the Creator by producing plenty from the soil and teaching a thorough understanding of creation. The result is blessing for all. But God's call to "be fruitful, multiply and fill the earth" is not just for humans. It is for all of creation! The implication is that this *entire* community will share the earth, not compete for it.

As in the Keetoowah story, Genesis narrates a "fall." When the serpent enters the garden and persuades the couple to eat from the tree of knowledge of good and evil, *shalom* is broken between God and humanity, between man and woman, and between humanity and the land. God gave humans instructions on how to use the land and explicit instructions on what not to do. Harmony is broken when humans use the land in a way God never intended. Thus the tree of the knowledge of good and evil symbolizes not merely human pride or disobedience (which the western European tradition focuses on), but also the abuse of the land. By misusing the land, human beings disregard God's authority as its sole owner. Humans think they can decide for themselves how it should be cultivated and used (as in the Keetoowah story). Adam and Eve seek to be like God, imagining that they own the garden and can decide for themselves how it should be used. This delusion breaks the intended symbiosis required to produce faith and God's blessing of the land. It throws creation and our relationship with the Creator out of balance. In the wake of this, the relationship changes between humans and animals. The harmonious community that God intended in Genesis 1 disintegrates into a number of distressing narratives—that is, Cain and Abel, Noah, and the Tower of Babel—which show how *shalom* has been fragmented at multiple levels. These stories all reinforce the need to understand and restore God's original design of harmonious reciprocity in the community of creation.

The Book of Creation

It is undeniable today that humanity must learn to share the land, water, and air with the rest of creation if the world is going to heal.

The world's glaciers are melting; land is eroding; there is a worldwide shortage of water; and animal and plant species are going extinct at an exponential rate. Humans must learn once again to make room for all God's creatures on the earth, to leave space for wildlife, domestic animals, birds, fish, trees, and plants, as well as other humans. What would it be like if the bears, or wolves, or big cats suddenly decided that they needed the whole earth for themselves? Many a horror movie has been made from such plots. Yet this is the original sin of humanity: seeing ourselves as more important than all other creatures, and by doing so, viewing ourselves as wiser than God! The Exxon Valdez spill, BP's Deep Horizon explosion, natural gas fracking, and nuclear disasters have become frequent occurrences—the new price we pay because of short-term, greed-based thinking.

Consider the Arctic National Wildlife Refuge (ANWR). It is the largest protected area in the United States, and is considered to be "pristine," comparable to the Grand Canyon or the Everglades. The Gwich'in people have existed for thousands of years in that place, living in reciprocity with the caribou, their primary source of food, clothing, tools, and medicines. Their stories and ceremonies reflect the ancient covenant they have made with these creatures; the Gwich'in say they share half their heart with the caribou, and that each looks after the other. Because they understand the natural rhythms of life in the Arctic, they know that drilling in the porcupine caribou calving grounds will decimate both the herd and their people.[3]

Alaska is one of the last places in North America where Indigenous peoples still survive on subsistence living. But their lifestyle, and the fish and game that support it, are now threatened by increased commercial fishing quotas (as well as illegal harvests);

---

3. It should be noted that not all Indigenous peoples in the area are on the same page: some Inupiat, who have a claim on coastal sections of the ANWR, have been open to drilling, believing that it will not negatively impact the adaptable caribou. Thus far, oil production has not resulted in "prosperity and affluence for the [Inupiat]," but has "brought about an acceleration in the loss of culture, in the rates of debt as well as creating greater economic dependence." T. Haller, A. Blochlinger, M. John, E. Marthaler, S. Ziegler, eds., *Fossil Fuels, Oil Companies and Indigenous Peoples* (Berlin: Lit Verlag, 2007), 213.

Members of the Gwich'in Nation protest the drilling of the Arctic National Wildlife Refuge in Washington, D.C.

sport hunters who fly in from all parts of the world to kill moose, bear, and other big game; the impact of mining pollution on rivers and streams; and significant commercial development. The natural balance of creation in Alaska has been deeply disturbed. As one Native man told me, "Alaska Fish and Game has allowed tens of thousands of moose cows to be harvested over the past decade. Now when I go to hunt for my own family and for the village elders, I can barely find a moose. What rancher in the lower forty-eight slaughters all their cows? No one who wants to remain a rancher; they slaughter their steers, not their cows!"

Remote areas like Alaska could serve as a wake-up call for the rest of North America, or they could be the last dominoes to fall. We still have a lot to learn from one another, from the earth, and from all her creatures. Humanity must learn to use God's space in more reverent ways that invoke community harmony, not individual (or corporate) greed. Each road we construct, each home we erect, each parking lot we build, is a moral decision. Urban areas need to be reimagined with community gardens, plant- and animal-protected areas, renewable energies, buildings that are reused or recycled, and large-scale water catchment and reuse. The earth is being exhausted through our exploitation of her natural resources: her waters are not given time to recharge, her air is polluted, her ozone layer wanes. Humans, if we wish to survive, can no longer afford to produce the wastes that poison air, earth, and water.

Settler Christians, Indigenous peoples and all those who are honest about what they see happening in creation have a great ethical and theological foundation for the pressing work of restoring the community of creation. It is articulated in all three ancient "Books": the primal words of Genesis, our sacred Indigenous origin stories, and the voice of creation. But we need ears to hear.

Talking Waters (continued)

It's Sunday
in downtown Saint Louis
riverfront abandoned
bright quiet hot

Flat-eyed buildings stand
shoulder to shoulder

Streets laid straight by master plainsmen
Ninety degree dry heat on every perfect corner

> *Secondly gentlemen: Multiply trading houses among*
>   *the Indians*
> *and place within their reach those things*
> *which will contribute more to their domestic comfort*
> *than the possession of extensive but uncultivated wilds*[1]

At field level
the prairie grasses
now are buried
pushed under
turned and tilled

> *We clear grasses and trees*[2]
> *We plow and carve the land*

> *Two thousand men and women*
> *scrabbling weeds*

> *Along the low wetlands*
> *along the dyke walls*

---

1. Thomas Jefferson, "Confidential message to Congress, 18 January 1803."
2. "'Clearing the Fields' in The Book of Songs," in *The White Pony: An Anthology of Chinese Poetry*, ed. Robert Payne (New York: John Day Company, 1947), 39.

Only the wind
still carries
seed names

Big Bluestem and Indian Grass
Switchgrass and Little Bluestem

> *In leading the Indian to agriculture*
> *to manufactures and civilization*
> *in bringing together their and our settlements*
> *in preparing them ultimately to participate*
> *in the benefits of our governments*
> *I trust and believe we are acting*
> *for their greatest good*[3]

The priest
smudges his thumb in chrism
he makes the sign of the cross
on the child's forehead

> *In nomine Patris et Filii et Spiritus Sancti*[4]

With his thumb the sun dancer
makes a stripe in blood
across the forehead and lengthwise
on each side of the buffalo skull

The same bloody mark
signs the dancer
to indicate
that he is adopted
by buffalo
as *hunka*
or relative by ceremony

---

3. Thomas Jefferson, "Confidential message."
4. "In the name of the Father, and the Son, and the Holy Spirit."

In spring the vast plains heave and roll[5]
like a green ocean
horse and rider upon them present
a remarkable picture
apparently extending into the air
forty-five to sixty feet high

I reach my hand
down
through the cold baptismal waters
pushing
the head of my godson
toward his false death

And when the waters recede?
When the rivers
again to themselves
become small?

When dry land is again
dry land?

Then houses will again go up
Farmers will plant again
Fruit trees will fruit
Flood plains again will be forgotten

> *Some of my relations*
> *said Short Bull*
> *have no ears*
> *so I have blown them all away*[6]

---

5. Sangres.com, "The Great Prairie Highway," http://www.sangres.com/
national-trails/santafetrail/ (accessed 1 January 2013).
6. From a sermon delivered by Short Bull, a Lakota resistance leader, at Red Leaf
camp on Pine Ridge Reservation, October 31, 1890, after he visited Wovoka,
the messiah who brought the Ghost dance. Short Bull's sermon quickened
the timetable for when God would bring about the next world (one without
whites). "My friends and relations: I will soon start this thing in running order. I

Outside
the picture clouds
the blue white sky
a horn sounds and blasts
and warns of the next flood stage

—Rose Marie Berger

---

have told you that this would come to pass in two seasons, but since the whites
are interfering so much, I will advance the time from what my father above
told me to do, so the time will be shorter. Therefore you must not be afraid of
anything. Some of my relations have no ears, so I will have them blown away."
The final phrase is reminiscent of Jesus: "Those who have ears, let them hear."
As quoted in James Mooney, *The Ghost Dance Religion* (Chicago: University of
Chicago Press, 1965), 30–31.

Circular Lifeways

Past, present and future.
I am told I must progress through one,
know I am in another and hope to live out the next.
When does one begin and the other end?
Beginnings and endings, one in the same.

Life did not begin with humans . . .
    nor will life cease to exist when we have passed to spirit
Origin stories tell of how Turtle Island came to be,
how Earth Mother was populated with beings . . .
    animal beings, plant beings, spirit beings, human beings.
Maheo'o was, is and will forever be.
A stagnant linear HIStory or "re-visioning" an ever changing reality.

—Vonåhe'e (Northern Cheyenne)

From Garden to Tower:
Genesis 1–11 as a Critique of Civilization and an Invitation to Indigenous Re-Visioning[1]

By Ched Myers

I will tell you something about stories [he said]
They aren't just entertainment.
Don't be fooled.
They are all we have, you see,
all we have to fight off
illness and death . . .

Their evil is mighty
but it can't stand up to our stories.
So they try to destroy the stories
let the stories be confused or forgotten.
They would like that . . .
because we would be defenceless then . . .
—*Leslie Marmon Silko (Laguna Pueblo)*[2]

O rigin stories matter. They tell us who we are, how we got this way, and what our responsibilities are to our collective past,

---

1. This is an abbreviated and revised version of a piece that appeared in *The Season of Creation: A Preaching Commentary, A: The Spirit Series*, eds. N. Habel, D. Rhoads, and F. Summers (Minneapolis: Augsburg Fortress, 2011), 85–91.
2. Leslie Marmon Silko, *Ceremony* (New York: Penguin, 1977), 2.

present, and future. They shape meaning and help us order life—
for good or for ill.

Randy Woodley's piece in this volume looks at origins by reading synoptically three "books": that of creation (nature), Scripture
(the Bible), and his own Keetoowah tribal traditions. We settlers
would do well to reflect in the same way. The problem for Christian
inheritors of the colonial project in the Americas, however, is not
simply that we are largely illiterate when it comes to "the book of
Creation." In the words of Leslie Silko, we have also become "confused" about the stories of Scripture, and have "forgotten" the old
traditional cultural stories that used to shape our identity. Thus
orphans, we tend to draw instead upon modern myths of our own
nobility and innocence that are rooted in the dominant "ideology
of progress" undergirding the European conquest of the Americas.

Origin tales such as the landing of pilgrims at Plymouth Rock,
or Simon Fraser's "discovery" of the Fraser River Valley, function
still to legitimate English expropriation of land and "settlement" of
the continent. Indeed, the powerful nineteenth-century narrative
of Manifest Destiny was a kind of creation story, as succinctly captured by John Gast's *American Progress* (ca. 1872). The westward
movement of militia, miners, and farmers—accompanied by the
goddess Columbia holding a school book and stringing telegraph
wire—proceeds inexorably from the rising sun of European civilization, while Native peoples (and wild animals!) flee west into the
darkness. Such prejudices continue to shape our modern imperial
mindset, legitimizing wars across the globe.

The prevailing modern worldview of human evolution, inextricably linked to the ethos of "social Darwinism," functions the
same way on a broader canvas. This scientific narrative asserts that
human history has, since the dawn of civilization, exhibited a slow
but steady climb out of primitive ignorance toward ever-increasing
technological, social, and economic sophistication. It holds as
a nonnegotiable article of faith that the cosmopolitan complexity of European-American society is superior to all that has gone
before. Moreover, this developmental process was *inevitable* and
is *irreversible*.

The primeval history of Genesis 1–11, which will be my focus
here, offers a very different origin story. On the one hand, it has

John Gast's American Progress, *ca. 1872*

resonances and parallels with some Indigenous creation stories, as Woodley points out. On the other, it contradicts *every key aspect* of the "salvation story" of Enlightenment Progress, as we shall see. It is not surprising, then, that this biblical creation narrative has been widely ridiculed in modernity as a prescientific and frankly irrelevant fable. In reaction, contemporary Christians tend to exhibit either defiant literalism or diffident embarrassment toward the Genesis account of origins. This confirms Silko's contention that, when older stories are "confused or forgotten," we are rendered "defenseless" against the myths of empire.

The reading of Genesis 1–11 offered here in brief outline has profound implications not only for our understanding of deep human origins, but for ecological theology, creation spirituality, and Indigenous-settler conversation—all of which we need to pursue passionately if we are to save the planet.

The two Genesis accounts of creation (chaps. 1 and 2), when read as a literary whole, narrate a world that was originally beneficent and bountiful, in no need of human genius to improve or control it. Humans are portrayed as deeply embedded in a living biosphere (Genesis 1), with a divine appointment to "serve and preserve" it (2:15). They are intimately *related* with other creatures: "Whatever the human called each living being, that was its name" (2:19f.). In one of many Hebrew word plays, "woman" (*ishshah*) is rendered from the body of "man" (*ish*)—a relationship of solidarity, not hierarchy (2:22f.).

However, this symbiosis is shattered in the tragic tale of Genesis 3. The equilibrium of Eden suffers an epochal rupture known in Christian tradition as "the fall." The "humus being" (Hebrew *'adam*) and the "mother of life" (*'ava*, 3:20) conspire to defy the divine taboo against grasping the fruit of the "tree of the knowledge of good and evil" (3:1-6).

This drama has long been read in our churches as a theological morality play about obedience, freedom, power, and/or sex. But it can also be understood as an archetypal explanation of the "break" in human consciousness that inaugurated our long history of alienation from the creation. In this reading, the "forbidden fruit" symbolizes the ancient human conceit that we, by employing our ingenuity, our technology, and our social organization, can *improve* on a world pronounced "good" by Creator (Genesis 1), but apparently not good *enough* for us.

Scholars believe that the Genesis accounts were produced by Israel's scribes, working with older sources (including some from non-Yahwistic Near Eastern traditions), probably during the Exilic period. In the aftermath of the failed Israelite monarchy, these sages attempted to understand their own history of decline, having seen their original wilderness traditions steadily eroded by royal exploitation, civil war, and eventual conquest and dispossession by more powerful neighboring empires. But Israel's scribes were also trying to discern the *roots* of this disaster, and thus offer deeper reflections on the root causes of all human oppression and violence. After all, the empires of the ancient Middle East had brought not only the Hebrews, but every other tribal people as well, to the brink of extinction. The problem, the scribes propose in Genesis 1–11, is thus not only moral or political, but *anthropological*. Something went fundamentally wrong in the deep human past, and Israel's national trauma was but a symptom of this more profound pathology.

The biblical creation and fall story can thus be seen as an ancient warning tale. As such, it faces the same kind of questions that Indigenous leaders throughout the Americas—from Cheyenne chief *Moke-tav-a-to* (Black Kettle) to Duwamish chief *Si'ahl* (Seattle)—had to confront in the wake of European conquest and colonization: What are the origins of the relentless tide of predatory violence and toxic alienation that is overtaking us? After all, only a diagnosis of the root causes of a disease can lead to true healing.

The deep anthropology of Genesis

The deep anthropology of Genesis deserves reconsideration in light of the fact that popular belief in the messianic fable of Progress is waning due to widespread disillusionment. The credibility of the narrative that Jacob Bronowski famously characterized as "the ascent of man" is being strained by our deepening environmental crisis, which now looks more like an "endgame."[3] Moreover, modern dogmas fail to square with recent anthropological research into human origins. Human life-ways prior to the rise of civilization are being radically revised and revalued, while modern assumptions about the intrinsic nobility of the civilizational project are being questioned.

The fact is, human beings lived for millennia in widely dispersed, bioregionally situated, clan-based, hunter/gatherer/horticulturalist cultures. These Pleistocene life-ways, according to paleoanthropologist Paul Shepard, were universal from "the beginning"—regardless of whether we think the story of *Homo sapiens* began 100,000 or 2.5 million years ago.[4] The work of scholars like Marshall Sahlins and John Gowdy has shifted anthropological assessment of both ancient and contemporary hunter-gatherer cultures almost 180 degrees.[5] "Pre-historic" (in the still-prevalent pejorative parlance) human life was *not*, as Thomas Hobbes contemptuously put it,

---

3. Bronowski, *The Ascent of Man* (New York: Little Brown & Co, 1976). See Derrick Jensen, *Endgame: Volume 1, The Problem of Civilization* (New York: Seven Stories Press, 2006).
4. See Paul Shepherd, *Coming Home to Pleistocene* (Washington, D.C.: Island, 1988); Colin Tudge, *The Time Before History* (New York: Touchstone, 1996).
5. See Marshall Sahlins, *Stone Age Economics* (New York: Aldine de Gruyter, 1972); John Gowdy, ed., *Limited Wants, Limited Means: A Reader on Hunter Gatherer Economics and the Environment* (Washington, D.C.: Island, 1998). See also Stanley Diamond, *In Search of the Primitive: A Critique of Civilization* (London: Transaction Books, 1974).

"solitary, poor, nasty, brutish, and short."[6] In fact, such traditional life-ways are now believed to have been healthier, freer, more leisurely, more materially satisfied, less anxious, and demonstrably more ecologically sustainable than modern industrial ones. While this assessment hardly comes as a surprise to Indigenous people, it fundamentally challenges some of the deepest assumptions of settler culture.

With the domestication of plants and animals in the late Neolithic period around 10,000 BCE, however, a slow but steady transformation in human habitation patterns commenced. This "agricultural revolution" led to increasingly sedentary village lifestyles and growing food surpluses, which in turn led to population increases. Social organization became steadily more complex, urbanized, and violent, as emerging command economies came under the management of ascendant military and political elites. The earliest archeological evidence for a walled city may be at Çatal Hüyük in Turkey around 6000 BCE; by the fourth millennium BCE we see full-fledged empires in Mesopotamia—which in the West are correlated to "the dawn of civilization."

Contrary to the myth of Progress, hunter-gatherers did *not* voluntarily embrace these new developments—no more than Native peoples rushed to join European colonizers after contact in the Americas. Rather, Indigenous people were forced into peasant servitude—directly through conquest and indirectly through loss of habitat—by more powerful and aggressive agricultural societies with a voracious appetite for land and labor. We know this process happened independently in several parts of the world over several millennia, including China, India, and Central and South America. But this process appears to have *first* triumphed in Mesopotamia, where delta waterways were harnessed for irrigated farming. The Semitic tribes to the west, therefore, had front-row seats for this unfolding drama—and were among its first victims. This suggests that the Genesis narrative, which preserved and adapted ancient traditions of memory, represents the world's first literature of resistance to the social and ecological disaster we now call civilization.

---

6. Thomas Hobbes. *Leviathan (With Selected Variants from the Latin Edition of 1668)*, ed. E. Curley (Indianapolis: Hacket Publishing Co, 1994), 76.

The Genesis story can be interpreted as a mythic memory of this deep history. Eden was when humans dwelled symbiotically with the biosphere, other living creatures, and the Spirit world. The fall, conversely, relates how what Sahlins called the "original abundance" of free hunter/gatherer/horticulturalists was lost. Farming societies that began by domesticating animals and "subduing" land for maximized production became aggressive, colonizing civilizations that tried to force non-agriculturalist tribes into serfdom. Those who tried to survive apart from this aggressive process were relegated to marginal lands—a case in point being the Israelites themselves. Under the leadership of wilderness prophets, this dissident movement escaped slavery under imperial Egypt sometime in the late Bronze Age (Exodus 1–15). They eventually took refuge in the dry, rocky soil of the Palestinian highlands, since the fertile lowlands were controlled by Canaanite allies of Egypt. Managerial agriculture thus portends the end of Eden (Genesis 3:23f.), sentencing each of the archetypal human beings to "forced labor" under farming regimes: 'adam must now struggle with 'adamah (earth, soil), which no longer bears its fruits so freely, while the woman must bear children in pain (due perhaps to the fact that they are physically larger because of the higher caloric intake).

This "curse" is further underlined by the first dramatic scene in Genesis 4: the archetypal story of Cain and Abel. Creator warns the farmer Cain (whose name means "spear"): "Sin is lurking at the door; its desire is for you, but you must master it" (4:7). The first use of the word *sin* in Torah, it implies there is now a power loose in the world that is predatory and addictive, which humans must recognize and resist (a diagnosis later echoed in Romans 5–6). Abel, on the other hand, seems to symbolize the remnant older, not-yet-fully domesticated life-ways of the pastoralist (nomadic forager?): he lives with animals outside the village, and seems to enjoy Creator's favor.

The primal murder takes place in a "field"—the farmer's domain (Genesis 4:8). As a result, humans are further alienated from the earth: "The blood [Hebrew *dam*] of your brother cries out from the soil [*'adamah*, 4:10f.]"; as Ellen van Wolde puts it, the ground is now "seeded" with blood.[7] For a second time, Creator pronounces that the natural fertility of the creation has been compromised by agricultural society's presumption over life (4:12). And again the consequence is exile, now intensified: Cain becomes a "wanderer and fugitive on the earth" (4:14). Indeed, as Wendell Berry often points out, industrial agriculture (in contrast to local horticulture) has no sense of home, wandering the world eager to exploit its advantage, displacing and destroying people of place.[8]

Cain's survival strategy is to build the "first" city (Genesis 4:17), which, as Jacques Ellul pointed out a half century ago, deepens the downward trajectory of the fall.[9] Tellingly, Cain names it after his son Enoch, whose name means "re-creation" or "inauguration" (Hebrew *chanakh*, 4:17). The vocation of the city indeed seeks to reengineer all of life according to the dictates of the built environment. Within four generations (4:18), Lamech (the progeny of civilization) announces the "politics of vengeance" (4:23f.). The Earth is soon "filled with violence" (6:5, 11f.).

This epidemic of domination is connected to the rise of the *nephilim*, an untranslatable Hebrew moniker sometimes rendered "giants in the earth" (6:4). The *nephilim* symbolize the warrior classes that had come to dominate Ancient Near Eastern city-states.[10] Anthropologists surmise that warrior societies may first have evolved from specialized hunting groups, who were physically stronger and more calculating than the rest of the clan, and who

---

7. Ellen van Wolde, *Stories of the Beginning: Genesis 1–11 and Other Creation Stories*, trans. John Bowden (Ridgefield: Morehouse, 1996), 84–85.

8. See Wendell Berry, *Home Economics* (San Francisco: Northpoint, 1987).

9. See Jacques Ellul, *The Meaning of the City*, trans. D. Pardee (Grand Rapids: Eerdmans, 1970).

10. *Nephilim* appears one other time in Scripture: in the report of the Israelite spies dispatched by Moses to do guerrilla reconnaissance on the fortified cities of Canaan (Numbers 13:17-19). That land, they say, "devours its inhabitants; and all the people that we saw in it are of great size. . . . There we saw the *Nephilim* . . . and we seemed like grasshoppers to them" (Numbers 13:32f.: see Joshua 14:12; 15:14; Judges 1:10). Thus the *Nephilim*—elsewhere called *Anakim* or *Rephaim*—seem to represent "larger than life" military opponents in Egyptian-controlled Canaan (see also Deuteronomy 1:28; 2:10f., 16-21; 9:1f.; 11:21f.; 14:12f.). Later, a heavily armed Philistine professional warrior (like Goliath, 1 Samuel 14:4-7) is called "one of the descendants of the giants" (2 Samuel 21:16).

became inured to killing. "Professional" hunters eventually became strongmen, then warrior chiefs, then kings with an appetite for conquest.

This is why the subsequent "genealogy of nations" identifies kingdoms with *innately predatory behavior*—they are all descendants of "Nimrod the hunter" (10:8-14). As one scholar concludes: "In a very real sense, 'true' warfare may be viewed as one of the more important social consequences of the agricultural revolution."[11] So began the essential history of civilization: relentlessly expanding empires conquering and exploiting the Earth and all who live symbiotically with her. It continues to our day, as the ever-shrinking land-base of First Nations is still coveted by industrial interests, from the tar sands of Alberta to the deep forests of the Philippines.[12]

Creator's strategic countermeasures

Throughout this depressing narrative of the fall, however, Creator is keenly cognizant of the deteriorating situation, and takes strategic countermeasures to mitigate the "curse" of civilization. The divine "council" that created the human being (1:26) convenes twice again to try to limit the damage, vignettes which neatly bookend the descent from garden to tower: In 3:22f., the human determination to reengineer creation pushes the council to expel them from Eden. Similarly, in the face of Babel's aspirations for omnipotence (11:6), the divine council recommends "deconstruction" of imperial monoculture in favor of the original vision of a dispersed, tribally diverse humanity (11:7-9).[13]

Two other crucial strategies of damage control occur within this frame. One is Creator's "mark" on Cain the murderer (4:15). On one hand, this "tattoo of taboo" warns people of the land to "watch out" for aggressive farming cultures. On the other, it cautions the reader

---

11. Andrew Schmookler, *The Parable of the Tribes: The Problem of Power in Social Evolution* (Berkeley: University of California Press, 1984), 79.

12. See Rex Wyler, *Blood of the Land: The Government and Corporate War against First Nations* (Philadelphia: New Society, 1992); Todd Gordon, *Imperialist Canada* (Winnipeg: Arbeiter Ring Publishing, 2010).

13. See Evan Eisenberg, *The Ecology of Eden: An Inquiry into the Dream of Paradise and a New Vision of Our Role in Nature* (New York: Vintage Books, 1998), Part 2.

against thinking that the problem of Cain can be solved simply by killing the murderer. The logic of retributive violence only begets a spiral of vengeance, a prospect already embodied by Lamech (4:23f.). The land of "Nod, east of Eden" is consequently designated as a place of "refuge for the guilty" (see also later Numbers 35:13-15 and Deuteronomy 4:41-43). Analogous practices of "sanctuary" can be found in many other Indigenous cultures, which similarly had to face the conundrum of how to contain the violent pathologies generated by the fall.

The other example is the Noah cycle, the major divinely authorized rescue project that lies at the center of the fall story like a fulcrum (Genesis 6:8–9:29). In our Sunday school trivializations of this tradition, we overlook the fact that the Ark provides shelter not just for fauna, but flora as well (6:19-21), including seed (7:3). But it is *only* "every living thing" (8:17) that comes aboard; aside from the boat itself, there is no indication that any artifact from human civilization is preserved. The Ark represents, in other words, original creation *regenerated*. But tragically, the renewal of the covenant (8:21–9:17) cannot prevent a second "corruption" (9:20ff.). So does the primeval history culminate in the dawn of full-blown empire (Genesis 10–11).

The "Plain of Shinar" (10:10; 11:2) is a symbol for the Fertile Crescent. The account of the Tower of Babel is a thinly veiled parody of the ziggurats that inhabited Mesopotamian, Sumerian, Babylonian, and Egyptian city-states. These ancient skyscrapers claimed to reach to heaven, but Creator had to "come down" to observe them (11:4-7). "Babel" is another Hebrew word play: *balal* means "to confuse," while the Akkadian *bab-ilu* means "gate of gods," an allusion to the temples that sat atop the ziggurat. The tower represents the fortress architecture of domination, and the centripetal project of social conformity (11:1-3). Imperial towers are thus frequently the targets of later prophetic denunciations (see for example Judges 8:9; Isaiah 2:16; 33:18; Ezekiel 31:10f.; Zephaniah 1:16). To the ancient Hebrews, these constructed heights ironically represented the *nadir* of the fall, the triumph of the wayward human impulse to reengineer the world in order to control and "improve" it.[14]

---

14. For more on the significance of the Babel story and its resonance with Acts 2, see my "Cultural Diversity and Deep Social Ecology: Genesis 11 and Acts

Yet Genesis does not end under the shadows of the archetypal tower in despair. On the heels of Creator's centrifugal scattering (11:8), Abram is called out of a Mesopotamian city and into the wilderness of Canaan. There Creator reveals to him an alternative future in a mystical vision under the branches of an ancient "teaching oak" (12:1-7)![15] Here commences the grandest divine rescue project of them all: the counter-narrative of redemption that stretches throughout the rest of the Bible. From Moses to Malachi, and from John the Baptist to John the Revelator, Scripture preserves the minority tradition of domesticated humans recovering their bearings in the wilderness. Jacob's dreaming (Genesis 28), Elijah's cave (1 Kings 19), and Jesus' desert "vision quest" (Luke 4:1-12) all remind us that the prophetic tradition never abandoned that primal symbiosis with Creation, and looked forward to its ultimate restoration after the final collapse of empire (for more examples, see Isaiah 14:3-8; 35:1ff.; Revelation 21–22).[16]

The bold, archetypal strokes of Genesis 1–11 name our settler history, however unsettling its critique may be to those still loyal to the Promethean fables of modernity. The biblical "fall" is not so much a cosmic moment of moral failure as a history of decline into civilization—exactly *contrary* to our mythic Western narrative of

---

2," in C. Myers and M. Colwell, *Our God Is Undocumented: Biblical Faith and Immigrant Justice* (Maryknoll: Orbis Books, 2012), Chapter 1.

15. "The Hebrew *'elon moreh* connotes a tree with sacred associations," writes Nahum Sarna; "*moreh* must mean 'teacher, oracle giver.'" *The JPS Torah Commentary: Genesis* (Philadelphia: Jewish Publication Society, 1989), 91. Under this sacred tree Abram pitches his nomad's tents and builds the first altar in the Bible. Similar scenarios occur repeatedly throughout the Abraham cycle (Genesis 13:18; 15:1ff. and 18:1ff.; 21:33), and again with the Israelite heroes Gideon (Judges 6:11) and Elijah (1 Kings 13:14; 19:4). The often overlooked "eleventh commandment" of the Covenant Code (Exodus 20:24-25) perhaps most clearly reasserts the ancient notion that communion with Creator requires only the *unreengineered* landscape of nature.

16. For more on these themes, see my essays "The Wilderness Temptations and the American Journey: Resistance and Contemplation in a Quincentenary Perspective," in *Richard Rohr: Illumination of His Life and Work*, eds. A. Ebert and P. Brockman (New York: Crossroad, 1993), 143–57; and "Everything Will Live Where the River Goes: A Bible Study on Water, God, and Redemption," *Sojourners*, April, 2012, http://sojo.net/magazine/2012/04/everything-will-live-where-river-goes (accessed 1 January 2013).

Progress. As a literary expression of resistance to empire, the primeval creation story rightly warned us of the social pathologies and ecocidal consequences that have intensified exponentially now for a dozen millennia.

As a result, our generation faces a threefold crisis:

1. The natural world has been increasingly demystified and subjected to ever more intense technological exploitation, to the point of collapse;

2. Hierarchical social formations, economic stratification, and war have proliferated to the point of perpetual class and national conflict; and

3. Human spiritual life and ecological competence have atrophied, resulting in our growing alienation from both nature and Spirit.

In light of this, the conversation represented in this book is crucial. Our settler churches need to learn from contemporary keepers of Indigenous wisdom—both Christian and non-Christian—about how to re-vision creation care and sustainable community. This includes exploring how a "Native hermeneutic" might help us re-read our sacred texts. But this will also mean challenging deeply held assumptions about the congruency between "Christian civilization" and the will of Creator for humanity and nature.

Furthermore, we Christians need to re-center our theology and practices in real landscapes, for which we take keen responsibility. In southern California, our educational work around what we call "bioregional discipleship" is grounded specifically in the Ventura watershed. We have come to understand that we can't save what we don't love, we can't love what we don't know, and we can't know what we haven't learned. So, we are committed to literacy, both in the ecology of our watershed *and* in the painful history and remnant culture of the First Peoples of this place. For us, this means experimenting with Native habitat preservation and restoration, and learning from Indigenous Chumash traditions of relationship to this landscape and habitat.[17]

---

17. Alongside conversations with local Chumash elders, we have learned from M. Kat Anderson's *Tending the Wild: Native American Knowledge*

It is impossible to argue, given today's ecological crisis, that the "civilized" life-ways of the last five thousand (or five hundred, or even fifty) years are as sustainable as those of the previous five hundred thousand. Let us settlers heed the ancient wisdom of Genesis 1–11, which may be "all we have to fight off illness and death." And let us "repent"—which is to say, struggle alongside Native communities to turn our *wrong*-way history around, and recover the *old* ways for which we were created.

---

and Management of California's Natural Resources (Berkeley: University of California Press, 2005) and Jan Timbrook's *Chumash Ethnobotany* (Berkeley: Heydey Books, 2007).

On BEING human

Are we ever really . . . something
Have we bought in and conformed, mutated
Our very BEING . . . human DOING
Spent time dissecting, columnizing . . . colonizing?
Only to find we are circular, not linear
Replacing our columns with parallels
We are still separate . . . but EQUAL
One road in the same direction but divided by the median

Crossing the forbidden median
Going to my comfortable to deal with YOU making me
    uncomfortable
        or did I make me uncomfortable.
Always the 3/4 cup intellect, 1/8 physical, 1/8 God . . .
    for good measure
        sum of 1. Solved. I'm still uncomfortable.

Maheo'o, Creator, I long to go beyond parallels
Let me live spiritually, emotionally, physically, and intellectually
Bring me back to Earth Mother, womb of all creation
Barefoot, connected and grounded, beyond roads and paths
To see the seasons change, knowing that you see the same
        differently, beautifully, Godly . . . without need for equal
        because we were never unequal
        We valued differently.
I pray for enthusiasm . . . En-theos, God within:[1]
        lived, that I may live my human journey . . . alive
Healing and connecting to my spirit, my reminder of Maheo'o in me
Help me exhale and inhale air fully, reminding me we share
        you and me—intricately woven, we rely on each other,
        we need each other
        Even to draw our parallels, I couldn't do it without you.

---

1. Richard Wagamese, *Quality of Light* (Doubleday: Toronto, 1997), 138.

Comfort me in my paradox that I may see the lines and
    envision circles
Back to whom you created me to be . . . a human BEING.

—*Vonâhe'e (Northern Cheyenne)*

Blind justice

Ts'leil Waututh, Chaytoose, Snauq'w, Coquitlam
The mountains rise behind my ancestors
And retreat from our care in the sale of them
Orchestrated by a department that seeks
Our vanquishment—$25.00 becomes millions in the blink of an eye
$25.00 becomes hunger cold in the next blink
Food becomes inadequate in the next blink
the murder of cedar, sea vegetables, ouske,[1] whale, and sockeye
crippled our ability to eat
we struggled to mature without food
Mr. Harper is sorry,
Me too

We could have recovered from smallpox
We had Xway-Xway[2]
We had medicine
We had healing songs and dances
But we were banned
From singing and dancing

We could have recovered
We had friends
Christian friends
But they were banned from helping us
My relations were banned from speaking
about land rights, fishing rights,
To raise our children
To educate them

Blind justice

---

1. Tsleil Waututh for baby seal.
2. "Place of the Mask"—an Indigenous village that was disbanded by the coloniz-ers of Vancouver in order to create room for what is now known as Stanley Park.

This is a call song
Settlers did not begin here as blind men
They witnessed our murder—some of them killed us
Some of them still kill us
They witnessed the murder of cedar
    Of sea vegetables
    Of Whale, seal, and sockeye
    The poisoning of our lands
Everyone is sorry now
Me too

We could have included you in our ceremony
    Of facing ourselves,
    Recovering ourselves
    Transforming ourselves
But our ceremonies were demeaned as devil worship.
Harper is sorry
Me too.

Still, I am not tragic
Not even in my addicted moments
    A needle hanging from the vein of my creased arm
    I was not tragic
    Even as I jumped from a skiff in a vain attempt to join
        my ancestors
I was not tragic

Even in my disconnection from song, from dance,
I was not tragic
    Even in seeing you as privileged,
    I found songs of justice to sing
    "Oh Freedom, over me, over me"
Even while you occupied my homeland, I in a homeless state
Did not begrudge you your privilege
Even as men abduct us as we hitchhike along highways
To disappear along this long colonial road
I found a way to stand up
And subvert colonial injustice

125

My body has always understood justice
"Everyone eats" is our law and so we included you
There is no word for exclusion in our language,
So your whiteness was never the threat
This is not the first massive death we have endured
as we died we girded up our loins,
Recovered and rebuilt

We are builders,
We are singers,
We are dancers
We are speakers
    We are still singing
    We are dancing again
    We are speaking in poetry
On paper, on metal and on plastic film

        —*Lee Maracle (Stó:lō)*

WHITE CHRISTIAN SETTLERS, THE BIBLE, AND (DE)COLONIZATION

By Dave Diewert

I begin by acknowledging that I am a white, male, Christian settler of European descent who lives and works on unceded Coast
Salish Territory, the lands of the Musqueam, Squamish, and Tsleil
Waututh peoples. I am a beneficiary of the brutal, genocidal
process of colonization that has secured for me legal rights and
privileges, access to wealth, and political and social status. The
nation-state that confers upon me such material and social goods
is a colonial power whose existence rests on fundamental policies
and practices of sustained violence, deception, and theft inflicted
on the Indigenous people of this land.[1]

I also acknowledge that my Christian religious heritage was
integral to the colonial project of European settlers. The mission
of civilizing and Christianizing the "savages of the new world"
was essential to the ideological framework that drove the colonizing enterprise. Métis writer Howard Adams, in his work *Prison of
Grass: Canada from a Native Point of View*, describes the key role
Christian missionaries performed in extending the domination of
European culture and political power. He writes:

> The part played by the priests in the colonization of native
> people was as destructive as that played by the soldier and the

---

1. For an account of Canada's past and present dispossession of the Indigenous,
and its relationship to global capitalism, see Todd Gordon, *Imperialist Canada*
(Arbeiter Ring Publishing, 2010).

Artist Edgar Heap of Birds reminds British Columbians that they live in occupied territory

fur trader. Missionaries were extremely effective in undermining the strength and spirit of the native society. Conversion to Christianity was a powerful force in the destruction of native culture and religion, and the imperialists fully understood how useful missionaries could be in subjugating colonized peoples.[2]

The establishment of Indian residential schools as a strategy of cultural assimilation was a lethal mechanism for asserting colonial state hegemony, and Christian churches and organizations fully participated in its implementation. The Canadian government saw in the churches a fit and willing partner in this colonial project of assimilation. Their theological and moral convictions carried the necessary European cultural norms, their proselytizing mission meshed with the "educational" objectives of the schools, and their religious zeal supplied the requisite courage and dedication. Catholic, Protestant, and Anabaptist denominations enthusiastically took on the main administrative and educational leadership of these "schools" (more accurately described, in many cases, as prison labor camps for Indigenous children and youth), where abuse, punishment, the relentless destruction of Native culture,

---

2. Howard Adams, *Prison of Grass: Canada from a Native Point of View*, rev. ed. (Saskatoon: Fifth House Publishers, 1989), 31.

and death were inflicted upon the bodies, minds, and spirits of the "students." The devastating fallout on successive generations of Indigenous families and communities is painfully evident in the over-representation of Native people among those who are homeless, incarcerated, and economically poor, as well as the high levels of abuse, violence, addiction, and suicide they experience.[3]

In addition, the establishment of Indian residential schools, with their objective of assimilation through the eradication of Native culture, and the implementation of the Indian reserve system, without treaty agreements in British Columbia, constituted a powerful two-pronged strategy for demarcating Native space, removing Natives from the land, and opening up vast territory for colonial settlement and capitalist enterprise.[4] Here, too, Christianity served an ideological and practical role. Back in August 1889, the superintendent of the Methodist Church, Alexander Sutherland, told his colleagues working with Indigenous people in western Canada, "Make the savage a Christian and he will settle peacefully on reserves. Teach him the scriptures and he will give up his claim to the land that we require."[5]

Scripture in the service of colonial power

The role of Christianity in the legitimization of oppressive colonial power, and its ongoing capacity to blind settlers to the violence and injustice that grounds their present state-sanctioned privileges, is deeply disturbing, and highlights the profound and urgent need to embark on the long and painful process of truth telling and self-examination. If there is to be a just and true reconciliation with the Indigenous peoples of this land, white Christian settlers must confront Christianity's role in colonization, past and present. We must interrogate our theological traditions, critique the ideologies that

---

3. John S. Milloy, *A National Crime: The Canadian Government and the Residential School System, 1879 to 1986* (Winnipeg: University of Manitoba Press, 1999). Suzanne Fournier and Ernie Crey, *Stolen from Our Embrace: The abduction of First Nations Children and the Restoration of Aboriginal Communities* (Vancouver/Toronto: Douglas & McIntyre, 1997).

4. For the constantly revised delineation of the reserve system in B.C., see Cole Harris, *Making Native Space: Colonialism, Resistance, and Reserves in British Columbia* (Vancouver: UBC Press, 2002).

5. Indian and Northern Affairs Canada, RG 10 Series R 7733.

support and justify political and economic domination, and inculcate new modes of thought and practice in the pursuit of justice.[6]

One area that requires critical attention in any attempt to dismantle Christian support for hegemonic power is the role played by the biblical text and the various ways in which it is read and appropriated. Scripture is an essential component in the formation of any theological understanding of Christian identity and mission. In the hands of those who wield political power or influence, it has been read as fundamentally buttressing the authority and control of the ruling class, and when viewed as absolute, universal truth, renders unassailable arrangements of asymmetrical power. As such, the biblical witness has often functioned as a bulwark in rationalizing colonial and imperial projects, serving to fuse religious orthodoxy with political mastery.[7] Scriptural texts have been incorporated into a theological architecture of timeless truths, wedded to European cultural practices, social structures, and political hierarchies, and imposed on Indigenous peoples with coercive force. In speaking of the eradication of the Indigenous populations of Turtle Island, Lakota/Sioux writer Richard Twiss states, "what makes the story most tragic is that so much of this was the result of the misappropriation of the biblical narrative that was co-opted as a tool of colonial imperialism."[8] The "good news" was enlisted into the service of death-dealing power.

Hungry for justice: the prophetic tradition in Scripture

I contend, however, that the biblical text is an unreliable and

---

6. On the challenge for white settlers in general to engage in processes of decolonization and just reconciliation, see Paulette Regan, *Unsettling the Settler Within: Indian Residential Schools, Truth Telling, and Reconciliation in Canada* (Vancouver: UBC Press, 2010).

7. Osage writer Robert Warrior maintains that the biblical conquest narratives, recounting the violent and at times wholesale destruction of Indigenous Canaanite communities, formed part of the ideological and theological justification for the colonial subjugation of Turtle Island (North America). Robert Allen Warrior, "A Native American Perspective: Canaanites, Cowboys, and Indians," in *Voices from the Margin: Interpreting the Bible in the Third World*, ed. R. S. Sugirtharajah (New York: Orbis, 1991) 287–95.

8. Richard Twiss, "All My Relations: An Indigenous Manifesto for Biblical Justice," *Journal of North American Institute for Indigenous Theological Studies* 8 (2010), 82.

subversive tool in the colonial construction of power, one that threatens to undermine and dismantle imperial interests. For the Bible also contains pervasive voices of dissent and nonconformity, narratives of defection, and counter-testimony to readings that seek to align it with domination. It bears witness to God on the side of the oppressed and outcast, in opposition to political oppression and economic exploitation. It foregrounds a God who mobilizes for the liberation of slaves, foreigners, and the poor. Its dangerous memories can and have fueled resistance to injustice, awakening visions of another more equitable and just world.

The biblical prophetic tradition, from Moses to Jesus, contains powerful currents of resistance and dissent.[9] In its passion for justice, it decries the machinations of state power and advocates for those most vulnerable to abuse, exploitation, and violence, those most susceptible to material deprivation. It advocates justice that is not limited to fairness in legal and judicial matters, but entails equitable access to resources, sufficient economic means for meaningful social participation, ensured personal dignity and mutual respect, and non-exclusionary community practices.

The prophetic witness presents the divine word in a vigorous adversarial stance toward repressive concentrations of political power. The prophet Amos, for example, passionately countered the soothing rhetoric of religious approval for the monarchy of Jeroboam II with a harsh and disturbing critique (4:4-5; 5:21-24). He denounced royal excesses (3:13-15), the overconsumption of the elite (6:4-7), and the ruthless oppression of the poor by the ruling class (2:6-8; 4:1-3; 5:10-13; 8:4-6). He announced the imminent downfall of the Israelite kingdom because of the lack of justice within its social and economic structures, and his words were understood as a threat to national political stability (7:10).

Perhaps the most paradigmatic narrative of God on the side of slaves and foreigners in opposition to brutal state power is the story of the exodus. This founding divine act of liberation from oppression was seared into Israelite consciousness and functioned as the touchstone of their identity, shaping thought and practices for

---

9. See Walter Brueggemann, *The Prophetic Imagination*, 2nd ed. (Philadelphia: Fortress Press, 2001).

centuries. At the same time, the exodus narrative cemented Egypt as oppressor *par excellence*, painting Pharaoh's regime as murderous and exploitative.

> Now a new king arose over Egypt, who did not know Joseph. He said to his people, "Look, the Israelite people are more numerous and more powerful than we. Come, let us deal shrewdly with them, or they will increase and, in the event of war, join our enemies and fight against us and escape from the land." Therefore they set taskmasters over them to oppress them with forced labor. They built supply cities, Pithom and Rameses, for Pharaoh. But the more they were oppressed, the more they multiplied and spread, so that the Egyptians came to dread the Israelites. The Egyptians became ruthless in imposing tasks on the Israelites, and made their lives bitter with hard service in mortar and brick and in every kind of field labor. They were ruthless in all the tasks that they imposed on them. (Exodus 1:8-14)
>
> The king of Egypt said to the Hebrew midwives, one of whom was named Shiphrah and the other Puah, "When you act as midwives to the Hebrew women, and see them on the birthstool, if it is a boy, kill him; but if it is a girl, she shall live." . . . Then Pharaoh commanded all his people, "Every boy that is born to the Hebrews you shall throw into the Nile, but you shall let every girl live." (Exodus 1:15-16)
>
> That same day Pharaoh commanded the taskmasters of the people, as well as their supervisors, "You shall no longer give the people straw to make bricks, as before; let them go and gather straw for themselves. But you shall require of them the same quantity of bricks as they have made previously; do not diminish it, for they are lazy; that is why they cry, 'Let us go and offer sacrifice to our God.' Let heavier work be laid on them; then they will labor at it and pay no attention to deceptive words." (Exodus 5:6-9)

These texts portray Pharaoh and the Egyptian empire as genocidal, deceptive, ruthlessly oppressive, exploitative, and fundamentally violent. The Egyptian king orders children to be systematically murdered and slaves subjected to conditions of bitter hardship. He propagates racist stereotypes of foreigners for political gain, he intensifies slave labor to increase his economic wealth, and he uses the constant threat of violence to maintain his domination and control. This depiction of oppressive state power is intensely vivid and discloses its horror with striking clarity.

Christians have typically read the exodus story as heirs of Israel. The God who orchestrated the liberation of Hebrew slaves is our God as well, and the founding figures of our faith were firmly embedded in this Israelite/Judean tradition. The exodus narrative itself significantly influenced the shape of the Gospel accounts of Jesus, and, abstracted and depoliticized, it has served as a model for various Christian theological constructions of salvation. So it seems entirely natural for us to engage the exodus account as our own story. We position ourselves imaginatively among the Hebrew slaves, and we view Pharaoh and his Egyptian regime as the personification of the tyranny and unjust oppression of the other.

We are Pharaoh, we are Egypt

But how shall we read the exodus narrative as white settlers of a colonial state? As a non-Indigenous "Canadian" of European descent, my heritage has much more in common with the Egyptians than the Hebrew slaves. Pharaoh's command to the midwives to kill the boys at birth has a disturbing resonance with the stated objective of the Indian residential school system: to "kill the Indian in the child."[10] Native people were used as instruments for settler

---

10. This is how Duncan Campbell Scott, head of the Department of Indian Affairs (1913–32), described the objective of the Indian Residential School system. The removal of 150,000 Indigenous children from their homes and communities and the concerted effort to annihilate their languages, customs, and spiritual traditions, along with the estimated deaths of over fifty thousand residential school children, easily fits within the UN definitions of the crime of genocide. The UN Convention on the Crime of Genocide defines this as "any of the following acts committed with intent to destroy, in whole or in part, a national, ethnical, racial or religious group, as such: a) killing members of the group; b) causing serious bodily or mental harm to members of the group; c) deliberately inflicting on the group conditions of life calculated to bring about its physical destruction in whole or in part; d) imposing measures intended to prevent births within the group; e) forcibly transferring children of the group to another group." See "UN General Assembly, *Convention on the Prevention and Punishment of the Crime of Genocide*, 9 December 1948," United Nations Treaty Series, 78, http://www .unhcr.org/refworld/docid/3ae6b3ac0.html (accessed 1

economic growth, first as resourceful guides for the fur trade and then as cheap labor within agricultural and resource extraction industries.[11] Indigenous lands were stolen through force or deception, and the richness of that land exploited for the accumulation of settler wealth. Racism was essential to the colonial myths of white superiority and Natives as primitive savages in need of civilization, and racism continues to function within the structures of ongoing colonial power and systems of state control over Indigenous lands, communities, and lives.

The truth of the matter is that, as white Christian settlers, we are much more aligned with the Egyptians than the Hebrews/Israelites, since we have benefited from a history of colonial violence, genocide, deception, exploitation, and racism.[12] We are firmly located among the oppressors, and this sets us fundamentally at odds with the God of the exodus, the liberator of the oppressed. This God is radically opposed to the brutal concentrations of wealth and power ascribed to the Egyptian regime in the exodus narrative, and, I would infer, opposed to the political and economic hegemony evident in the construction and consolidation of the colonial Canadian state. In the effort to ensure superiority and domination, Christian settlers have readily enlisted the biblical God among the endorsers of expanding accumulation of political power and material wealth, completely suppressing the understanding of God as Creator and humans as creatures living in harmony and humility with other creatures and the earth, a truth firmly embedded within the sacred traditions of Indigenous culture(s).

For ancient Israel, acts of rupture and departure were necessary for its liberation from the violence of Pharaoh's empire and its self-determination as the people of Yhwh. Breaking patterns of normalized domination and leaving its confinement within the Egyptian state were essential for establishing alternative, self-governing

---

January 2013).

11. George Walkem, premier and attorney general of B.C. (1874–76), was particularly keen on pushing Native people into the workforce rather than into schools or onto reservations. See Harris, *Making Native Space*, 87.

12. I am deeply grateful to Laurel Dykstra for opening up and exploring this perspective with clarity and insight. See Laurel A. Dykstra, *Set Them Free: The Other Side of Exodus* (New York: Orbis, 2002).

Israelite communities.[13] According to the biblical account, Hebrew liberation would come at a considerable cost, especially for the Egyptian elite but also for the Egyptian people in general. As white Christian settlers, we are challenged to read the exodus account from a place among the Egyptians, knowing that our God is at work on the side of those we have murdered, oppressed, and deprived of dignity and self-determination, and that their liberation will cost us. So where do we go from here?

Remarkably, there were Egyptians in the exodus narrative who refused to participate in the genocidal and oppressive dictates of Pharaoh. The death-dealing ways of the Egyptian empire were thwarted, at least on certain occasions, by the noncompliance of its citizens. The midwives Shiphrah and Puah rejected Pharaoh's orders to kill the boys and instead let them live (1:17).[14] Pharaoh's own daughter saved a young Hebrew male child rather than toss him into the river, and raised the child within the royal court (2:5-10). Moses himself, though not ethnically Egyptian, was raised and recognized as such, and yet he rejected his place of privilege and power in Pharaoh's palace and stood among the Hebrew slaves, acknowledging them as his people and eventually joining them on the path of emancipation. Other unnamed Egyptians aided and abetted the Israelites' departure, and helped supply them with goods for the journey (3:21-22; 11:2-3; 12:35-36). All of these beneficiaries of state power refused to extend its violence onto the bodies of foreign slaves and their families, and in one way or another cooperated in their liberation.

Not reform—recognize, resist, and dismantle

For white Christian settlers, situating ourselves among the Egyptians ought to be profoundly disorienting and disturbing to the

---

13. For an inspiring articulation of Indigenous pathways of revolt and resurgence, see Taiaiake Alfred, *Wasáse: Indigenous Pathways of Action and Freedom* (Peterborough, Ontario: Broadview Press, 2005).

14. There is some debate on the ethnic identity of the midwives. The Hebrew phrase *hamyalledōt hā(ibriyyōt* in the Massoretic text clearly identifies the midwives as being Hebrew/Israelite, but the unpointed text could be read as "midwives of the Hebrew (women)," suggesting their non-Hebrew, possibly Egyptian, status. Their access to Pharaoh's presence, knowledge of Egyptian women in childbirth, and the expectation that they would kill Hebrew infants are suggestive of their identity as Egyptians. See Dykstra, *Set Them Free*, 163–64.

usual ways of seeing ourselves in the text and using it to justify our power. It calls into question a simple, unconditional alignment with ancient Israel in our interpretation and appropriation of the biblical text. Moreover, it produces an anxiety and suspicion around any effort to employ biblical hermeneutics and theological arguments in order to buttress the political and cultural domination of others. The abiding truth of the exodus account is that aligning ourselves with God means aligning ourselves with the work of liberation and life for those who are oppressed and vulnerable to abuse, and against political systems of violence that enslave, exploit, and destroy human lives.

Within the history of Canadian colonization there were white settlers who resisted various colonial policies and practices. Father C. J. Grandidier, an Oblate priest in Kamloops, British Columbia, opposed the provincial Native land policies and the province's theoretical assumptions about property rights that sought to diminish Indigenous access to land.[15] Dr. Peter Bryce, Chief Medical Officer for the Department of Indian Affairs (1904–13), was a relentless recorder and critic of the deadly health conditions in Indian residential schools and the policies that shaped their operation.[16] Neither of them, however, was antagonistic to the colonial project per se; they just thought that its implementation in these cases was unnecessarily brutal. Within their time and place, their resistance was noteworthy, but their critique seemed to be that the harshness and inhumanity of the policies made the ultimate objective of assimilation more difficult. Father Grandidier thought the reserves should be larger so Native people could be more successful farmers, but not that the idea of reserves was unjust. Dr. Bryce didn't question the existence of residential schools, but he was convinced that they needed to be run more humanely. Our great challenge is to recognize, resist, and dismantle the structures of oppressive power, not just reform their most harmful policies.

White Christian settlers have a responsibility to engage in hard processes of truth telling and sustained practices of decolonization

---

15. Harris, *Making Native Space*, 76–80.
16. Megan Sproule-Jones, "Crusading for the Forgotten: Dr. Peter Bryce, Public Health, and Prairie Native Residential Schools," *Canadian Bulletin of Medical History* 13 (1996): 199–224.

alongside our Indigenous sisters and brothers, to learn from them the insidious dynamics and devastating impacts of systemic racism that we cannot see, and to stand in solidarity with them in their struggle for justice and self-determination, regardless of the cost. Decolonization for white settlers will inevitably require a deepening understanding of past and present colonial violence, and a relentless refusal to reproduce that violence through consistent practices of solidarity. The biblical witness can be a source of encouragement and inspiration on this path of healing and liberation as we nourish our imaginations from the stream of prophetic voices passionately summoning us to justice.

Blind Justice (continued)

In the many millennia of life here we have learned there
    are constants
        The tide surges, retreats faithfully
        Threatened fishes struggle to return
        The epidemic dead always return
Plants, the trees, the animal world will always struggle to recover
We may endure another Hayaluq[1] of the sort that nearly killed
    us all
We may endure earthquakes and storms
But the plants, the people and the animals
will return

I am your witness
Inspired by the earth's response to her desecration
The waters will cleanse the earth
Hurricanes will rearrange rivers
Earthquakes will object, but the earth will do her duty
And we will too.
We will all have to face ourselves
And our sense of justice
We will need to nourish our imagination
And summon our souls, our hearts and our minds to a justice,
which includes all life—together
So I call you
Come, hear this song,
Sing with me.

I am not the only vulnerable one here
Our sharing is not our weakness but our strength
I have been waiting for you all these years
Waiting for you to see me, to hear this call song
I am not the only one that needs help here

---

1. Lushootseed (the language of the Lummi) for the big wave, tsunami, floodwaters.

The sharing of my country with us
Defines your humanity
You need us as much as I need you.

       —Lee Maracle (Stó:lō)

Composting in Iraqi Kurdistan

Lots of vegetable and fruit refuse was headed for the landfill, and though the daily garbage pickup presented an easy way to put it quickly out of sight and mind, I couldn't do it. Life in Iraqi Kurdistan used far too much plastic, paper, and packages to also send compostable matter into the mound of garbage. So I wracked my brain and searched the city of Suleymaniyah for something to use as a compost bin. I needed something to contain the food scraps as they decayed and were transformed into the nutrients for new life.

To my surprise (and for good reason, I later learned), this seemed to be a foreign concept to many urban Kurds, the Indigenous peoples of northern Iraq. There certainly were not any ready-made, black-lidded, conical-shaped compost barrels to be found in the bazaar. And our small courtyard was made of solid concrete, so I couldn't just make a pile of the stuff.

As I took my daily walks, I looked around and tried to think beyond conventional compost-bin ideas. A large garbage can? No, given the eating habits of the six members of our Christian Peacemaker Team, that would fill up in days. Build a bin with concrete blocks? No, I wanted something easy to dispose of if we had to move someday.

A large electrical facility was being built near the CPT house, and one day I walked through the construction zone. I knew it as soon as I saw it: a very large, abandoned wooden packing crate. But who could I ask if this was available for the taking, and how would I get it home to our courtyard? I turned to my friend Mohammed Salah; he knew Kurdish and he had a truck. When I asked Mohammed, he was willing to help. But there was a problem. "What exactly do you want to do with this heavy crate?" He could not even imagine the concept I tried to explain to him.

Then I thought of nature's prime example of vegetative matter turning into rich earth. "Mohammed," I said, "you know when you are walking through a leafy forest and at the foot of the trees you find a thick layer of rich, dark earth under the layer of recently fallen leaves? Well, that's the compost made of leaves from many years back. Those leaves have rotted and formed the nutrients the trees require to continue growing."

I noticed a very puzzled look on his face. Obviously my picture was not helping. Then I suddenly remembered. Mohammed had told us stories of the trees that used to be on the mountains surrounding Suleymaniyah. These trees had provided shade for picnics and, later, as Saddam Hussein began his attacks on the Kurdish people, a sanctuary for rebel fighters. In retaliation, Hussein had all the trees cut down so the rebels would not be able to hide. So, no, Mohammed did not know about leafy forests. How could he?

Mohammed told me that he would just watch and wait. He wanted to see the black earth, the life that I promised would come from decaying vegetables, fruit, and shredded paper.

—Kathy Moorhead Thiessen

THEOLOGICAL COMPOSTING IN ROMANS 8:
AN INDIGENOUS MEDITATION ON PAUL'S RHETORIC OF DECAY

By Laura E. Donaldson (Cherokee)

I consider that the sufferings of this present time are not
worth comparing with the glory about to be revealed to us.
For the creation waits with eager longing for the revealing of
the children of God; for the creation was subjected to futility,
not of its own will but by the will of the one who subjected
it, in hope that the creation itself will be set free from its
bondage to decay and will obtain the freedom of the glory of
the children of God.

—*Romans 8:18-21*

The world continually draws sustenance from decay . . . life's
appearance of permanence is deceiving.[1]

—*John Borrows*

I t would be difficult to find a more magnificent declaration of the
divine-human relationship than in Romans 8. Paul's rhetorical
talents reach a pinnacle in poetic statements such as the one ending the chapter:

---

1. John Borrows, *Canada's Indigenous Constitution* (Toronto: University of
Toronto Press, 2010).

> For I am convinced that neither death, nor life, nor angels, nor
> rulers, nor things present, nor things to come, nor powers, nor
> height, nor depth, nor anything else in all creation, will be able
> to separate us from the love of God in Christ Jesus our Lord.
> (vv. 38-39)

Countless Christians have been comforted by these powerful words
in times of suffering and oppression. And critical to the reassurance
that Paul offers in this text is the metaphor of a woman in labor that he
employs a few verses earlier, a vivid metaphor to express his anticipa-
tion of humanity's new life in Christ. While the Jewish and Christian
traditions had long employed the trope of childbirth to dramatize
the cosmic misery that would accompany God's final judgment,[2] Paul
uses it to emphasize the joyous redemption that this pain enables:

> We know that the whole creation has been groaning in labour
> pains until now; and not only the creation, but we ourselves,
> who have the first fruits of the Spirit, groan inwardly while we
> wait for adoption, the redemption of our bodies. (vv. 22-23)

Like the chapter's final verses, this trope of childbirth has
inspired many with the hope that "the creation itself will be set
free"—and for Paul, this includes the physical resurrection of the
human body, as well as the body of creation, or the natural world.

In his commentary on Romans, Paul Meyer notes that verses
22-23 constitute the only place in the New Testament where the
natural world becomes the explicit focus of eschatological attention: "For the creation was subjected to futility, not of its own will
but by the will of the one who subjected it, in hope that the creation
itself will be set free from its bondage to decay and will obtain the
freedom of the glory of the children of God."[3] A central part of this
liberation is from the chains of *douleias tes phthoras*, the shackling
of creation to the inevitability of death. In biblical Greek, the term
douleias denotes the condition of slavery, with particular reference
to degradation and unhappiness,[4] and *phthoras*, the susceptibil-

---

2. Paul W. Meyer, "Romans," in *The Harpercollins Bible Commentary*, 2nd ed.,
ed. James Luther Mays (San Francisco: Harper, 2000), 1059.
3. Ibid.
4. William D. Mounce, *The Analytical Lexicon to the Greek New Testament*
(Grand Rapids, MI: Zondervan, 1993), 152.

ity to corruption, decay, and destruction.[5] While the NRSV uses "bondage to decay" to render the Greek, the KJV chooses "bondage to corruption." Both are reasonably accurate translations, although "bondage to decay" conveys the more literal sense of the phrase. Meyer interprets *douleias tes phthoras* as creation's vulnerability to the ravages of time.[6] Although *ravages* is a violent word, it does highlight the negative implications of Paul's joyous message. For Paul, decay—the inevitability of death and decomposition—represents a process that must be overcome and ultimately suppressed if one is to enjoy true Christian freedom. I would argue that this rhetoric of decay has significantly contributed to a view of creation that is not only unsustainable but also devastating in its social and environmental implementations.

In contrast to Paul, Indigenous cultures offer a much more positive context for understanding that decay is the enabling condition, rather than an obstacle, to creation. One finds a compelling example of this in stories such as "Moldy Head," an oral narrative widespread throughout the Native American, Alaskan Native, and First Nations cultures of the Pacific Northwest. In the version of "Moldy Head" told by Yukon elder Mrs. Angela Sidney, a young boy lives in a community whose sustenance depends upon the salmon that return every year to spawn. The boy cries for food at night, so before bed his mother usually gives him the head of a salmon to eat. One night, however, the boy asks his mother why the salmon head is always moldy. He rejects the moldy salmon and throws it away. The boy's words and actions offend the salmon spirits, upon whose good graces the livelihood of his community rests. So, the next time he goes to the place where the village dries their fish, the boy falls in the water and his family believes that he has drowned. Moldy Head has not drowned, however. The salmon people have captured him, and they spend the period until the following spawning season teaching the boy the meaning of respect. He is reunited with his family when his mother catches a salmon wearing a copper necklace just like the one her son used to have. After the ministrations

---

5. Sakae Kubo, *A Reader's Greek-English Lexicon of the New Testament and a Beginner's Guide for the Translation of New Testament Greek*, New rev. ed. (Grand Rapids, MI: Zondervan, 1975), 140.
6. Meyer, 1059.

of a spiritual healer, the boy is restored to human form and rejoins his community. According to Mrs. Sidney, "that's how they know about fish" (Moldy Head brings new knowledge about the salmon to his community) and "that's why kids are told not to insult fish" (members of the community need to learn respect for that which sustains their lives).[7]

Nora Marks Dauenhauer (Tlingit) and Richard Dauenhauer have remarked that origin stories are inherently theoretical because they are "human creations after the fact," that is, they codify and transmit cultural messages orally and in writing.[8] Origin stories construct frameworks for understanding human experience and articulate "people's opinions about the origin and meaning of the world and life as we know it."[9] While the Dauenhauers focus specifically on the genre of creation stories, one could make a similar claim about the Moldy Head story. It articulates people's opinions about the origin and meaning of the human relationship with the salmon that are so essential to their survival.

It also offers a framework for understanding the meaning of decay. In the story, Moldy Head is taught to respect not only the spirits of the salmon, but also the natural processes of decay and the biological transformation of all life. The story provides a social and spiritual "imaginary" (a term coined by philosopher Charles Taylor) in which mold, a symptom of the ongoing decomposition of matter, functions as a crucial component of creation's cycle (and circle). I only wish that Paul—and much of Christian theology after him—had similarly learned not to reject the salmon's moldy head!

A different way to understand the lessons of Moldy Head is through what soil biologist Elaine Ingham has identified as the "soil food web."[10] According to Ingham, what many people pejoratively call "dirt" is actually a web woven by an incredible diversity of organisms:

7. Julie Cruikshank, *Life Lived Like a Story: Life Stories of Three Yukon Native Elders, American Indian Lives* (Lincoln: University of Nebraska Press, 1990), 78.
8. Nora Marks Dauenhauer and Richard Dauenhauer, "Tlingit Origin Stories," in *Stars Above, Earth Below: American Indians and Nature*, ed. Marsha Bol (Niwot, CO: Roberts Rinehart, 1998), 29.
9. Ibid.
10. Elaine R. Ingham, "The Soil Food Web," http://urbanext.illinois.edu/soil/SoilBiology/soil_food_web.htm (accessed 15 May 2012).

They range in size from the tiniest one-celled bacteria, algae, fungi, and protozoa, to the more complex nematodes and micro-arthropods, to the visible earthworms, insects, small vertebrates, and plants. As these organisms eat, grow, and move through the soil, they make it possible to have clean water, clean air, healthy plants, and moderated water flow. . . . As organisms decompose complex materials, or consume other organisms, nutrients are converted from one form to another, and are made available to plants and to other soil organisms. All plants—grass, trees, shrubs, agricultural crops—depend on the food web for their nutrition.[11]

Since the soil food web also nourishes the animals, birds, and countless other species comprising the world as we know it, one could say that its complex material transformations also support life in general. It literally renews the earth and enables a resurrection of the earth's body by transforming old matter into new life.

Unfortunately, many Christian theologians have failed to recognize this insight. For example, Pauline scholar N. T. Wright has called Romans 8 "Paul's most spectacular piece of creation-theology, a bursting out of a fresh reading of Genesis 1–3, coupled with the exodus narrative of liberation from slavery and the journey to the promised inheritance: creation itself will be set free from its bondage to decay, to share the freedom of God's children."[12] While Wright, one of the most eloquent and prolific reinterpreters of Paul, never resorts to the old dualisms between spirit and flesh to achieve his "fresh" perspective, he nevertheless leaves Paul's view of decay unchallenged. For Wright, the apostle's rhetoric of the Christian journey to freedom refigures the Jewish exodus story. Wright argues that, for Paul, the end of exile, or the undoing of creation's bondage to decay, will be inaugurated in the new covenant represented by Christ and the Holy Spirit. However, this very interesting attempt to embody Paul's rhetoric within the context of the Jewish traditions of covenant and creation falls short precisely in its uncritical embracing of freedom as *dis*embodied. To be free, one must still transcend matter's vulnerability to degradation and the processes of decay.

---

11. Ibid.
12. N. T. Wright, *Paul: In Fresh Perspective* (Minneapolis, MN: Fortress Press, 2009), 31.

A story by legal scholar John Borrows (Anishinaabe) offers a counterpoint to Wright and, more importantly, a provocative model of how decay motivates life. In this story, Nanabush—trickster, shape-shifter, and world cocreator—assumes the form of an otter and goes hunting for fish. After finding some silver herring, Otter/Nanabush quickly devours it before other predators can steal his catch. Through the death of this fish, Nanabush renews his own life: "Death demands this exchange; nourishment ever arises from decay."[13] Further on in his journey, Nanabush (this time as himself) sees a limestone cliff rising up from the bay, across the sound before him:

> It looks permanent, ever constant, until you see it through the corridor of time. Nanabush remembers that it was once a complex living being, a coral reef. Thousands of tiny creatures made it their home as they built on each other's death. This was the time when the earth was covered in water, when he had to take refuge on the turtle's back. The divers plumbed the depths for him then, retrieving small particles of soil, so he could grow this present world. Muskrat died bringing mud to the surface. That was many years ago, but life had always demanded death, even at that time. The world continually draws sustenance from decay. Like the escarpment, life's appearance of permanence is deceiving.
>
> Now the escarpment basks in the rising sun and reflects on the shimmering waves. Its ancient death still feeds life. Cedar, birch, and poplar grow from the old rocks. They host a thousand species under their expansive green canopies. Sea life has turned to stone, and eventually turned into trees, birds, and insects. Animals feed on each, and humans follow this same pattern. Transformation is the law of life.[14]

The Moldy Head and Nanabush narratives construct a radical alternative to the rhetoric of freedom in Romans 8. In these Native stories, decay embodies transformation rather than enslavement, and dynamic law of life rather than an obstacle that humans must overcome.

---

13. Borrows, *Canada's Indigenous Constitution*, 284.
14. Ibid., 285.

In his book, *Caring for Creation*, evangelical theologian Calvin DeWitt has identified Indigenous knowledge about living sustainably and cooperatively on earth as one of the most important antidotes for the poison of the world's current eco-crisis.[15] In the narratives I have presented, such healing knowledge includes how the movement and exchange of death and decay form a necessary part of the greater life spiral: life begets death, which in turn begets life, albeit in a different form. Redemption is ongoing, not a future state that leaves behind biological existence. Moldy Head and Nanabush offer a much more sustainable vision for the planet than that implied by the disembodied eschatology of Romans 8. These stories testify that creation has always already "obtained its glory," and that it is only our ability to perceive this that is lacking.

---

15. Calvin B. DeWitt, *Caring for Creation: Responsible Stewardship of God's Handiwork* (Grand Rapids, MI: Baker Books, 1998), 19.

Personal Encounters with Paul's Decay

My first serious engagement with Paul's letter to the Romans came in my Pauline Studies course at Canadian Mennonite Bible College back in the late 1970s. One of the most inspiring thoughts I took away from that class was the idea that, for Paul, the salvation accomplished in the life, death, and resurrection of Jesus included not only human beings but all of creation. As communicated to me by my professor, the apostle's grand vision of the salvation of all things only made sense within the context of a renewed earth. Any thoughts I had entertained about the necessity for the world's complete destruction and reemergence vanished and never returned.

The inconvenient detail about creation's "bondage to decay" never concerned me. But as I reflect on Paul's words today, my mind is incapable of even conceiving of any kind of creation without the presence of decay. Does not a renewed creation imply growth and flourishing? And does not growth in the natural world imply decay and even death, as Laura's essay states? The idea that a renewed creation could be static, somehow frozen in time and "disembodied," is not only senseless but abhorrent to me.

Is it possible, then, that Paul was using the rhetoric of decay as a hyperbolic metaphor to describe a whole new way of thinking about the transformation of creation? Or was Paul serious about viewing creation's "bondage to decay" as an "obstacle that humans must overcome," yet referring not to the natural life-giving process of decay but—and this is the key—to the human-made decay of creation so evident all around us in the twenty-first century? God's wonderful earth is gradually being destroyed day after day by the insanity of humans who view it as a resource to be exploited for the sake of acquiring wealth, for the sake of more and more stuff, and their personal comfort. Such decay and death is not life-giving, but life-stealing. It is a bondage from which creation must be freed, and it is up to us, the ones who are responsible for the bondage, to free creation from the stain of projects like the oil sands extraction in northern Alberta, gas fracking in the Balkan fields of Saskatchewan and North Dakota, and the hydro mega-developments in my northern Manitoba backyard.

If Paul was referring to a human-initiated decay, then his words could not be more timely. But where does that leave us in considering the renewed creation awaiting us? If that renewed creation includes decay and death, what are the ramifications for salvation theology? And how does this relate to Jesus' words (as recorded in John) that, "unless a grain of wheat falls into the ground and dies . . . [how can it bear fruit]?"

Laura's essay leaves me with many exciting thoughts and questions, yet few answers. The stories of Moldy Head and Nanabush offer a "sustainable vision" for the future of creation, and we must wrestle with them as we re-vision Romans 8. But I wonder whether Paul would really have seen them as presenting arguments opposed to his letters. Perhaps he would have welcomed and embraced such stories as one way to grapple with the profound mysteries of life.

—*Vic Thiessen*

O Kanada

"*alles will leben*,"
my Oma used to say.
everything wants to live.

alles will leben,
she grins, shaking her head
her knees in the dirt
her thumb and fingers
a deathgrip around this brown taproot
the dandelion
plunging away from her
deep into the earth but not deep enough
or the same saying
the same thumb and fingers
crushing a potato bug

the dandelion, like herself, is non-native here
an "invasive species"
the potato a gift
from indigenous farmers

she knows none of this
her tight thumb and forefinger
are thinking about the pinch
of planting potato eyes in the last years
in South Ukraine
only the eyes
the only thing left uneaten
year after year, nothing but skins
and eyes turned into the ground
all flesh hollowed out
and consumed

every summer life rose again
out of those weak and wrinkled eyes
and made a smaller crop
and every winter hunger
scraped a little more
of the insides
out
of the village

here, *Dank Gott*, there is no Machnov
no angry bandit to raid her cellar
here, there is the RCMP, who are honest
here she plants generous potato chunks
plump and crisp
smooth and round in her palm
like the cheeks of this big-eyed grandson
here, promise rises tall and green
here, she laughs at the little bandits
staining her thumbnail orange-
red

alles will leben, she smiles, for
she is not among the crushed
here, the sun is in her brown hair
and on her red babushka kerchief
with the bright and blotchy flowers from South Ukraine
and on the potatoes from Peru
and on the *dent de Lyon* from France
and on the beetle from Colorado
and on her gardening jeans from K-Mart
and on the dirt from here
from here
from here
from here.
O Kanada, O Kanada, she sighs.

—*Marcus Rempel*

9

THE EARTH IS A SONG MADE VISIBLE:
A CHEYENNE CHRISTIAN PERSPECTIVE[1]

By Chief Lawrence Hart (Southern Cheyenne)

In this age of ecological crisis, I am convinced that traditional Native American perspectives regarding the earth can help all peoples—both settler and Indigenous—discover ways to counter the increasing destruction of the environment. Of course, many in the environmental movement, in progressive circles and churches, and within Native communities, are well aware of these traditional views. We know that the earth is sacred. We know that all things are interconnected in the circle of creation. We know that if you damage one part, you do damage to all forms of life within that delicate balance. Yet despite that knowledge, many, if not most of us, struggle to live lives in harmony with it. How can we change that and live into a better way?

One way to connect traditional knowledge to the depths of our hearts, bodies, and everyday practice is through sacred ritual, ceremony, and song. Traditional Indigenous knowledge has always been embodied knowledge—embodied in cultural customs and observed by whole communities. That knowledge was never meant simply to be known and passed down through oral or textual tradition. It was to be taken up through ceremony and reverential acts

---

1. This chapter is a significantly revised version of an essay I published in Calvin Redekop, ed., *Creation and the Environment: An Anabaptist Perspective on a Sustainable World* (Baltimore: John Hopkins University Press, 2000), 170-80.

of respect and reciprocity. That's where its power has been and is made manifest—power to transform us, sustain the earth, and even re-create the world in which we live.

What if settler and Indigenous peoples found and/or rediscovered ceremonial ways, respective to their different traditions and communities, to annually, seasonally, even daily, honor the sacredness of earth? Could that enable us to live in a more respectful fashion with "all our relations"?

In this reflection, I'd like to summarize some of the basic differences that I see between Native American and mainstream American views with respect to the earth, and then describe a few of the ways in which my people, the Cheyenne, have practiced these views. I'll conclude with some explorations as to what this might mean for those of us who no longer live so close to the earth in traditional and sustainable ways (i.e., those of us who drive our gas-filled vehicles to the local store to buy the three sisters—corn, beans, and squash).

Native American views regarding the earth

Beliefs that Native Americans hold with respect to the earth are often in conflict with the views held by the majority of other peoples in Turtle Island. A brief focus on a few of these will be sufficient to highlight the dissimilarities.

First, in contrast to the rugged individualism espoused by mainstream society and much of Christianity, there is a strong *peoplehood* concept amongst Indigenous peoples. Community is, in a sense, everything, and this belief—prevalent throughout the hemisphere—greatly impacts our relation with the land. For the Indigenous, thought and action tend to begin from the first-person plural. As an individual, I may use the personal pronoun. However, I can never say "I" without being cognizant that I am a Cheyenne. My identity as an individual Native American is connected to and deeply rooted in a particular tribe. Individualism is a foreign concept to Native Americans (though it has made inroads through colonialism and policies of assimilation). An individual Native American born into a tribe will immediately have an identity with a subgroup, which may be an extended family, a clan, or a society of the tribe, and that connection continues throughout life. The tribal subgroups have a function to benefit the whole. If a group fails to perform a function, the whole suffers. If it succeeds, the whole benefits.

What this vision of peoplehood means for the Indigenous relationship to the earth is that it is not individuals who hold a particular view of the land and the creation, but whole tribes and whole groups. The earth is for the circle of people. And since the earth is for the whole, no one individual can own any part of it. The earth belongs to the Creator,

A Cheyenne woman points a ceremonial pipe towards the earth, ca. 1910.

and is gifted to peoples. This isn't Indigenous "romanticism." Plenty of historical accounts testify that Native Americans objected to European notions of earth as property to be owned and sold. Many tribes have resisted this in various ways, and the older generation still de-emphasizes land ownership.

Sacredness. This is another significant value that separates the Indigenous from many other peoples. We believe the earth has a sacredness about it, especially that part of the earth in which the Creator has chosen to place our particular community. Yes, it is true that the Jewish and Christian Scriptures talk about the earth as a creation of God, and proclaim that the whole earth is holy. But more often than not, the European inheritors of those texts have not translated that belief in the holiness of the world into concrete practices where the land is recognized as such. For example, when non-Native Christians gather for church in Chicago, Seattle, or Toronto, they typically don't acknowledge the land on which they gather. By words or physical action, they do not attempt to recognize or connect with the very place on which they are privileged to gather. The liturgy or worship service is "placeless"—not "placed" in Toronto or "placed" in Seattle. But Indigenous peoples typically do "place" their worship. In my territory, the Cheyenne priest begins all ceremonies by touching the earth four times. One cannot conduct an action or speak without first acknowledging the earth.[2] Or consider the pipe ceremonies in Cheyenne, Cree, Anishinaabe, and Lakota communities. Traditions vary, but the pipe will often be pointed in seven directions. The first is toward the Creator/Father Sky. The second always to the land/Mother Earth. This ritual or invocation must take place. Without it, we have desecrated the sacred. There's a much different view of land at work in these Indigenous communities. And it can nurture a different relationship to the land—a sense of rootedness, connectedness, reverence, and respect.

I understand why some Christian groups, like the Anabaptists— my Christian family—have taken the position on land that they have. During the Reformation, the Anabaptists pushed against Catholic beliefs, which held certain objects, words, days, persons, *and places* to be sacred. They saw certain abuses at work, and were concerned about a lack of biblical support for such. Much of that was valid. But did they lose something in that radical resistance in regards to place? Perhaps it is time for a rethinking of the particular lands we inhabit. Perhaps God has gifted the original peoples of this land with a view of place that can help reform the church's understanding today?

Cheyenne practices

Cheyenne peoples have a variety of practices to honor their relationship with the earth. A central one is ritualistic singing. Many

---

2. Similar practice was (and still is) observed amongst the Northern Cheyenne. Tribal historian, John Stands In Timber (1884–1967), describes how the elders in his community would always begin a story or teaching by physically recognizing/respecting the land on which they lived: "An old storyteller would smooth the ground in front of him with his hand and make two marks in it with his right thumb, two with his left, and a double mark with both thumbs together. Then he would rub his hands, and pass his right hand up his right leg to his waist, and touch his left hand and pass it on up his right arm to his breast. He did the same thing with his left and right hands going up the other side. Then he touched the marks on the ground with both hands and rubbed them together and passed them over his head and all over his body. That meant the Creator had made human beings' bodies and their limbs as he had made the earth, and that the Creator was witness to what was to be told. They did not tell any of the old or holy stories without that." As quoted in *Cheyenne Memories* (New Haven, CT: Yale University Press, 1998), 12.

routine activities of life involve a song or songs, and most have lyrics that recognize the earth. This tradition is still prevalent within Native American church life and is still practiced in cultures where Native Americans have not been swayed by strong forces of acculturation and assimilation, including influences from some quarters of the church. Here are a few examples.

In preparation for tilling, a common practice by many tribal groups was to sing a song before the earth was broken. This was done because tilling was valued as a God-ordained task. Despite the words of Genesis 2:15, which connects the impact of sin to plowing of the ground, we acknowledge the fundamental goodness of this relationship.

Another song was sung before planting seeds, and there were songs for the harvest, too. These were common rituals. Indeed, for every occasion in Cheyenne life, let alone Native American life, there was a song—songs at birth, songs for life's everyday activities, and songs at death. Singing of songs by Native Americans was simply a part of the rhythm of life, and in my reading was not all that different from the practice of the Hebrew people in both the Old and New Testaments. When I hear Indigenous songs sung today, especially those sung by women, I am reminded of the song sung by Miriam after crossing the Red Sea, that of Hannah when God granted her wish for a son, the Magnificat sung by the chosen Mary, or songs sung when the early church gathered (Philippians 2:5-11).

When Christian missionaries first arrived, the Pueblo people still sang before planting the special varieties of corn they had developed. Unfortunately, new converts were expected to cease practicing this and other cultural traditions, and as a result there were profound cultural conflicts. Cultural conflicts still exist on that reservation today. Yet some Indigenous Christians and missionary workers have suggested that the sacred practices of the Pueblo should be viewed as analogous to that of the Old Testament period. Christian workers and Pueblo Christians could presumably build upon this "Old Testament culture" and add to it the Good News of the New Testament. These ancient songs could still be sung, could still bring life to the people and the land in which they walk. Sadly, this excellent recommendation has yet to be followed.

In spite of that, ritualistic singing is still practiced by many tribes and reflects the strong connectedness to the earth that was shared by all tribes. And this tradition has impacted the life of the Cheyenne churches, too. Many Cheyenne Christian songs reveal tribal understandings of the land, and the hymns thereby gain greater meaning.

Consider the Cheyenne translation of the classic European hymn "Silent Night" (ca. 1818). This well-known and internationally used Christmas carol has no reference to the earth in the original German, nor in the English. But Rudolphe Petter, a Swiss linguist who studied Cheyenne culture and language in Oklahoma and Montana at the turn of the century, did something very interesting with this hymn. He added a reference to *ho'eva* (the earth), and in doing so captured the rich meaning of the incarnation (the Great Spirit become flesh).

> 1. Pavetaa'eva nehe'xoveva *Tsexho'ehnese ho'eva,*
> Jesus Vo'estanevestomanehe. Ehvo'estanetsehestaotsehoo'o
> Tsexho'eotsestomotahaetse Vo'estanevehahtsestotse.

> 2. Ahaa esheeva nehe'xoveva *Tsexho'ehnese ho'eva,*
> Jesus Vo'estanevestomanehe, Tsehvo'estanevehatano'toetse
> Netao'o haveseveva, Tsehveno'ohaetse.

Translation:
1. It was a good night then, *When he came to earth,*
Jesus the Savior. He became a person
When he brought us Salvation.

2. It was a blessed day then, *When he came to earth,*
Jesus the Savior, When he wanted to save us
From all sin, When he rescued us.

By using *ho'eva*, Petter and his Cheyenne language informant were able to communicate the birth of Christ in a way that connects it to the redemption of the entire creation, and honor that which has central importance for a people whose culture is inextricably linked to the earth.

What if today's Cheyenne, other Indigenous Christians, and settler Christians did something similar? What if they purposefully translated and reworked their songs and hymns to reflect a more earth-centered theology? Most of our worship liturgy and praise lack song and ritual that connect us to the place in which we live, the dirt from which we were given birth, the soil that God has blessed and made sacred. We need to do what the Cheyenne "Silent Night" does . . . *and go even further* to make thicker connections with Mother Earth. The places in which we worship—church sanctuaries, for example—often distance us from the environment by keeping us indoors and removed from the elements. What if we learned from the Indigenous and did our ceremonies by the rivers, the trees, out in the sun, and so on? That's a tradition many of the biblical mothers and fathers practiced. Abraham, for example, planted a tree in Beersheba so he could worship Yahweh (Genesis 21). What I am inviting us to do is to rediscover and practice an Indigenous value that is also, in many ways, a biblical value, but one that has been largely lost.

One of the most profound songs is that sung by the Cheyenne peace chief White Antelope. On November 29, 1864, during the Sand Creek Massacre, he sang the following death song:

> Father have pity on me, Father have pity on me,
> The old men say, only the earth endures.
> You have spoken truly. You have spoken well.
> Nothing lives long, only the Earth and the Mountains.
> Nothing lives long, only the Earth and the Mountains.

It's clear that White Antelope (and his people) had a special relationship with the earth. Yet again I say, this is not something that's totally foreign to the Jewish-Christian heritage. If we listen closely, we can hear a parallel to White Antelope's song in the Hebrew Bible. In Psalm 90, the poet tells us that human beings are finite creatures of dust, that the mountains were "born" long before we came around, and that everything is wholly dependent on the mercy of the Creator. In Psalm 119, we are assured that God has established the earth and that it stands firm. The Bible does have "indigenous" voices, voices attuned to the land.

Seeking a second discovery

The time has come for a second discovery of America, one that comes about through attentive listening to the voices of Native

Americans, and collective action on our common wisdom. Thomas R. Berger, a distinguished jurist from Canada, writes the following in his book, *A Long and Terrible Shadow*:

> The culture of Native people amounts to more than crafts and carvings. Their tradition of decision-making by consensus, their respect for the wisdom of their elders, their concept of the extended family, their belief in a special relationship with the land, their regard for the environment, their willingness to share—all these values persist in one form or another within their own culture, even though they have been under unremitting pressure to abandon them. . . . This is still the age of discovery, a discovery of the true meaning of the history of the New World and of the Native People's rightful place in that world. This is a discovery to be made in our own time should we choose it—the second discovery of America.[3]

Not too long ago, a Christian anthropologist was commissioned to study the cultural conflicts between people in the church, both non-Indigenous Christian workers and converts, and a traditional Pueblo people on their reservation. Historically, it had been expected that the converts would put off all their cultural practices, for they were seen as pagan. Ironically, these were the very people who, through their agronomy, had produced a variety of corn whose stalk was short in height but produced a long cob that could reach maturity in a few weeks. The Pueblo people produced many corn varieties, including the famous blue corn. Certain types could withstand arid conditions and, in a short time with little moisture, produce more than enough to meet their needs. The Pueblo's ability to do such remarkable things with this plant is derived from their deeply spiritual relationship with the land and its Creator. Can we Christians, settler and Indigenous, not learn a few things about the land from their spiritual traditions and practices?

The Pueblo sing songs about the land and for the land, because the land is very good. The biblical story in the first chapter of Genesis invites us to do the same: "God saw all that he had made, and pronounced it good." From a Native American perspective, the

---

3. Thomas R. Berger, *A Long and Terrible Shadow: White Values, Native Rights in the Americas, 1492–1992* (Vancouver: Douglas & McIntyre, 1991), 160.

created earth is a song made visible . . . the song of the Creator. We should be so inspired by her (Mother Earth) that we sing, too!

Over the past three decades, our worship liturgies have undergone significant change. I have been encouraged that language and lyrics have become more inclusive, and I thank the women who have led this change. More recently, ritual is gaining some acceptance and usage. Today, we need creative poets, composers, liturgists, and others to explore how to root our worship in the land. We need to sing the land, to experience it, to be transformed by its power, and so glorify God. We need the Spirit to help us envision imaginative practices that can help us live alternative, more radical lives in balance with creation.

To treat the earth as a sacred gift of God, it is important that we have plenty of knowledge and understanding and lots of good science. There's no doubt about that. But in order to treat the earth as sacred, we also need the gift and grace and energy and courage of the Creator. Some of that can come through the spiritual means of communal worship, ceremony, and ritual. Indigenous peoples know what some of that might look like from our traditions. Yet those traditions need to be renewed and applied today to help our communities navigate a context in which many of us are living much like the dominant society, struggling to live in balance.

Settler peoples and settler Christians need to learn from the traditions of the lands in which they live, and thoughtfully create rituals and liturgy that can foster a more communal, intimate, and personal relationship to the earth. If we all do this, perhaps the groaning of which the apostle speaks (Romans 8) will break into a song of liberation. May it be, and soon.

Potato Prayers

I remember kneeling once on the earth as a song made visible, as Chief Lawrence Hart speaks of it. I remember planting potatoes with Madeleine, an elder at Doig River Reserve, in northern British Columbia. Every potato she planted Madeleine blessed in the name of Jesus.

My grandmother prayed over her potatoes, too—once they were peeled, boiled, and steaming on a well-laid table. Somehow, for my people, who are a deeply pious, prayerful lot, our instincts to pray run indoors. Once we're all in our good clothes around the white, square tablecloth, once the potato has been safely removed from the living womb of earth and sanctified into pure white starch, we solemnly bow our heads.

I wonder: if my people had had prayers and spiritual teachings for planting and hilling potatoes, for picking potato bugs, and for digging potatoes up, as Aboriginal people seem to have for every contact they make with the living things of earth, could we have ever turned our family farming heritage over to "agribusiness"? Winkler, Manitoba, is home to the official "potato lands" of this province, and also the heart of the Mennonite Bible belt. It is a land of such loamy fertility that, even in these days of "farm crisis" (How far back do these days go? When will we see their end?), farmers there can still get rich, none more so than the large-scale potato farmers. I have a colleague who grew up working on one of these farms. The high-tech methodologies, the incredible production statistics he describes—thirty thousand pounds per acre this year—stagger me. The pesticide regime required by McCain's, their singular customer and lord, terrifies me. Toxic dowsings occur almost weekly.

But the potatoes on the plates of my people still look much the same, and so we bow our heads and thank the Lord. But who is now our Lord of the harvest? It is surely not a grandmother laying the name of Jesus on each potato that accounts for the thirty thousand pounds of potatoes per acre that will be reaped on Winkler's two- to three-thousand-acre megafarms this fall. Surely we should bless the wisdom of McCain's, and laud the wizardry of Monsanto?

Does that sound idolatrous? How could it? That is business, and work, which belong outside and which our Jesus has nothing to do with. Inside the four walls of the church and around the ordered square of the dining-room table, we still pray in Jesus' name, Amen. So, all is well in our house. And safe. And sterile. And nearly dead.

I'd like to go outside and see if I can find Madeleine's Jesus. He is in the earth, with each potato, with each worm, in every living member of the living soil. He is there, receiving Monsanto's biocides, chemically burned, lashed, exhausted. And he is there holding Madeleine's blessings and bringing forth life.

Broken and blessed. His body. Our bread.

Madeleine the Potato Blesser holds out a communion to us. Chief Lawrence Hart intones a Cheyenne Mennonite earth-sky harmony line. Might we join in these, and make of our farming yet a Eucharist?

—Marcus Rempel

PART 3

VOICES OF CHALLENGE AND PROTEST

beginning . . .

god   and the devil
hooked up on social media recently and
still caught in a colonial time warp
decided to start everything over again
by meeting in the church parking lot
to shoot craps to decide who would create whom
and despite his omnipotence
god kept rolling ones, but putting his
most articulate doctrinal spin to work
claimed one plus one is three
(to try to get a little advantage)
but the devil rolled two twos
laughed
danced off his disguise
shape-shifted into coyote and
bull-elk and saguaro and iron,
and said, two plus two—is thirteen blessings,
just like you and me, land and sea,
day and night, sky and earth
corn and lightning, raven and
sapling, and winners
and losers becoming losers and winners
—two is the truth
even of us!
but god turned pink with disbelief
said, "don't give me that Potawatomie gift economy crap!"
became a white man and started killing everything in sight
until he finally killed himself
and then the earth said to the sun
"burn the flesh off
so we can gather all the relatives
gamble with the bones
and see what comes next!"

—*Jim Perkinson*

10

WHY I DO NOT BELIEVE IN
A CREATOR

By Tink Tinker (Wazhazhe/Osage Nation)

W*hat is your word for God? What do you mean you have no word for God? Everyone believes in a Creator, don't they?* Our more liberal-minded White friends always want to know more about us, so they naturally come with questions. Thirty-five years ago, a Native elder from northern California told us a creation story. Long ago, Coyote was floating through the air and wanted some place to rest. So he created the earth—although it was just an accident. So is coyote God? *The* Creator?

As we have learned from the world of physics, even scientific observation changes what is being observed (i.e., the "observer effect"). In this case, the very question that any White person (say, an anthropologist) asks a Native person shapes her answer in decisive ways. Whatever the Native person has to say about the matter must now use the language categories of the colonizer. In this case, the key problematic words are *god, creator,* and *believe.* The question itself shapes the reality that the Native person must try to describe. Now she must struggle to use colonial language of god, creator, and belief to interpret her own world back to the well-meaning colonizer, who seems to assume that everyone in the world is similar to himself. The more these euro-christian friends hear about Coyote, however, the clearer they are that crazy Old

Man Coyote is not exactly what they mean by the word *god*—even if he created something.[1]

It must sound quite incredulous and heretical to announce a disbelief in a creator, since talk of a "creator" and a "creation" has become second nature in the euro-colonized world, as liberal Christianity attempts to reclaim a theology rooted in what some call its "First Article" doctrine (i.e., beginning with the creator and creation, as in the Apostles' Creed). My objection to creator/creation language, however, is vitally important to preserve the coherence of an American Indian worldview. My concerns include both linguistic complexities involved in any translation and the imposition of categories of cognition in the colonizer's language as though they represent some level of normative universality in this late colonial world. This is *necessarily complex*, and requires some detail in explanation.

The up-down image schema

In this case, creator and creation are key categories of presumed universality deeply embedded in the "social imaginary"[2] of euro-colonial people in north America as normative truth. As such, they get too easily imposed on the vanquished Aboriginal owners

---

1. My use of the lower case for such adjectives as *english, christian, biblical*, etc., is intentional. While nouns naming religious groups might be capitalized out of respect for each Christian—as for each Muslim or Buddhist—using the lower-case *christian* or *biblical* for adjectives allows readers to avoid unnecessary normativizing or universalizing of the principal institutional religious quotient of the euro-west. Likewise, I avoid capitalizing such national or regional adjectives as *american, amer-european, european, euro-western*, etc., and decline capitalizing the *n* in *north America*. It is important to my argumentation that people recognize the historical artificiality of modern regional and nation-state social constructions.

Quite paradoxically, I know, I insist on capitalizing *White* (adjective or noun) to indicate a clear cultural pattern invested in Whiteness that is all too often overlooked or even denied by american Whites. Moreover, this brings parity to the insistence of African Americans on the capitalization of the word *Black* in reference to their own community (in contra-distinction to the *New York Times* usage). Likewise, I always capitalize *Indian, American Indian*, and *Native American*.

2. A phrase coined by the Canadian philosopher Charles Taylor (Catholic) that refers to the set of symbols and values that construct a society's field of understanding and determine what is thinkable and doable.

of the land as though the euro-american metaphoric imagination were so concrete and tangible, a presumably obvious "first principle," as it were, that all peoples must inherently find some way to talk about this colonial christian imaginary—even if in their own discrete language. First of all, the word necessitates a couple of other cognitional categories that I am increasingly disavowing. Those two categories include both the notion of a "creator"—that is something euro-westerners would call "god," usually with a capital letter—and a much more pervasive cognitive model we might call an up-down cognitive image schema (using the language of cognitive linguistic theorists). This image schema then identifies a whole social imaginary that organizes everything from political realities (even in a "procedural" democracy) to theologies (from conservative to liberal). Identifying a creator as a super-personality who is responsible for creating all things, a "god on high," is a euro-colonial hierarchic imaginary that lends itself both historically and presently to euro-christian notions of hierarchy and inequality.

Here, I am not simply objecting to the language of god and creator as language embedded in a european worldview or christian ideology. It is much more crucial to notice that imposing these religious metaphors of a hierarchical divine as an overlay on Indian cultures irredeemably distorts the Native culture and destroys the intricacies and the beauty, that is, the coherence, of the Native worldview. An up-down linguistic cognitive image functions to structure the social whole around vertical hierarchies of power and authority.

Largely unnoticed by those who are immersed in it, an up-down image schema is an ever-present american conceptual metaphor, one that creates the hierarchic notions that dominate our euro-colonial world of christian conquest. It puts some over others, and someone always seems to be "in charge." The up can be a king or a president, but that person is the One, the top of a hierarchy. Until recently, european theorists explained White as the superior form in their racial hierarchy with a descending rank according to the darkness of skin color. While man is "head of the household" in european gender hierarchy (the so-called "order of creation" that suppresses women into a lower status; see Genesis 2 and 1 Timothy 2:11-15), children are always thought to be subservient to the parents (to be "seen and not heard"). This order-of-creation mentality then evolves politically into the valorization of "meritocracy" as a norm in American political, intellectual, and socioeconomic culture. Especially beginning in the sixteenth century, humans come before all the rest of creation. Since trees are far down the hierarchy of being, clear-cutting a forest for human profit is an easy thing to rationalize. Capitalist economies function with a clear up-down hierarchy of command, as do modern military "chains of command." Up-down lends itself especially to the language of ruler and sovereignty, words that lack any ancient counterpart in Native languages. And in the euro-christian worldview, there must be a spiritual power (higher power) who rules over humans and over all creation. So people generally talk of a god who "looks over them."

In other contexts I have noted that the Indigenous worldview is primarily spatial, while the euro-western worldview is primarily temporal. That may seem a bit paradoxical in my description, here, of what seems to be a spatial up-down euro-christian imagery. The temporality that is so characteristic of the euro-western worldview is somehow morphed into this physical-space image of the up-down deity. There is a hierarchical "geography" that is attached to the euro-western temporal worldview, resulting in this up-down, spatial imagery (or imaginary) that gets populated with all kinds of concrete objects that inhabit actual space—such as a kingdom, and a white-haired, bearded god sitting on a throne in a heavenly palace. It is indeed spatial imagery—everything in it has a "footprint"—but the spatial here is "located" in a way-off, distant, abstract place. The up-down image schema seems to be inherently temporal and only subordinately spatial.

A clear and particularly disastrous use of the up-down image schema in relation to Native Peoples is the use of "Great White Father" to refer to the U.S. head of government and "Great White Mother" in Canada, in reference to the Queen of England. The language does not come from Natives themselves, but was the vain attempt of White colonial functionaries on the frontiers to name both White superiority and the authority of the political leader of the european invaders, whether Washington or Ottawa. The hierarchy is obvious: White conquistador (White superiority) over savage, uncivilized Natives.

An American Indian worldview, to the contrary, generates a social whole that eschews up-down hierarchies in favor of lateral social constructs that are much more egalitarian and predicated on balance and harmony. The important distinction, here, is that "lateral" does not imply "neutralizing," or a dismissal of the uniqueness of persons (whether two-legged, four-legged, winged, or all other forms of living and moving persons) within the greater whole. In other words, it is not a worldview that could be equated with the euro-western notion of "communism."

Imposing an up-down cognitive schema overlay on an Indian collateral worldview not only fails to allow for the expressing of Native realities, it is ultimately very destructive of those Native realities. And it certainly does not matter that many, if not most, Native People have made—under the duress of sheer survival—the concessive move to adopt those cognitional categories as somehow meaningful in their own postcolonial contexts. Ultimately, this new euro-christian colonial imaginary, imposed on Native Peoples and their lands over the past centuries, grossly distorts what is left of Indian cultures, and remains an impediment to continuing any egalitarian relationship between Peoples (using *Peoples* as a legal technical term). More to the point, I would argue that this newly imposed euro-christian worldview is ultimately destructive to the earth and all our relatives here on the earth, and thus imperils all Peoples, including those who live within the euro-western worldview.

The key problem is that the deep structure realities of the two worlds, those of euro-Christianity and American Indians, are inherently opposite to one another. Or, as Seneca scholar Barbara Mann puts it in *Iroquois Women,* "[I]n the european/Iroquoian instance, *none of the metanarratives of the two cultures coincide.*"[3]

Collateral-egalitarian image schema as community-ist

The worldview that traditionally pervaded all Native communities in the Americas embodies a cognitive model we might call a

---

3. Barbara Mann, *Iroquoian Women: The Gantowisas* (New York: Peter Lang, 2000), 63. Note also Vine Deloria's comment in the introduction to his *Metaphysics of Modern Existence*: "The fundamental factor that keeps Indians and non-Indians from communicating is that they are speaking about two entirely different perceptions of the world" (San Francisco: Harper and Row, 1979), vii.

collateral-egalitarian image schema, which is more of a community-ist model. As noted above, this is distinct from what the euro-west too easily imposes on Native peoples as a communist model. To understand the radical difference this model embodies, we need to begin with the numbers one and two and unpack the difference culturally. Mann rightly insists that Indian people are dualistic, in the sense of paired reciprocity, and that two represents the number of balance and wholeness. The number one, she insists, is dysfunctional. We need to see the number one as extractive rather than reciprocal. Value is placed in the One as superior, and the euro-west cannot envision a distribution of value or meaning across multiplicities of Two. In the euro-western, christianized mind, this kind of distribution dilutes value. There is only a monolithic image of power and value of the one, which is static—and superior. Two, in the American Indian context, is necessarily dynamic and lends itself to reciprocity.

For Indian peoples, this duality inherent in the number two is the balance of two paired halves necessary to make a whole: light and dark, male and female, sky and earth, night and day, sun and moon, etc. This American Indian reciprocal dualism of paired halves is the opposite of what she identifies as the Manichaean oppositional dualism, an up-down image schema that fuels euro-western political and religious ideologies. So, first of all, the notion of a single creator immediately participates in the dysfunctionality of the number one, signaling a hierarchical order of creation. The dualistic opposite, rather than a feminine co-participant, is then abject evil, or the Devil, something entirely lacking in Indian cultures until it was read back into our traditions by missionaries who needed to find (and still do) an equivalent evil to fit their own theologies. For Indian folk, the notion of a single, male sky god is decidedly unbalanced and leads to chaos, competition, male supremacy, racial hierarchy, and competing notions of a single (doctrinal?) truth over against falseness, heresy, and evil. It immediately allows for an anthropology that is decidedly anthropocentric and elevates the human (superior) over all other life-forms (the inferior), and equally allows for the elevation of male over female—since it is the male/man/ *adam* who is particularly made in the image of the christian, male sky god.

Indians, creator, god, and the colonization of the mind

"Wait a minute there!" some colonialist critic might insist, "I hear Indian folk call on Creator in their prayers all the time." Yes, it is true that many Indian folk and even national communities have today fallen into using Creator language, and I must admit to having fallen into that usage myself in some previous writings. Yet this reflects a couple of postcolonial realities. First, Indian minds have been so deeply colonized into colonial discourses—even discourses about ourselves—that we have come to believe what the missionaries have told us about ourselves. Even those of us who claim to have rejected the imposition of colonialist language and cognition can find ourselves slipping into euro-christian colonialist usage at the strangest and most unguarded moments.

Under the intense colonizing pressure of the invader governments (i.e., Canada and the United States) and the steady stream of euro-colonial missionaries, too many Indian folk have simply capitulated to Christianity in the guise of one denomination or another. To use creator language instead of missionary-god language helps these Indian folk feel a little more Indian-like, since all our traditions do acknowledge a variety of powers that brought about our present world. Second, many Indian folk have held on to something of their traditional ways, but those ways have been effectively altered along the way by euro-colonial interpreters (missionaries, anthropologists, elitist tourists and adventurers, etc.) in processes that Mann usefully calls "euro-forming." In this process, even our traditional ways are persistently reshaped particularly to exclude the feminine and to replace reciprocal dualism with the masculinist oneness of a sky-god.

wako^{n}da, the colonial missionaries have long told us, must be the Osage word for "God." Osages, and other Natives, must necessarily have some innate sense of a monolithic high god (read hierarchic/up-down god). The necessity, of course, is for affirming the self-identity and cosmology of the conquering colonizer and to coerce the Native into the new cultural modality of singularity and hierarchy of the up-down image schema imposed by the colonizer. The first step, then, is to erase women, erase the feminine, entirely. So, what was a powerful reciprocal duality of collateral balance becomes a male-dominant monotheistic modality. *wako^{n}da* *mo^{n}shita ski wako^{n}da udseta*, Life Maker Above and Life Maker Below, Grandfather and Grandmother, all get reductively suppressed into "Dear heavenly Father." And that dear heavenly father, we are assured by the missionary voice, is the english equivalent of the original Native *wako^{n}da*. *What a tragic loss, a loss of cosmic balance.* The power of the old Osage traditional experience of the world, and of every Native community of the Americas, was its implicit and explicit sense of balance and harmony. That collateral image schema of balance and harmony, then, is replaced by the multiple euro-western cultural image schema of up-down (masculinist) hierarchy. The co-lateral, community-ist image schema of interrelationship ("we are all related") is replaced by hierarchy and ultimately of domination. The role of the feminine in our experience of the cosmic energies is erased in favor of male supremacy; the collateral image schema of cosmic (and personal) balance is instantly discarded in favor of the new up-down image schema of power and control. Not only is the masculine high god fully in charge, a masculinist clergy is vested with full authority to interpret the will of that one. And that has become the predominant Osage reality today after more than a century of intense missionization.

Cosmic duality and balance (expressed in *wako^{n}da mo^{n}shita* and *wako^{n}da udseta*) are as much at stake as are personal and community-ist balance. These spiritual energies are dual and reciprocal, mutually reinforcing of one another and vitally necessary for balance. In my wife's dissertation about Indigenous Andean mining, she describes the Andean view that everything under the surface of the earth was not "evil," but rather held a different kind of energy that needed to be respected when going underground. Those underground or subterranean energies are absolutely necessary for balance in all of the universe, but they must be approached and interacted with differently. As Aaron Running Hawk listened to her description, he said that from a Lakota perspective, the unearthing of minerals and bringing them up to the surface for modern industrial use was creating a huge imbalance of the earth. One can picture the sphere of the earth becoming distorted in shape and wobbling out of its spin and orbit. Also, during the Latin American celebration of Carnival, the purpose of the event is to momentarily reverse the duality in order to preserve balance. Thus, the Andean procession of dancers wearing fearsome masks of the underground powers is exactly meant to maintain balance. "El Diablo" (the post-Christianizing name for Tio or Muki) is brought into the light of day for a little while, but then one would presume from this that the above-earth powers become subterranean for a little while. Then it all shifts back to the way it was. This has incredible contemporary relevance. For within the Indigenous Andean worldview, which respects both powers above and below, the very minerals of the earth are considered to be the veins and blood of this living, animate earth. And thus, modern industrialization is committing extraordinary personal violence by leeching all that blood to the surface in order to satisfy the monotheistic imaginings and desires of those who live by the "Protestant ethic" of capitalism and prosperity theology.[4]

Indian "creation" stories

While all Indian people have stories of origin—called "creation stories" in euro-talk—these stories differ significantly from the euro-west's. Osages remember that the dry-land portion of this world was made in the long ago by *o'po^n to^{n}ga*, the bull elk. So, why can't we just say that Bull-Elk is the Creator and leave it at that? The first problem with that choice is that human people and, at least, elk already existed. So did the earth. When the sky people/humans came down from the stars, they were brought down to the earth by the eagle (another creator figure?) but found it covered with water. It was Elk who then created the dry ground and all kinds of living things to help the humans to be able to survive. Once these sky people began to make their way around *mo^{n}sho^n*, then they discovered another community of humans, the earth people, who were already here. So, Elk shared a role and responsibility in making the world the way it is—as did Eagle. But neither one is the sort of monotheistic "creator" like the one brought over the waters with the christian european invasion. Indeed, recall that the world and people already existed—particularly the oak tree in which the sky people first landed. Namely, there are no credible, historical American Indian

---

4. See Loring Abeyta, *Resistance at Cerro de Pasco: Indigenous Moral Economy and the Structure of Social Movements in Peru* (PhD diss., University of Denver, 2005).

stories that tell of a creation *ex nihilo,* a creation from nothing. Nor is there a super-personality who is ultimately in charge. This same structuring of beginnings plays out in all Indian traditions. As Barbara Mann describes the Iroquois traditions, for instance, there are pairs of individuals who contribute to the making of the world— Sky Woman, her daughter Lynx, and Lynx's two sets of twins, one male and one female. Writing in correction of the euro-formed version of Iroquois traditions, which labels the male twins (Flint and Sapling) as one good and one evil, she insists, "Flint was not a 'destroyer,' nor Sapling a lone 'Creator.' Instead, both Twins were creators of life abundant—as were their female elders before them."[5] Mann's point, here, relates exactly back to Indigenous Andeans' understanding of Muki as a separate spiritual power source, as well as explaining carnival's misuse of Muki as a christian devil figure. Here we could add one more note of difference. While there is no garden of bliss in Aboriginal American traditions, all these stories tell of balancing the world from the beginning, without any aspersions of human fallen-ness or sin, and without any notion of an evil influence in the process. That only comes with the christian euro-forming of our traditions.

We are all related

In terms of euro-christian theological notions, the contemporary and more liberal idea of stewardship continues precisely this notion of hierarchy in an anthropocentric modality that is antithetical to an Indian worldview and the values that emerge from that worldview. Since our experience of the world is one of interrelationship, we cannot conceive of a human superiority to any of the other living things of the world. They are all "relatives." And to put ourselves somehow in charge seems to Indian peoples to be a very dangerous move, which puts the balance of the whole in great jeopardy.

Experiencing all non-human persons as relations generates an affect or way of life in which there can be no hierarchy of being, either among a human community or between the different categories of persons in the world: two-leggeds, four-leggeds, flying ones, or what we call the living-moving people, for example, trees,

---

5. Mann, *Iroquoian Women,* 89.

corn, rivers, and mountains. All of these persons are our relatives and need to be attended to with appropriate relationship behaviors. If we are all related, then the ideal that every Indian community strived to achieve was and is harmony and balance with all life around us, that is, with all our relatives. And this epitomizes the collateral-egalitarian image schema. Even an up-down hierarchy of human/non-human proves destructive to any ideal of cosmic balance.

Disruptions of balance (from personal to cosmic) occur daily, so they must be mitigated with ceremonial reciprocity. Whatever we human beings acquire or receive, we must give something back. So, if we take an animal relative's life—for example, the buffalo—there must be a ceremony to restore balance in our relationship with the buffalo and with the earth. The ceremonial giving back might include, for instance, a sprinkling of corn pollen (Navajo or Pueblo traditions). Then, when we harvest agricultural goods—for example, corn and corn pollen—there must likewise be a reciprocal ceremony of giving something back. Perhaps the gift might be one of tobacco, but harvesting tobacco likewise requires us to give in order to maintain balance even as we disrupt balance by taking. So, we are constantly reminded that the people whose lives we disrupt by taking are indeed our relatives: corn, buffalo, tobacco, and all other living beings. None of these people are there merely for human consumption or at-will usage. Rather they inhabit the earth along with us and have intrinsic value equal to that of humans. And our response to disruptions we necessarily create, in order to eat and live, requires a constant cycle of ceremony intended to restore balance.

In our living room, we have a lovely lithograph by Hopi artist Dan Namingha titled *Ceremonial Night*, a scene with the moon rising over a Southwest pueblo. The irony of the title, of course, is that there is never a single ceremonial night. The ceremony includes all the nights and days leading up to and preparing for the ceremonial night, and then includes all the nights and days afterward spent fulfilling the obligations, which are communicated from the spirits in the ceremony itself and which lend themselves to maintaining community balance. This hardly accords with the drive for efficiency that is the reality of our modern-day, post-industrial, digitalized twenty-first century.

Even under the conditions of conquest, generations of propa-gandizing residential schools and missionaries, and the radical urbanization of many contemporary Native folk, we still try to pay attention to this need to maintain balance. At urban powwows or community ceremonies, someone always takes responsibility for making a "spirit plate" to set aside for our ancestors and for the spir-its, something that many of us do even as we cook in our high-rise condominiums or apartments. There is constant travel from north american cities back to reservations and reserves just to maintain the ancestral connections. The land here takes on a continuing importance in the self-identity of people. For some national com-munities, there is still a tradition of taking a baby's umbilical cord back to the home territory (now usually reduced to a reservation) to be buried there in order to maintain a life-long ceremonial tie to that place.

In this spirit, our responsibility as humans, and the responsibil-ity of every other life form, is to help maintain harmony and balance in the cosmic whole around us. While we can destroy that balance and have a responsibility to help maintain balance, we are never conceived as being in charge in some hierarchical chain of being. This is very different from the story our colonizers tell.

How our White relatives might join us in this cosmic task of maintaining harmony and balance, I cannot even begin to suggest. Sorting out that task after centuries of living out of the up-down hierarchic worldview is something that these relatives must sort out themselves—even though we Natives can certainly help inform that process along the way. But the up-down metaphoric conventions of life that seem so natural and intuitive to all euro-christian folk must give way to a new notion of collateral-egalitarian balance. From our experience with the modern economics of power politics, especially around the use and abuse of Native lands (think Alberta tar sands), to the United States' reliance on foreign policy modalities that rely so heavily on the threat and use of violence (including economic vio-lence in this late colonial period), to the startling realities of global warming and climate change, it seems that two-leggeds are being given a strong message about the way of life that has come to domi-nate the earth. Up-down theologies of domination have not served the world well. Even the more liberal and entirely post-modern the-ologies of "stewardship" are still stuck in that up-down schema that inordinately privileges the human being in an anthropocentric hier-archy. All this points to the need for a serious rethinking of the one, cosmic, male creator god who rules all things. Talk of creation and the single creator it implies is not possible for those of us who take seriously collateral-egalitarian balance and community-ist living.

jumping from heaven
and landing on the ground

white settler eye in my head
seeing "god" at the dead-body end of bread
broken in hand, sands of time falling towards the end
sending prayers up, and life down, on the ground
again
red people's red blood like abel's
still weeping in the loam
buffalo roaming through the heart
no longer on the land
salmon canned to be served on the table
sandwiched between the spam and the lamb
larder waiting fat to be carved from the cow
bowed at the knee like an our father to
the cleaver
drink my beefeater!
but   a kettle drum reverb fevers
        my nightmare dreams of dread comeuppance
            like a rasta head learning arawak tricks of survival
                    staring straight through my fear
        maroon croons from the outback of florida
            seminole red leading renegade white and escaped black
                    to repel the 1816 anglo-attack, and jesus now
        broken back into native roots and corn mothers
            frybread and bison head dragged
                in honor of sun, moon eye glowing from a height
        even god fears, deer and leering fox, eagle drift
            like a smoke signal over south dakota rock imprisoned
                in a jeffersonian deadpan face, waiting rivers racing
        with climate change waters to climb the sky, rain
            on the unblinking eye, ice the cracks with slow-flaking
                truth about the lie, undoing missionary hubris that
    it all began in the impossible mathematics that zero plus one . . .
            can equal anything other than "dead."

there is nothing sacred about three when the holy is
    a multiplicity
of twos bartering bull-elk scat and pollen
into everything
and the ceremony that "saves"
is a red version of instructions
given from the belly
of coyote's never ceasing
laughter!
and i awake softer, and wanting
finally
to listen.

—*Jim Perkinson*

Nopiming Canoe Song[1]

This is where we first understood what love is,
Grand golden light drifting down through
The flickering trees' leaves
And shining on the pines' green gilded needles.

This is where the river sang to us,
Its bass underground cadences mingling
With the treble notes of water kissing air,
Slight breeze rippling across sparkling waves.

This is where the rocks whispered their
Secret rose-veined granite promises,
Remembering fire and offering joy,
Deeply nestled in the solid earth.

You showed me how to imitate the chickadees' *dee dee dee*,
For a funky interspecies competition and duet.
You showed me the tracks of moose and rabbits,
The mysterious spiral grass nests of deer.

---

1. What would a hybrid, dialogic, Mennonite-Canadian, traditionalist, ecopo-
etic, postmodern, gendered, intercultural, interspecies, settler indigeneity—of
the sort Cree-Canadian bard and world traveler Tomson Highway challenges
us to envision in his evocative (and provocative) essay—look like? Here are
two attempts at such envisioning from a fellow traveler and similarly (and
also differently) hyphenated poet world citizen, at present gratefully living in
southwestern Manitoba, the very heart of North America, the magical center
of Turtle Island, traditional land of the Dakota-Sioux and Métis nations, now
a gathering place for refugees and dreamers of nations and traditions from
around the world. This first poem is dedicated to Errol Black and Jan Chaboyer,
who inspired it, and was written in support of the Pimachiowin Aki Project,
which aims to have a portion of the boreal forest east of Lake Winnipeg in
Manitoba and Ontario designated a UNESCO World Heritage Site. The poem
premiered at the 2012 Brandon Folk Music and Art Festival, and was previously
published in *Prairie Fire. Nopiming* is an Anishinaabe word meaning "in the
woods" or "entrance to the wilderness."

You showed me the scar on your left arm.
You drew charcoal stars around my name
On birchbark. I sang you a dream tree lullaby
In the old language of my grandmothers.

One day our canoe glided through a field of
Skeletons, charred stumps of burnt trees
Weeping against the bereft sky.
We turned to each other, stricken, then,

And held each other close for consolation,
The bright purple fireweed rising impertinently
From the grass proclaiming against all logic
Hope for regeneration in another season.

One morning we woke to the sight
Of an eagle circling, keen-eyed, regal,
Above the forest's crown. Our spirits
Rose up then, in gratitude and greeting.

This is where we came to know what love is,
Grand golden light drifting down through
The flickering trees' leaves,
And shining on the pines' green gilded needles.

—Di Brandt

11

Inside or Outside Eden?
The Gods Who Give Us Language and Story Our Place

By Tomson Highway (Cree)

The variety of languages is not merely a variety of sounds and
signs, but in fact a variety of world-views.

—*Wilhelm von Humboldt*

Come near, friends, and listen to a story of beginnings, a story
of place and home, a story about the gods and our attempts to
speak them, know them, live them, even here . . .

I was born under the most miraculous of circumstances. Coming
from a family of nomadic caribou hunters who roamed the area just
south of what is now the Manitoba-Nunavut border, I was born
in a snow bank. To be exact, in a tent, pitched in one awful hurry
in the month of December in the middle of a snow bank. Strictly
speaking, that part of the country is so far north that it's no longer
Cree territory but Dene and, in fact, almost Inuit. And no European
language existed up there back in those days—the 1950s—as they
still don't to this very day. There was Cree, then one step north,
Dene, then another step north, Inuit. And by then, you are in the
true polar Arctic.

Cree, my mother tongue, is an Algonquian language that is
related to Ojibway, Blackfoot, and other Native languages, much
as French is a Latin language that is related to Spanish. Dene, on
the other hand, is an Athaspaskan language that is related to Slavey

and other Native languages of the Northwest and Yukon territories, much as Russian is a Slavic language that is related to Polish, Ukrainian, and so on.

In any case, my father, in his wanderings as a young man, had fallen in love with the beauty of that extraordinary land and so moved in with the Dene. He learned their language, as did my mother, and as did we, their twelve children (some to a greater extent, others lesser). My parents, in particular, were thus truly bilingual. An equivalent situation would be an Anglo-Canadian from Rosedale, Toronto (one of the most privileged neighborhoods in Canada), speaking fluent English and Mandarin, a truly virtuosic-not-to-mention-high-class act. But my father was not only bilingual. He was quadrilingual, as he also spoke some Inuit—that's how far north he roamed when he was younger—and, later on in life, would teach himself his own form of pidgin English, self-taught, yes, for he never went to school (for there were, and are, no schools up there).

This part of the world of which I speak is a part of Canada no Canadian has ever seen for the simple reason that it is inaccessible except to those of us who come from there. It's also the most beautiful land on the planet, unimaginable, for one thing, in its vastness. Did you know, for instance, that Nunavut alone has the same square kilometrage as all of Western Europe, an area that includes Finland, all three Scandinavian countries, Germany, Holland, Belgium, England, Italy, France, Spain, and Portugal? And yet, that part of Europe alone has a population of some 300 million—about a third of a billion—where Nunavut, by comparison, has a population of only 40,000? And that's just one territory of Canada. Imagine Germany, which has a population of some 80 million, with a population of 2,000. Imagine England (70 million) with 1,500 people. Our friends here in France (where I live winters) cannot grasp such a concept. Now, imagine your family having all of Lake Ontario to itself. Or all of Muskoka. Or all of Prince Edward Island. To itself. Well, that's how I grew up. My father was the king of this enormous domain. And we, the last three of his twelve children, the last three of his five sons, grew up his princes.

There are, for one thing, thousands of lakes, some the size of ponds, some the size of seas, the water so clean and clear and blue that you can drink from it with your cupped hand. When was the last time you drank water straight out of Lake Winnipeg? Or Lake Ontario? And the islands in those lakes. Imagine Lake Erie with a thousand islands, most of them ringed by gold sand beaches or surfaces of granite that slope into the water like slides. And no people. Just you and your family. And the rivers—endless rivers—and the rapids and the waterfalls that no person has ever seen, but us. When you fly over that region by bush plane, you realize that northern Manitoba is actually more water than land. And the trees may get shorter as you approach the tree line, but the forests—of spruce, pine, birch, poplar, tamarack, willow—are endless. And the hills get higher until they become eskers. Eskers? Ridges of land that were formed by Ice Age glaciers scraping the Earth's surface as they receded, leaving hills as high as eighty meters, hills that are treed almost to the top, leaving the top itself a surface of fine, powdery, golden sand with islands of inch-high, bunch-thick, earth-berry bushes—*askeemina*, we called them; to this day, I don't know the English name, but the word translates as "earth-berries"—so that these eskers looked like golf courses, fifty kilometers long. And no one there to walk there and pick those berries but us—me and Mom and Dad and my two brothers. Then there were the wild cranberries, blueberries, cloudberries—called "bake apple" in Newfoundland—raspberries, *mitheecheemina, peethigoomina, oocheepawnee-imina*, more berries for which I don't know the English names.

And then there were the fish! Trout the size of five-year-old children, pike even bigger, whitefish, pickerel. And then there were the geese, ducks, loons, ptarmigans, the last a kind of Arctic pheasant whose feathers turn snow-white in winter, tastier than *foie gras* in Paris. And then there were the fox, wolf, mink, marten, wolverine (all inedible), and the moose, rabbits, porcupine, beaver, muskrat (all edible). And the great herds of caribou ten thousand strong that came thundering down from the high Arctic in midwinter to feed on our miles of mint-green reindeer moss, which they dug up from under blankets of snow that was so white it blinded people if they looked at it too long. And air so clean it makes lungs gasp audibly as their owners alight from planes just landed from the south and its big-city air. And the silence of that north is so immense you swear you can hear the Earth breathe. Silence that immense exists nowhere—nowhere—in the south.

So, my father was driving his dogsled in this place, from the Nunavut border area some three hundred kilometers south to the village of Brochet, the First Nation of which we are registered members. He was going to trade in our furs (my father was a trapper in winter, a fisherman in summer), renew our supplies, and celebrate the Christmas season with extended family before we made our way back up north for the second part of winter. But imagine driving a sled pulled by eight huskies through the most pristine landscape human eyes have ever seen: mile after mile after mile of spruce and pine forest laden with the purest, whitest snow, frozen lake after frozen lake covered with this same snow a foot thick. And you're driving through this landscape sometimes in sunlight, sometimes in snowfall with flakes the size of quarters, sometimes under a night sky where the stars outnumber the grains of sand in the Sahara Desert. Or under a full moon the size of a pie.

Well, that's what my parents were doing, driving through this Garden of Eden when my mother, nine months pregnant and sunk into a goose-down duvet inside the sled, went into labor. Fortunately, my father, with three other children in that sled—the rest had either died as infants, flown the coop to start their own families, or were away at boarding school—had just reached an island on this one lake, some one hundred miles north of Brochet, where stood a Dene encampment with a woman, luckily, who had midwife experience. Once at the other end of that island, which was some four square miles in area, he pitched our tent.[1] And by the light of a kerosene lamp, the space heated by a little tin woodstove that we never traveled without, I was born, the floor under my mother nothing but spruce boughs piled over snow. In the early morning hours of the sixth of December, 1951. So, if my mother spoke fluent Dene and the midwife only Dene, then the first words I heard when I came into this world were not English, not French, not Cree, but Dene, a language I still speak some of to this very day.

I've since, of course, become fluent in English and French (and am quickly moving on to Spanish). But as I age, I never cease to be astonished at the difference in structure between the European

---

1. We lived there the summer I was eight and the summer I was thirteen, so I remember what it looked like.

languages and the Native languages of North America. I live in France six months of the year, just ten kilometers from the Spanish border, and have crisscrossed Europe a hundred times. I've also crisscrossed all three Americas more times than I care to remember. The differences between European and Indigenous languages are striking, and, of the many differences in structure, the most arresting has to do with gender.

European languages are obsessed with gender. Gender, moreover, that is arranged in a hierarchy, a vertical straight line. Consider English. You've got *he* at the top, followed by *she*, followed by *it* (or *him*, *her*, and *it*). In French, it's more pronounced with its *il* and *elle* or *le* and *la*. A table is a *la* but a desk is a *le*. Air is masculine but water is feminine. Sorrow is feminine but happiness is masculine. A vagina—get this—is masculine whereas a prostate gland, contrariwise, is feminine. Go figure! In German, things are even more pronounced with their *ders*, *dies*, and *dasses*. And so on, and so on. Structurally, in all these European languages, it's a straight line with God as "He" at the top, then man as "he," then woman as "she," and nature as "it," with one level having power over the next. The implications of this are profound. The sad history of Western heteropatriarchy bears witness. Women and Mother Earth haven't fared too well.

Where does this obsession with gender and hierarchy come from? Is it too simplistic to say that we need not look much further than the prized, dominant mythology of Western society? There are plenty of different definitions of mythology. But for European languages, mythology belongs in the book, and that book is the Bible, and in that book God is Male, not female.

While the European worldview divides the universe according to this hierarchy of gender, with God as Male at the top and nature as "it" at the bottom, the Native languages of North America (to name but one America) divide theirs not into genders but into that which is animate and that which is inanimate . . . that which has a soul and that which doesn't. The key words are the articles *ana* (for animate) and *anima* for inanimate: *ana iskwew* (the woman), *ana napew* (the man), *ana seeti* (the tree), *ana asini* (the rock). All these "creatures" have living, breathing souls, equal in power, equal in status. But take the soul out of that woman and she/he becomes *anima meeyow* (the corpse). Ditto for the man. Take the spirit out of that tree and he/she becomes *anima teetaapoowin* (the chair, which, of course, is made from the wood of that tree). Take the spirit out of that rock, crush it into cement, and it becomes a side-walk (*anima meeskanow*). Can you see it? There is no hierarchy. If in the European languages the design is a vertical straight line (a phallic design), then in the Native languages the design is a circle (a yonic, that is, a womb-like, design). There is no *he*, there is no *she*. We are all *he/shes* or *she/hes*. And God is a *he/she*, which is where the idea of "divinity" in female form has a foothold—a concept that somehow disappeared from European thought at some point in its history (for a reason). But the argument for female divinity goes one step further in Indigenous thought.

All the parts of the body, by themselves, are inanimate. The head by itself is inanimate. The hand has no soul. The stomach has no soul. Even the heart has no soul. Even the penis, interestingly enough, has no soul. There are only three parts of the human body which, by themselves, have a soul, and those are the breasts, the vagina, and the womb. And that's where the concept of God as female rests as solid as rock.

Certain sacred books and the languages birthed by them have at their core the story of eviction—an eviction from a Garden due to an act committed by a woman. Other sacred books and their languages do *not* (Buddhism, for instance, does not, or so I understand). To some languages, a place like Canada—and the Manitoba-Nunavut border area I described above—is a living hell. To others, it is a para-dise, a garden from which *man*kind has *never* been evicted, least of all due to an act committed by a woman, an act for which she—and her relations—have paid dearly, both in myth and in everyday life. The statistics are gruesome.

Rape, wife battery, and abuse are daily occurrences, even in a country as "civilized" as Canada, and certainly here in France, worse in Spain. In Brazil, which has a population of 150 million, the fifth largest in the world, statistics say that a woman is hit by her hus-band or boyfriend once every fifteen minutes.

My brother and I went to school with Helen Betty Osborne. She's from northern Manitoba. I'm from northern Manitoba. Helen Betty Osborne is the seventeen-year-old Cree girl from Norway House in

Helen Betty Osborne,
1952–1971

northern Manitoba who, one snowy night in November 1971, was abducted by four young, white, heterosexual men. One of them ended up ramming a screwdriver fifty-six times up her vagina, leaving her there, in the bushes, to bleed to her death. And got away with it.

How could they get away with it? How could the men who perpetrate such acts not *really* be considered sick? Could it have something, anything, to do with the "sacred book" from which comes the thinking of these men's societies?

A good chunk of that book celebrates raw, patriarchal, abusive power. And the male God leads the way, ravaging the many women who stand against him.

> The Lord will afflict with scabs the heads of the daughter of Zion and the Lord will lay bare their secret parts. (Isaiah 3:17)

> You adulterous wife! You prefer strangers to your own husband. . . . Therefore, you prostitute, hear the word of the Lord! . . . I will gather [your lovers] against you . . . and will strip you in front of them. . . . Then I will deliver you into the hands of your lovers, and they will tear down your mounds . . . tear off your clothes . . . and hack you to pieces with their swords. (Ezekiel 16:35-40)

Of course, God is not really male, we are told, and the violated women are "just a symbol" of something else (some "real evil" that deserves divine vengeance). But perhaps this language isn't helpful. Perhaps it bleeds beyond the symbolic. Perhaps it has real life, deadly implications for how we relate to the Creator, relate to each other, relate to this earth, our mother.

Christianity's most influential thinker, the apostle Paul, certainly thought that the sacred words of a male God were more than symbolic. They were divine. They decreed how life should be ordered.

> Now I want you to realize that the head of every man is Christ, and the head of the woman is man, and the head of Christ is God. (1 Corinthians 11:3)

Language shapes. It really does. As Mary Daly said, "If God is male, then male is God."[2] And that's why Helen Betty Osborne's killers were just healthy men out doing what healthy men are supposed to be doing: hanging out with the girls on a Saturday night. Think of it this way: if those four young men were to have gone into those bushes and made love to each other instead of doing what they did to Helen, then—and only then—would they be considered sick. (It's crazy . . . who is having a good time here and who is not?)

This has been going on for far too long. Since 1492, I think. That's the year the male God of Christianity arrived in the Americas, there to meet, for the first time in some two thousand years, his female counterpart. We know what happened to her, don't we? It was also the year, the decade, the epoch, when the witch-burnings of France, Spain, England, and Germany were at their very height, when as many as one hundred thousand women lost their lives to a very male god, a crime for which the church, for one, has never apologized or made amends.[3]

Bluntly put, the dominant way of thinking—embraced not by all, but by many Christians, and a good chunk of Western society— asserts that existence on Planet Earth is a curse from an angry male God, which will one day be escaped through a hereafter. Another way of thinking, more life-giving, proposes that earth is Eden, our intended home, a blessing, a gift from a benevolent female god. Unilingualism (and uni-religious thinking) has a tendency to engender uni-dimensional thinking. That is its danger; take it from one who speaks five languages. In this day of global burning, where the Indigenous and poor especially suffer due to the rape of the earth, we need to start looking at our planet as a Garden, or it will, indeed, be taken from us sooner than we think. We need to try with all our might to get outside the language(s) that tell us that we have been evicted from the Mother's womb, punished by God for an act of pleasure engaged in by a woman. Sisters and brothers, think of our grandchildren. Think of *their* grandchildren.

---

2. Mary Daly, *Beyond God the Father: Toward a Philosophy of Women's Liberation* (Boston: Beacon Press, 1973), 19.

3. Carol P. Christ, "Rebirth of the Religion of the Goddess," in *Encyclopedia of Women and Religion in North America: Volume 3*, eds. Rosemary Skinner Keller, Rosemary Radford Ruether, and Marie Cantlon (Bloomington: Indiana University Press, 2006), 1205.

Jubilate Brandon, July 2011[1]
after Christopher Smart

For I will consider the city of Brandon.

For Brandon is a jewel of a city, an emerald, a diamond, at least in the summer, nestled shyly among the scenic hills and valleys of southwestern Manitoba, the famed parkland of the prairies.

For at the first glance of light each morning, Brandon sparkles with birdsong, robin's chirps, sparrow's chatter, the raucous caw caw of ravens, saluting our Lord Sun.

For these same raucous ravens have taken over Clark Hall and become university dons, overseeing every intellectual transaction with indignant commentary.

For the rabbits who used to hide in the alleyways have become bold and nibble our lettuces in broad daylight.

For the Assiniboine River has generously overrun its banks, swallowed up the duck pond and the geese nesting grounds and the deer paths among the trees, remembering its ancient glory days as a great lake. The geese and ducks are happy for their much expanded pond, the deer trying to figure out where to hang out now, should they urbanize like the rabbits and raccoons or should they retreat back up country?

---

1. In celebration of your visionary (inter)cultural teachings, Tomson Highway, about language, about land, the "animate," about transformation and the divine feminine; for setting such an inspiring example for us in your writing, compositions, and performances of courage, love, beauty, music, drama, laughter, joy— spiritual shapeshifting in its most elegant forms; in gratitude for our friendship and creative dialogue over many years, from your Manitoba Mennonite "twin," *megweech, dank schoen, ki-sa-ki-hi-tin, eck lev dee.*

For the children have taken up skateboarding from morning to night, defying gravity with brave leaps and twirls and smashing down, and getting up and doing it again. And again.

For the people, young and old, have taken up poetry, and musical instruments, and play them with such grace and skill, the trees on Princess Avenue have taken up dancing, have you seen them? Especially on Tuesdays.

For the evening breeze at sundown is so delicate, so fragrant, so colored with the ambience of lilacs and prairie lilies and wild roses, it sometimes hurts our hearts.

For sometimes in the winter the trees of Brandon are covered with filigrees of sculpted lace snow, transforming the grey streets into a delicate fairyland in the hushed dawn. But let's not talk about winter.

For Richard the Red patrols the back alleys in his muscle shirt and leather pants, dubiously defending the weak with his enthusiastic freckled fist.

For the Lady of our Wheat City, all dressed up for partying in her astonishing bristly wheat-sheafed skirt, has waited patiently at City Hall since 2006 for someone to want to take it off.

For every evening mothers and fathers and their young children, wives and husbands, grandmothers and grandfathers, lovers, people of all ages, and races, gather in the parks for picnics, and walk along the streets, holding hands. This is what peace looks like.

For our Lady of the Lake no longer has to explain what she's doing here in the hot dry prairie of southwestern Manitoba, Vivianne, Elaine, our own bright Lady of the Harbour, queen of rhubarb pie and lemon meringue, now considering investing in boats.

For our new Lady Mayor, Her Lovely Worship, has revivified the black and white six o'clock news with hot pink jackets and headbands. And sandbag corridors laced with jazz.

For the robin in my front yard decided last summer to investigate the mirrors in my garden. All summer long he pecked experimentally at the mirror robins, and the mirror robins cheerfully pecked back at him. Sometimes he rushed at them, one at a time, with ferociously outspread wings, and they rushed obediently, one after another, back at him.

Sometimes he hid between mirrors and leaped out unexpectedly at them. They did the same.

O give it up silly nephew, sang his uncle from a high branch in the ornamental sour apple tree. Don't we red-chested birds have better things to do than gaze at ourselves in glass mirrors for godsake.

O but he wouldn't. He wouldn't. He kept at it all summer. While his young wife robin worked so hard to construct their new nest and then sat patiently on the eggs for weeks, and later spent every daylight hour digging for worms in the grass to feed the new chirping hungry babies, and the great uncle robin sat regally on his high perch keeping watch over the neighborhood, our artist bird patiently and meticulously kept up his daily mirror investigations.

Peck peck peck. Peck peck peck. Peck peck peck. O it was such a mystery, such an obsession, such an absorbing game. Peck peck peck. Peck peck peck.

This summer he came back again, from wherever robins go in the winter, ready to get at it again. But by then the ravens had taken over the neighborhood. Such scavengers they are! Such thieves! Such noisy bosses! Caw caw caw caw.

One of the ravens of keener sight, impressed with the robin's mirror game, tried it a few times himself. But he just didn't have the finesse for it, he shouldered the black mirror bird rudely, and was simultaneously disgusted and bored when the rude mirror bird shouldered him back.

The sparrows, undeterred by a pushy crow or two, or indeed, in other seasons, by our impressive midwinter temperatures of forty or fifty below, tried it a few times, but they also didn't have that same fine scientific robin's mind, that same poetic finesse, that robinic obsession.

Where do robins go in the winter? I know where the sparrows go, they hide in my woodshed, decorating the wood with bright white strips of sparrow poop. I know where ravens go, they head straight back up into their respective mythologies: creator, trickster, stealer of the sun. *Tis some visitor, I muttered, tapping at my chamber door—Only this and nothing more.* Tell it like it is! Tell it like it is!

This robin I guess figured out the mirror game well enough, having leapfrogged so successfully into the middle of this poem, which is trying to sing the praises of Brandon.

For it is indeed a most exquisite little jewel of a city, an emerald set with diamonds, in an extraordinarily beautiful landscape, blessed by the gods, overseen by angels, how lucky we are to be able to call this "home," despite its tumultuous history, its variously mixed deeds, shards of glass sometimes lying on the sidewalk, morning evidence of terrible midnights, broken hearts, yet miraculously touched by grace, cosmic harmonies singing through us, and in us, all of us together here, fashioning willow canes into baskets, and harpsichords, learning to live in greater love, reaching for light.

—*Di Brandt*

Feel the Pull

Oh white man, white man, always fighting
Your mind is a mind of war
Dichotomous thinking of either/or
Oh white man, white man, always wond'ring

Don't draw me into your white man argument
Into that simple black and white of unreality
You see and hear me but you're still speculating
Arguing inside your head never really engaging me

When you see us on our continuum
You still segment us by your divisive mind
Your search for neat intrinsic categories
Belies reality of extrinsic sensibilities

Your dialogue really doesn't include me
You are talking to some idealization of us
When we don't fit your tidy labels
Then you wrestle till you can assign me

Why don't you just ask the elders what they think
Or the parents who have to feed their kids?
Why not just listen to the whole community
And stay there long enough till you weep?

Then you'll lose your pejorative
And not speak of cashing in
You'll feel the pull of necessity
And forget thoughts of complicity

—*Adrian Jacobs (Cayuga)*

12

Chief Seattle Syndrome:
What to Do about Indigenous
Bulldozer Operators

By Will Braun

Chief Seattle—the storied leader of the Duwamish tribe and the man for whom a relatively progressive West Coast city is named—was either a figure of commanding physical stature or a short man with rounded shoulders; it depends on which version of the facts you choose. And it is not just his physique that has proven historically malleable.

Long after his death in 1866, Chief Seattle was turned into a minor prophet of the environmental movement. His name appears under quotations on T-shirts and posters of the type stocked by lefty bookstores—quotations like: "Man did not weave the web of life, he is but a strand in it" and "Every part of the earth is sacred to my people; every shining pine needle, every sandy shore, every mist in the dark woods . . ."

The chief's words speak incisively of the sacredness and inter-connectedness of the earth, themes that are foundational to many of us who advocate for the health of the planet. His words resonate deeply with me. The catch, though, is that they are likely not his.

Most of the wisdom attributed to Chief Seattle dates back to a speech he is believed to have delivered in 1854. No transcript of the speech exists, but in 1887—thirty-three years after the fact and twenty-one years after the chief's death—Henry A. Smith printed his English reconstruction of Chief Seattle's words based on notes he had taken at the speech. Scholars, including Duwamish researcher Thomas R. Speer, discount the authenticity of this version, in part because it speaks about the prairies, with which the chief was not familiar, and about multitudes of Indigenous people fleeing settlers, which was contrary to the chief's experience.

Then in 1972, a white professor, Ted Perry, adapted Smith's adaptation of the speech for a film with ecological undercurrents. The film version also blended in material from a letter Chief Seattle purportedly sent to the U.S. president. The origins of this letter are even more dubious than those of the speech.

Most of the quotations we see today are from this movie version of Chief Seattle, removed from the original by two or more white writers, at least one environmental agenda, and sometimes a gender-sensitive poster editor.

Tellingly and awkwardly, the website of the Duwamish tribe says much about the great chief but does not mention the speech or letter (though one short quotation from the latter appears in a sidebar).

By most credible accounts, Chief Seattle was a strong orator and a leader whose authority was recognized by Indigenous and non-Indigenous alike. He presided over the tumultuous period of white settlement and sought peace and interaction with the settlers. The only well-documented words of Chief Seattle are brief, and make no mention of shining pine needles or mist in dark woods. "We are the friends of the Americans," he said in a speech to a U.S. representative in 1855. "We look upon you as our Father."

Despite a lack of evidence, certain writers and poster makers have been unable to resist the urge to project onto Chief Seattle their vision of what I would call a "noble environmentalist"—an idealized, primitivized hero-symbol of the fight to defend the earth against industrial development.

Like those who have posterized Chief Seattle, American photographer Edward S. Curtis couldn't resist the impulse to mold reality to fit his vision of Indigenous nobility. Curtis, who worked from the 1880s through the 1930s, gained international acclaim for his iconic photographs of Indigenous people. But he has been criticized for removing traces of Western culture from subjects, and paying them to wear historically or culturally inaccurate clothing. Ironically, his first Indigenous subject is believed to have been the daughter of Chief Seattle.

Curtis and Chief Seattle are emblematic of the urge to impose an idealized narrative on Indigenous people— Curtis as reviser and Seattle as unwitting subject. I think of this urge as Chief Seattle Syndrome, a syndrome I have found prevalent in Indigenous-settler dialogue on creation-related issues.

For much of the past fifteen years, I have been privileged and blessed to work on environmental issues and Indigenous rights, much of the time in a faith context. I have seen the Indigenous-settler dialogue on creation issues play out in classrooms,

Postcard of Chief Seattle, ca. 1900

church basements, conference sessions, articles, and books. I would distill the common gist of the discourse as follows: (1) Indigenous people have an exemplary, conservation-oriented reverence for creation; (2) settler culture has a bulldozer-oriented worldview that underlies the current destruction of the planet; and (3) people need to be convinced of these truths. There are elaborations and twists, but that tends to be the general thrust.

I have been informed and inspired by this dialogue. A profound alternative to the dominant ideology of limitless economic growth is vital. Hearing Aboriginal presenters speak about their worldview during my university days is what set me on the path that has led me here.

While I am immensely grateful for the Aboriginal teachings that have shaped me, I have come to see the usual dialogue about Indigenous worldviews and creation as simplistic and romanticized.

Consider the following realities: Indigenous-owned companies cashed in on more than $1.3 billion worth of work in the Alberta oil sands (or "tar sands," if you prefer) in 2010, with more than 1,700

Indigenous people working in oil-sands-related jobs. Further north, three of the four regional Indigenous governments in the vicinity of the proposed Mackenzie Valley Pipeline have formally teamed up with the world's largest oil companies to push for the $16.2 billion natural gas pipeline.

Mining companies have also found cooperation from many Indigenous governments. The Canadian Mining Association—which displayed an Inuit *inukshuk* prominently on its website when I visited it—says the mining sector is the largest private-sector employer of Indigenous people in Canada, with more than 170 agreements between Indigenous people and mining companies.

In the hydroelectric power sector, the Innu Nation of Labrador is backing the proposed $6.2 billion Muskrat Falls hydro dam and the larger Gull Island Dam. In Quebec, the James Bay Cree have consented to large-scale hydro developments (in exchange for cancellation of other large projects, among other provisions). And in my home province, five hydro-affected First Nations are partnering with Manitoba Hydro on construction or proposed construction of $14.5 billion worth of large dams. Another four First Nations are expected to actively support renewal of the fifty-year license of the Grand Rapids Dam, a particularly destructive older dam that floods 115,700 hectares.

In most of these cases, Indigenous influence has altered or will alter project designs to reduce environmental impacts, but that doesn't change the fact that these are industrial mega-developments founded on the Wall Street dogma of continual growth.

Of course, a segment of the Indigenous population in each of the places listed above opposes development. And in other places, Indigenous governments are resisting developments. Examples include British Columbia's proposed $7.9 billion Site C hydro project and the proposed Northern Gateway Pipeline from the Alberta bitumen sands to the B.C. coast. But even in cases like these, Indigenous opposition is not necessarily Seattle-esque rejection of industrial development per se, but rejection of particular projects for particular reasons.

While I worked for the Pimicikamak Cree, they opposed hydro development on highly principled grounds, but were cautiously open to a large titanium mine in their homeland. The Haisla First

Nation, at the West Coast end of the proposed Northern Gateway Pipeline, resolutely oppose the transport of bitumen through their territory but are actively involved in a project to export liquified natural gas, some of which would come from controversial fracking operations further north. Many similar examples could be cited.

Often Indigenous people oppose projects because benefits do not outweigh environmental costs in their assessment, or because proponents have simply not taken them seriously.

In my experience, Indigenous-settler dialogue often skirts the fact that many Indigenous people are open to industrial development. The Edward S. Curtis within us tends to remove the hard hats and bulldozers from the scene before creating an image of Indigenous reality. But the reality of Indigenous industrialization is too widespread to ignore. It challenges the simple dichotomy between Indigenous and settler worldviews. It precludes any notion of a single, prevailing Indigenous view. And it throws a monkey wrench in the standard gist of Indigenous-settler creation dialogue.

How should people concerned about Indigenous rights and ecological health respond to the extent of Indigenous participation in major resource development? I've heard people respond by asserting that the traditional worldview, as it is sometimes called, is the only true or legitimate Indigenous perspective—thereby dismissing the views of Indigenous people who are open to industrial development. Often these dismissals are harsh and categorical.

I've heard people refer to Indigenous leaders who partner with industry as "John Wayne Indians." The implication is that they are the ones who, in exchange for safety and pay, ride with the white guys to help them catch Indigenous people. A comparable term is "house slaves," which refers to the slaves who resided in their masters' mansions and who, in return for better treatment than the field slaves, gave their allegiances to their owners rather than to the cause of freedom.

One noted Indigenous scholar, whom I have long admired, told me recently that when Indigenous leaders accept environmentally destructive projects it shows they have succumbed to "colonization of the mind," a concept that various Indigenous scholars have written about. When I mentioned my conversations with Indigenous leaders in Manitoba who speak about ceremonies to ask permission of the plants and animals to build huge hydroelectric dams, this person said there is no ceremony by which you ask your grandmother for permission to rape her.

Like this commenter, I too have difficulty with placing a cloak of sacredness over a project that pours cement into the very heart of a river, but I am also uncomfortable with these fervent denunciations of people with differing views. My reasons for discomfort are twofold.

First, we are all entangled in the industrial machinery of our age, and this should temper our views. The most ardent Indigenous environmental advocates I know are just as beholden to the energy-intensive, ecologically damaging economic system as the average member of society. They fly, drive, use ethically tainted personal communications gadgetry, leave their office lights on all night, and happily eat whatever the agro-food industry packages up for them.

To fly regularly is not the same as actively pursuing a major resource extraction project—nor does it negate the frequent flyer's message—but it does mean that there is something more at play than drawing clear lines between the good guys and bad guys. It's messy. The bad guys are not all bad and the good guys are not all good. We're all complicit in a complicated mess. I believe Indigenous-settler dialogue has greater value when it starts with an acknowledgement of complicity and complexity rather than with simplified dichotomies.

Of course, Indigenous people would not be participants in the complicated mess had the colonizers not shown up. This informs the current reality in a critical way, but it does not change the messiness or basic fact of it.

My second reason for discomfort with the dismissal of development-minded Indigenous people is that I think they have something valuable to contribute to the dialogue. Rather than vilify the "bad" Indigenous industrializers, the dialogue on creation issues should seek their inclusion, either in person, when possible, or at least in the form of a serious grappling with the perspectives they have shared publicly.

I have been privileged to interact with Indigenous people all along the spectrum from conservation to industrialization. At times, these interactions have been difficult. I have written articles that some Indigenous leaders have not appreciated. I have been chastised publicly for questioning hydropower, which some communities expect to rely on for their future well-being.

In suggesting more inclusive dialogue, I am not naive to the forces that surround big projects. In Manitoba, the government-owned utility has paid First Nations (with a combined population of about ten thousand) $194 million in negotiation and process costs related to three hydropower projects over about fifteen years. This flow of money—for which no one is required to give a detailed public account—creates unhealthy dynamics. Similarly, the alignment of Indigenous interests with corporate interests means that the Indigenous voice becomes partially subservient to the pro-development public relations machinery.

For a time, I was involved in informing church groups in the U.S. Midwest—which imports billions of dollars of hydropower from Manitoba—about the socio-environmental impacts of northern dams. One First Nation that wanted to partner on new export-dependent dams, and thus needed to protect the reputation of Manitoba hydropower, hired a Washington D.C.-based PR firm to advise them on how to communicate to U.S. church groups.

The firm said in a briefing paper that the U.S. audiences in question were "made up of guilty white liberals." It said these people "like to rail against the corporate culture" and want to "protect what they see as the pure way of life of the Indian people."

"Play to their guilt," they advised. It was good advice. In many cases it worked to neutralize church opposition to industrial development. It worked, in part, because people were caught in a simplified, idealized narrative.

My inadvertent discovery of this tactic did not make dialogue with this First Nation easier, but it didn't end it either.

What then might dialogue with Indigenous development proponents look like? What can be learned? I interviewed Fred Carmichael for a 2011 article about Indigenous participation in industrial megaprojects. He is the former head of the Gwich'in Tribal Council in the Northwest Territories and the current chair of the Aboriginal Pipeline Group, the entity that has partnered with the two largest oil companies in the world (in their Canadian incarnations) to push for construction of the Mackenzie Valley Pipeline.

The pipeline would carry natural gas from the far north to the Alberta bitumen sands and other southern markets.

Carmichael is no fan of environmentalists, whom he blames for killing off the fur industry without offering anything to replace it. He has little use for environmentalists who object to the pipeline project with no regard for the fact that his people are "proud people" who don't want to "be dependent on government" but have few economic options.

Carmichael, who has been a businessman all his life, also points out that the southern environmentalists who oppose the proposed Mackenzie project benefit from other pipelines. "If they're so concerned [about pipelines]," he says, "then hey, let's shut all the pipelines down, every one of them in Canada. Let's see what Toronto says. Why does it apply to us and not them?"

He's brash, but he makes a point—one that would likely not be heard in a typical Indigenous-settler dialogue.

But his strongest point goes back to the importance of livelihood. Speaking to me by phone from Inuvik, Northwest Territories, he again addresses his comments to the environmentalists:

> Okay fine, this pipeline might not be the best for the environment . . . but you know we're taking every step possible to make sure we do the best job possible to make sure that it doesn't harm the environment any more than need be. But if that's not good enough for you, don't just come here and take away our bread and butter from our children; you come here and you find us another alternative to the pipeline.

Carmichael's point about alternative livelihood options is critical. No group should have to choose between acute poverty and a megaproject that "might not be the best for the environment." The absence of options is an advantage for corporate developers seeking Indigenous consent.

Indigenous poverty and lack of options represent a monumental failure of Canadian society. Many decades of overtly assimilationist government policies, sinister dispossession of Indigenous lands and resources, and a general ongoing failure to honorably and equitably share the wealth of this nation with Indigenous people have backed Indigenous peoples into a corner.

But this is a delicate point to make. Fred Carmichael could easily take offense. Indigenous leaders who sit at negotiating tables with huge companies would not necessarily welcome public discussion of the weaknesses of their people or their bargaining position. They emphasize the strengths they bring, which are significant.

Fred Carmichael has sat at those negotiating tables. He now has allies among the most powerful companies on earth. He will never be turned into a Chief Seattle figure, but his is a voice that needs to be heard. Though he is combative, he is also candid, intensely practical, and honest about the ethical greyness of society—all helpful antidotes to the idealization syndrome. In the end, I was grateful for the chance to speak with a leading Indigenous industrial apologist.

A lengthy interview with Ovide Mercredi provided similar insights, though his tone differed considerably. Mercredi is the former national chief of the Assembly of First Nations, and when I spoke with him in 2010 he was chief of Misipawistik Cree Nation in northern Manitoba. Now he is a band councillor.

He grew up next to an ecologically disastrous hydro dam, and over the years he has been a vocal advocate for the health of the planet. But he has undergone a subtle shift. He and his people are actively pursuing participation in a nickel mine, something he says he never would have imagined himself doing back in the 1960s.

Like Carmichael, part of his motivation is something near economic desperation. He spoke about the fatigue that comes from constantly dealing with his people's poverty. "That's a full-time job," he says. The weight of his duties is evident in his voice and posture as we sit in the comfy chairs of the coffee shop in his favorite Winnipeg bookstore. "We're always looking for ways to create jobs," he says with a sigh.

Mercredi admits there is "a certain amount of sadness" involved in considering a major project because he says it would require "compromising basic principles" of Indigenous culture.

Mercredi is no house slave. His considerations cannot be dismissed. He says a mine would only proceed if specific environmental protections could be guaranteed and if stringent regulations were in place. A significant Indigenous ownership stake would also be required, thereby guaranteeing Indigenous control and economic opportunity.

Mercredi says in some ways his thinking has shifted, even though he says he's still motivated by idealism. He doesn't hold to the view that his people were ever "pure environmentalists." He believes that if Manitoba Hydro had come to the community in the 1960s and treated his people respectfully, "they would have learned from us that we're not opposed to the idea of hydro development."

"We probably would have accommodated them," he says, if they would have agreed to a considerably smaller, less damaging dam.

Earlier this year, Mercredi and his colleagues accepted $58 million over fifty years in exchange for withdrawing their staunch opposition to renewal of the fifty-year licence of the dam in their territory.

Mercredi does not fit neatly on either side of the development debate, but I find his perspectives, as ethically murky as they are at points, more helpful than predictable idealizations or demonizations. Like Mercredi and Carmichael, participants in the Indigenous-settler dialogue need to grapple with the practical, imperfect realities of this world as it is.

We are all on this planet together—conservationists and bulldozer operators alike—and we need to spend more time humbly reaching across the lines that divide us and less time accentuating those lines. Polarization itself is a threat to the environment. We need to get out of our camps.

We also need to be informed by the practical realities of environmental issues as they play out in the world. This is part of the lesson of people like Mercredi and Carmichael, who are forced to deal with practicalities, such as employment.

I get impatient with the often-theoretical nature of Indigenous-settler dialogue. Perhaps the theoretical and theological considerations could flow from the practical ones, rather than the other way around, which seems to be the commonly assumed order. Rather than delving abstractly into matters of worldview, or dwelling on the rightness of one view over another, I would like to see more dialogue about how society can realistically address the demand for the energy and resources that we all depend on. And, as Mercredi and Carmichael would add, how can we realistically address Indigenous livelihood needs at the same time? Economic opportunity for Indigenous communities must be part of the creation dialogue.

I believe the holistic, balanced worldview articulated by some Indigenous people (and on certain T-shirts) is of great value, especially given the persistent dogma of economic growth. But I think it should be applied in a practical, inclusive, non-polarized, and realistic fashion. The best way to do this is to dare to include a broad diversity of Indigenous voices, diligently resisting the urge to bend Indigenous reality to fit our preferred vision.

Sherman Alexie, the noted Indigenous writer from Seattle, says, "white people only like Indians if we're warriors or guardians of the earth." I wish Chief Seattle had really uttered the magnificent words often attributed to him. Though even if he had, the urge to idealize him would have hit a different obstacle. As per the custom of various West Coast Indigenous peoples, Chief Seattle most likely owned slaves. Reality is never as simple as we'd like it to be.

We do better to welcome this awkward fact than to succumb—like modern-day Edward S. Curtis's, creating tailored images of Indigenous people—to Chief Seattle Syndrome. Curtis worked in black and white; we need to work in gray.

12: Response

Laughter will come

Why does suffering inspire such art?
Jesus, you know
Why do my tears tear you apart?
Jesus, you know

Why are we marked by such pain?
Creator, you know
Why do they look on us with disdain?
Creator, you know

Why is our beauty now so abused?
Spirit, you know
Why are our elders so broken and bruised?
Spirit, you know

I see a place where pain is soothed by a tender hand
I see a place where tears are wiped away with soft leather
I see a place where we are no longer put to shame
I see a place where the proud bow in weeping chagrin
I see a place where elders, women, children and men laugh again!

—*Adrian Jacobs (Cayuga)*

Hymn of Remorse

We covered over your colorful earth with gray cement.
We cut down trees and stripped the soil wherever we went.
We scarred the hills for gold and coal,
Blind with greed inside our soul,
Our goal: to have complete control.

Lord, have mercy. Can we be restored?
Lord, have mercy.

What of the lands of tribes and nations who lived here first?
Who took the best with broken treaties, and left the worst?
By whom were slaves bought, used, sold?
Who valued humans less than gold?
Who told us racist lies until our hearts went cold?

Lord, have mercy. Can we be restored?
Lord, have mercy.

The noise of traffic is drowning out the songbird's song.
Your voice within us is telling us that we've gone wrong.
You call us from our selfishness,
To be blessed—and to bless
To turn to you, to begin anew.

Lord, have mercy. Can we be restored?
Lord, have mercy.

—Brian McLaren

13

A Serpent in the Garden:
An Unholy Worldview on Sacred Land[1]

By Waziyatawin (Dakota)

Indigenous scholar Jack Forbes writes, "The 'cosmology' or 'world-view' of a people is closely related, of course, to all of their actions. *The world-view influences actions and, in turn, actions tell us what the world-view really is!*"[2] If this is indeed true, then what do the actions of Christians (broadly speaking) have to tell us about their worldview in the 520 years since the first invasion of the Western Hemisphere?

What happened, for example, to the brown-skinned people of Hispaniola (modern-day Haiti/Dominican Republic) whom Columbus first encountered, a people who were so peaceable, so accustomed to sharing, and so unaccustomed to iron weapons of war that, according to the colonizer's own record, they accidentally cut their hands on the sword shown to them?[3] They were wiped out by the genocidal campaign that Columbus and company launched against them. As the Dominican friar Bartolomé de Las Casas

---

1. This language plays upon Christian understandings; it is not reflective of North American Indigenous worldviews. Indigenous people value serpents— even in our gardens!
2. Jack Forbes, *Columbus and Other Cannibals* (New York: Seven Stories Press, 2008), 20. Emphasis added.
3. From Columbus' logs: "They do not bear arms, and do not know them, for I showed them a sword, they took it by the edge and cut themselves out of ignorance," as quoted in Howard Zinn, *A People's History of the United States* (New York: The New Press, 1997), 3.

1892 U.S. stamp celebrating the four hundredth anniversary of Columbus's landing

wrote, "Here *those Christians* perpetrated their first ravages and oppression against the native peoples. This was the first land in the New World to be destroyed and depopulated by *the Christians*."[4] The people of Hispaniola had their lives unjustly and savagely taken by professed Jesus followers, and they were not, as we all know, the only ones to meet such a fate. Millions of their Indigenous sisters and brothers on Turtle Island were killed at the hands of other Europeans, as nation after imperial nation, bearing Christ on their lips and crosses on their military standards, followed suit.

In his book *American Holocaust*, historian David Stannard asserts, "The pace and magnitude of their obliteration varied from place to place and from time to time, but for years now historical demographers have been uncovering, in region upon region, post-Columbian depopulation rates of between 90 and 98 percent with such regularity that an overall decline of 95 percent has become a working rule of thumb."[5] Many have argued that the mass death of Indigenous populations was primarily by disease, and as such, was inadvertent and inevitable. Stannard argues, however, that

---

4. Bartolomé de Las Casas, *Devastation of the Indies: A Brief Account* (Baltimore: Johns Hopkins University Press, 1992), 32. Emphasis added.
5. David Stannard, *American Holocaust: The Conquest of the New World* (New York: Oxford, 1992), x.

microbial pestilence—*some of it deliberately spread*[6]—and purposeful genocide worked together as "interdependent forces acting dynamically—whipsawing their victims between plague and violence, each one feeding upon the other, and together driving countless numbers of entire ancient societies to the brink—and often over the brink—of total extermination."[7] Estimates vary as to how many Indigenous people were decimated in the Western Hemisphere.[8] Conservative numbers are around six to ten million. Others persuasively argue that upwards of one hundred million died. Either way, the catastrophic losses created by an invading population bent on land and resource theft are mind-numbing and beyond comprehension. And what did these invaders have in common? To answer this question, Stannard reminds us of the words of Elie Wiesel, Nobel laureate and survivor of the Jewish Holocaust:

> All the killers were Christian. . . . The Nazi system was the consequence of a movement of ideas and followed a strict logic; it did not arise in a void but had its roots deep in a tradition that prophesied it, prepared for it, and brought it to maturity. That tradition was inseparable from the past of Christianized, civilized Europe.[9]

Just as the perpetrators of the Jewish Holocaust were Christians, so were the perpetrators of the Indigenous Holocaust in the Americas,

---

6. The most frequently cited instance of purposeful bioterror is Commander in Chief Sir Jeffrey Amherst's recommendation to use smallpox to reduce Native American tribes hostile to the British. Writing to Colonel Henry Bouquet, Amherst said, "Could it not be contrived to send the smallpox amongst those disaffected tribes of Indians?" In June 1763, one of Amherst's subordinates, Captain Simeon Ecuyer, did just that, giving blankets and a handkerchief from a smallpox hospital to a local Indigenous community. See Claudia Card, *Confronting Evils: Terrorism, Torture, Genocide* (New York: Cambridge, 2010), 260. There is much speculation that such methods of war were practiced by the Spanish against the Inca in South America during the fifteenth century, and even in the late nineteenth century in British Columbia against the Tsilhqot'in.

7. Ibid., xii. Stannard notes that on just the island of Hispaniola what had been a population of eight million in 1492 essentially became extinct by 1535, making it larger than any examples of twentieth-century genocide (74–75), and that was just the beginning.

8. See Joy Porter, *Land and Spirit in Native America* (Santa Barbara, CA: Praeger, 2012), 119–21.

9. Quoted in Stannard, 153.

all following a zealous conviction (or logic) of European, Christian superiority.

I can hear the cries of protest—"Surely not all?" Of course, some Christian nations weren't as bad as others. Some Christian churches, communities and individuals were not as directly involved in the ethnic cleansing, intentional dispossession, and/or assimilation of Indigenous nations. Some did not plunder the land as much as others. But as Daniel Castro has demonstrated in his recent book on de Las Casas—that "patron saint" of Indigenous rights, the one routinely lifted up as an advocate for the humanity of Native peoples— even the best of the Christians were, more often than not, "another face of empire."[10] Imbued with notions of religious paternalism and racial superiority, the "good Christians" did not seek to dismantle the oppressive systems, institutions, and ways of Christian colonialism, but merely to reform them, making them gentler systems of oppression.

Hear me right: I fully recognize that Christianity is not a monolithic whole. It was and is diverse, often made up of conflicting realities. And so I am aware that a certain violence is committed when speaking generically about it. But sometimes we must speak in such terms, especially when dealing with larger powers. Elie Wiesel was close friends with French Christian writer Francois Mauriac—a resister of the Nazi movement. Wiesel knew of Le Chambon, a French Christian village that went to incredible efforts to safeguard Jews. Yet Wiesel still asserts that Christianity (or the "Christian-civilization complex," if you will) was a dominant force that led to the destruction of millions of innocents. *And it was.* Likewise, I am aware of exceptional Christians who resisted the Indigenous Holocaust (a few, like Reverend Jeremiah Evarts, are highlighted in this book). I also recognize that there is a difference between that form of Christianity in which church and state walk arm in arm (as in yesterday's Spanish Conquest or in today's American Evangelical religion), and those forms on the other side of the spectrum that tend towards anarchism and resist state violence (like the Quakers). Nevertheless, Vine Deloria was right when he said that Christianity

---

10. Daniel Castro, *Another Face of Empire: Bartolomé de Las Casas, Indigenous Rights, and Ecclesiastical Imperialism* (Durham: Duke University Press, 2007).

has "a track record" that "bring[s] fear into the hearts and minds of non-Christian peoples."[11] In the name of Christ, this land and her peoples (human and nonhuman) have been repeatedly crucified, and the more benign forms of Christianity have done little to stop it. Most Christians—as in the Nazi Holocaust—have gone along with the system, enjoyed the unjust benefits passed on to them, and refused to question or raise their voices in significant protest.

So what happened to the terrestrial paradise—*and it was paradise compared to today's ecologically and culturally devastated realities*—that Columbus and his men invaded? One Spanish observer noted that in only two decades after Columbus' landing there was "neither paper nor time enough to tell all that the [conquistadors] did to ruin the Indians and rob them and *destroy the land*."[12] The Spanish release of European pigs and dogs wrought havoc on the delicate island ecology, and the assaults on the land continued through harmful agricultural practices (starting with sugar plantations in the early sixteenth century worked by imported slave labor) and massive deforestation, both of which have continued to the present day. Spanish invasion and colonization disrupted Indigenous life-ways and set into motion centuries of destructive land practices. Haiti, for example, is now considered an "environmental disaster" and a "human catastrophe." The 60 percent of Haiti that used to be covered in lush forests has been deforested to such an extent that now less than 1 percent remains. These factors have led to 90 percent soil degradation and wide-scale desertification.[13]

Similar environmental destruction has followed wherever European, Christian colonizers landed. In the United States today, 98 percent of the prairies are gone to support monocrop agriculture, and Canada has destroyed 99 percent of the original humus (i.e., the stable organic matter in the topsoil of mature soils).[14] In my Dakota homeland of *Minisota Makoce* (Land Where the Waters Reflect the Skies), we have experienced unprecedented environmental loss

---

11. Vine Deloria, *God is Red* (CO: Fulcrum, 2003), 189.
12. Quoted in Stannard, x. Emphasis added.
13. Vereda Johnson Williams, "A Case Study of Desertification in Haiti," *Journal of Sustainable Development*, 4:3 (June 2011), 20–31.
14. Lierre Keith, *The Vegetarian Myth: Food, Justice, and Sustainability* (Crescent City, CA: Flashpoint Press, 2009), 3.

since colonization. In the span of less than two hundred years, the colonizers have destroyed 99 percent of the prairies, 90 percent of the wetlands, 98 percent of the white pines, and 98 percent of the Big Woods of southern Minnesota. Moreover, mining, manufacturing, energy production, industrial agriculture, and animal feedlots have polluted our land, water, and air at life-threatening and life-destroying levels.[15]

The problem is not just with a land-base here and a land-base there. It's everywhere. We are now facing global catastrophe, with CO_2 emissions threatening runaway global warming—one recent study said that by 2100 global temperatures will have increased by sixteen degrees Celsius[16]—and through environmental destruction on such a scale (think tar sands and fracking) that our planet may become uninhabitable—think 90 percent of large ocean fish gone, think ten times as much plastic in the ocean as phytoplankton, think two hundred species gone forever every day.

None of this was an issue prior to invasion. Indigenous peoples could drink from non-toxic waters, breathe clean air, and provide for ourselves with abundant food sources. It was paradise. Derrick Jensen writes:

> Early European accounts of this continent's opulence border on the unbelievable. Time and again we read of "goodly woods, full of Deere, Conies, Hares, and Fowle, even in the middest of Summer, in incredible abundance," of islands "as completely covered with birds, which nest there, as a field is covered with grass," of rivers so full of salmon that "at night one is unable to sleep, so great is the noise they make," of lobsters "in such plenty that they are used for bait to catch the Codd fish." Early Europeans describe towering forests of cedars, with an understory of grapes and berries that stained the legs and bellies of their horses. They describe rivers so thick with fish that they

---

15. For more info on this, see my *What Does Justice Look Like? The Struggle for Liberation in Dakota Homeland* (St. Paul: Living Justice Press, 2008), 135–46. Winona LaDuke also describes the ecological devastation in Minnesota in her books *All Our Relations: Native Struggles for Land and Life* (Cambridge, MA: South End Press, 1999), 115–34 and *Recovering the Sacred: The Power of Naming and Claiming* (Cambridge, MA: South End Press, 2005), 167–210.
16. Lierre Keith, Andrew McBay, and Derrick Jensen, *Deep Green Resistance* (New York: Seven Sisters, 2011), 13.

"could be taken not only with a net but in baskets let down
[and weighted with] a stone." They describe birds in flocks so
large they darkened the sky for days at a time and so dense that
"a single shot from an old muzzle-loader into a flock of curlews
[Eskimo curlews, made extinct by our culture] brought down
28 birds."[17]

Prior to colonization, Indigenous peoples were not, as Thomas
Hobbes surmised, eking out an existence that was "nasty, brutish and short."[18] Our ancestors lived in a world of copious riches,
and had been doing so for thousands and thousands of years.
Maintaining good relations with all of creation, we educated our
children in our own way, prayed and carried out ceremony in our
own way, and spoke our own land-based languages. Yet in less than
a few centuries, our lands were ripped up and raped, toxified and
exploited, and our peoples and cultures did not fare much better.

Can we blame Christianity for the death and destruction of
Indigenous peoples and lands? If Christianity is the fundamental
worldview underlying these destructive *actions*, then the answer
to that question is "yes." Of course, industrialism, modern technology, and transnational, capitalist corporations should be held liable,
too. Yes, hetero-patriarchy, Enlightenment ideology, and secular
science must shoulder responsibility. But Christianity must bear
considerable blame, because (1) its worldview has helped midwife
and/or bless the abovementioned "isms," ideologies, and movements, (2) the colonial system in this land has been overwhelmingly
Christian, and (3) a vast majority of colonizers, both past and present, have embraced particular Christian beliefs that are damaging
to Indigenous life-forms.

What is it, in particular, that allows Christian communities,
societies, and nations to wage a kind of all-encompassing war
against Indigenous peoples, Indigenous creatures, and Indigenous
ecosystems? Why are all these forms of life perceived to be inferior?

---

17. Derrick Jensen, *A Language Older Than Words* (White River, VT: Chelsea
Green Publishing, 2004), 85–86.
18. Aric McBay writes: "We're often told that civilization was a step forward
which freed people from the 'grind' of subsistence. If that were true, then the
history of civilization would not be rife with slavery, conquest, and the spread of
religious and political systems by the sword." Keith and McBay, 36.

Perhaps the most devastating teaching from the Bible (from the viewpoint of non-Christian life-forms) is the Genesis hierarchy, which has led to an extreme notion of anthropocentrism. Essentially, this hierarchy is a form of "human supremacist" thinking, where human beings believe themselves to be the central and most significant entities in the universe, or they assess reality through an exclusively human perspective. Genesis 1:26 states, "Then God said, 'Let us make humankind in our image, according to our likeness; and let them have dominion over the fish of the sea, and over the birds of the air, and over the cattle, and over all the wild animals of the earth, and over every creeping thing that creeps upon the earth.'" Then in Genesis 1:28 we read: "God blessed them, and God said to them, 'Be fruitful and multiply, and fill the earth and subdue it; and have dominion over the fish of the sea and over the birds of the air and over every living thing that moves upon the earth.'"

Subdue it. Rule over. It's the language of control and domination. And this notion of human superiority over the rest of creation is not tangential to Judeo-Christian thinking, but is deeply rooted in it. Beyond the Genesis narrative and those Original Instructions that God is said to have given the first human beings, we find the teaching repeated and affirmed in, for example, the book of Psalms and the prophets Jeremiah and Daniel.

I recognize that there are different understandings as to what this notion of "dominion" means and how it should be lived out. Though millions of Evangelicals would affirm megachurch pastor John MacArthur's brazen convictions that "the creation mandate commands human beings to . . . dominate the earth," for "the earth we inhabit is not a permanent planet . . . [but] a disposable planet," many liberal or progressive Christians would shudder at such words.[19] The latter have attempted to recast this dictum to subjugate all other life by rejecting the language of domination and reinterpreting it as "stewardship." But that is still highly problematic. "Stewardship" is loaded with anthropocentric ideology, implying that humans, and Christians in particular (since they have more power than the Jewish and Muslim communities that share this "creation mandate"), know best how to organize or care for other

---

19. John MacAurthur, *Right Thinking in a World Gone Wrong* (Eugene: Harvest House, 2009), 148.

beings. Thus, Christians know best how to serve as stewards of the land, stewards of the sea, stewards of the animals, stewards of the plants, and stewards of the non-Christians.[20]

Theologian Paul Collins is one of the few Christians who is prepared to admit that the Bible does contain such disturbing anthropocentric and dominating voices within it, and that the church has not—to this day—seriously grappled with them. He asserts that the "stewardship" reading, though popular, cuts against the plain meaning of the text.[21] *Dominion* comes from the Hebrew verb *radah*, which means "to force" or "to keep another under one's authority," and "is clearly used in Genesis to indicate human power and control over the world." *Subdue* is even harsher. Coming from the Hebrew *kavash*, it "refers to the actual act of subjugation, the act of putting the foot of the master on the head of the slave or the subdued enemy." This isn't material that one would want to highlight in a "Green Bible." The Genesis text unabashedly affirms human domination and use of the environment for human benefit.

For Christians to continue to believe and proclaim such convictions today is frightening, for if there is one thing that they (broadly speaking) have demonstrated, it is that such views are harmful to life—and not just a little harmful: the kind of genocidal harmful that makes species go extinct and ecosystems collapse. Christians need to acknowledge and deconstruct those core aspects of their faith that elevate and prioritize humanity over and against the earth. This will be a massive undertaking. As Collins laments, the church

> ... still has a long way to go before a thoroughgoing ecological approach is integrated into theology and belief.... The bottom line for the tradition of Christian theology inherited by the churches is the emphasis on the absolute priority of humanity

---

20. Here is one example of Christian "stewarding of non-Christians," passed on to me by editor Steve Heinrichs. His denomination, the Mennonites, were both formally and informally involved in the Indian day and residential school system. Touched by paternalism in their beliefs about and practices toward Indigenous peoples, many were persuaded that it was their "calling" to direct and guide Natives into a better way. Hence one denominational leader could say, in 1963, "We feel that saving the Indian out of his squalor, ignorance and filth is step one in bringing him to the saving knowledge of Jesus Christ."

21. Paul Collins, *Judgement Day: The Struggle for Life on Earth* (New York: Orbis, 2011), 142.

over the rest of creation. In this tradition, everything in the world plays a secondary role to humankind and its needs. No matter what their rhetoric about environmentalism, the mainstream Christian churches are still crippled by an anthropocentrism that dominates their unconscious reactions and guides their value judgments.[22]

The only Christian teaching that rivals the destructiveness of the "dominion mandate" is the great commission, rooted in the particularity of Christ's exclusive saving power. According to John 14, Jesus declares, "I am the way, the truth, and the life. No one comes unto the Father but through me." The problem with this teaching—affirmed by all orthodox Christians—is that it disallows the possibility of multiple, equally valid, spiritual truths, and renounces all other traditions as, at best, incomplete and in need of fulfillment, or misguided and in need of correction. At worst, other religions are false or of the devil. Again, there are those who have tried to recast the gospel's teaching in more inclusive and pluralistic directions, and thus find a way so that people of other faiths and spiritualities (or just plain good people) can be saved.[23] But in the end, Christ, seen or unseen, is always privileged as the Way, for "every knee will bow, and every tongue will confess" (Philippians 2:10). Couple this restricted vision of truth and salvation with the missionary directives given in Matthew and Mark—the great commission—and the result is deadly. According to the imperative of these sacred texts, the rest of the world must also be converted or assimilated into the Christian way. Matthew 28:19-20 has Jesus saying, "Go and make disciples of all nations, baptizing them in the name of the Father and of the Son and of the Holy Spirit, and teaching them to obey everything I have commanded you. And surely I am with you always, to the very end of the age.'" In Mark 16:15-16—a disputed text, but accepted by most Christians through the ages—Jesus instructs, "Go into all the world and preach the gospel to all creation. Whoever

---

22. Ibid., 10, 17–18.
23. For an Evangelical perspective, see Terrance L. Tiessen, *Who Can Be Saved? Reassessing Salvation in Christ and World Religions* (Grand Rapids, MI: InterVarsity Press, 2004); for a Catholic perspective, see Jacques Dupuis, *Christianity and the Religions: From Confrontation to Dialogue* (New York: Orbis, 2002).

believes and is baptized will be saved, but whoever does not believe will be condemned."

If you are struggling to grasp the imperialistic nature of these commands, just imagine that these texts were from the Qur'an or from Marx's *Communist Manifesto*, and directed at "pagan" Christians. Do you see it now? Up until recently, the great commission has been non-negotiable: Christians are to seek and save "the lost"—a requirement that fuels a sense of righteousness and superiority that has resulted in the most appalling actions and behaviors against Indigenous peoples, with dire consequences to our communities. Some Christians may have shelved the call to proselytize. But most have not.

Believing they are doing "God's work," Christian missionaries and churches have relentlessly targeted Indigenous populations to "kill the Indian, and save the man," (as Captain Richard Pratt, architect of Native boarding schools, once put it), seeking to eradicate Indigenous spirituality and cosmology, replacing them with Christian religion and values. Not only has this devastated our spiritual traditions, it has also systematically undermined our sense of community (with peoples and all other life-forms) by focusing on the individual. Indigenous theologian Tink Tinker has pointed out that Eurocentric Christianity's emphasis on personal salvation exemplifies one of the profound differences between our clashing worldviews:

> To remove individuals from the communitarian whole through the process of conversion affects the community whole and not just the individual, even though only the individual makes a self-conscious choice. Eventually the pressure of missionization destroyed the ceremonial life of the community, because so many Indian ceremonies require the participation of the whole community for their success.[24]

Not coincidentally, Christian mission has also facilitated governmental and corporate aims, for through the destruction of our cultures and spiritualities we have lost significant capacity to effectively resist the theft and destruction of our homelands. Moreover, it should be noted how those responsible for this devastation

---

24. George E. Tinker, *American Indian Liberation: A Theology of Sovereignty* (New York: Orbis, 2008), 9.

have consistently targeted the most vulnerable in our communities—the children—as a way to assimilate us and dispossess us of Indigenous identity and lands. The Canadian residential "schools" and the U.S. boarding "schools" are the most obvious examples of the ways Christians worked hand in hand with governments to facilitate colonialist aims, but there are many others.[25] Of course, most followers of Jesus, imbued with "good intentions" thought it was the right thing to do. They still do. Colonial-style missions are prevalent throughout the Americas, and many remain utterly silent (or critically ignorant) of the injustices and ongoing ethnocide in which they partake.

"But they weren't/aren't real Christians!" That's the classic response of the church, and even the progressive Christian ally, when confronted with this litany of crimes: to assert that the perpetrators were not truly Christian or that they were "misinterpreting" and "abusing" true Christianity. And while it may be true that those Christians "back then" read their Bibles differently, in ways that some contemporary Christians do not, the fact is they still read those Scriptures, prayed in the name of Jesus, went to church, taught Sunday school, supported proselytization, and so on. They were Christians. And they were part of dominant Christian nations, just as Christians are today.

Some Christians might believe that they live in a post-Christendom world, but the United States and Canada are still Christian nation-states. More than 77 percent of the population continue to claim some affiliation with Christianity, and more importantly, the systems and institutions of these countries are clearly rooted in Christian traditions—as represented by the Doctrine of Discovery (the fifteenth-century papal bull that gave Christian nations the right to dispossess Native peoples of their lands) and the ideology of Manifest Destiny, both of which are embedded in law and practice (that is, they impact present-day realities). The occupying powers of Turtle Island are firmly founded on these unjust church traditions,

---

25. For example, in the Dakota context, when the colonizers imprisoned Dakota people in concentration camps or forcibly removed us from our homelands, missionaries were always present to seek converts among the desperate and weary—all the while actively occupying our lands, colonizing our people, and participating in policies of ethnic cleansing, cultural genocide, and land theft.

which assert that "civilized" peoples had (and have) the right to dispossess and/or rule over "savage" Native peoples. In the last few years, some denominations have repudiated such traditions, like the Anglican and United churches, but it is largely a rhetorical move, lacking deeds to match words. Where are the examples of Christian institutions and individuals turning over their landholdings and homes to Indigenous nations? Where are the examples of good Christians working to dismantle the very systems and institutions of colonialism that are inherently unjust? No, more often than not, the vast majority of good Christians, who want to separate themselves out from those bad Christians of the past and present, want to remain beneficiaries of the colonial occupation, never challenging their participation in the institutions that are foundational to that privilege.

Let us contrast the dominant Euro-Christian worldview and its impact on Indigenous peoples and lands with Indigenous cosmologies and worldviews. Certainly there were a few pre-Columbian Indigenous societies that were imperialistic, hierarchical, and damaging to the environment, but they were the exceptions. Most Indigenous societies existed for thousands of years on the same land-base—that is, they lived the meaning of "sustainability." Their *actions* demonstrated that they possessed a cosmology that valued life. In Dakota culture, that cosmology is best encapsulated in the phrase *mitakuye owas'in*, or "all my relations." Other Indigenous societies have similar phrases within their own languages. Our ancestors recognized the spiritual essence, sentience, and intelligence of all forms of life, and we sought to maintain good relations with this universe of spiritual beings; we understood that we were part of creation. Rather than seeking control over other life-forms, we sought reciprocity and balance. Indigenous intellectuals Vine Deloria Jr. and Daniel Wildcat have discussed this in terms of "power and place," which were and are foundational concepts within Indigenous knowledge: "power being the living energy that inhabits and/or composes the universe, and place being the relationship of things to each other."[26] Our spiritual practices were dedicated to

---

26. Vine Deloria Jr. and Daniel Wildcat, *Power and Place: Indian Education in America* (Golden, CO: American Indian Graduate Center and Fulcrum Resources, 2001), 23.

constantly renewing these relationships and our ceremonial life was dedicated to celebrating and completing these constructive and cooperative relationships.[27] That we maintained these practices within our homelands over millennia without destroying them is a testament to the existence of cosmologies that support life.[28] Further, because most of us have origin stories rooted in our land-base, we are Indigenous to the land in the same way that each kind of plant, animal, or tree is also Indigenous. And we understand that we have the responsibility to cherish and protect these places that have birthed us.

In comparison with the violence wrought by Euro-Christian "civilization," I cannot imagine a more ecologically sensitive and beautiful way of being in the world than living Indigenous values of reciprocity and balance. As Indigenous communities across the Americas and the globe seek resurgence, it is not Christianity that will show us how to live in a good way on this land, but our own ancient and sacred traditions. We need to put all our energies and focus there. Christians have demonstrated that there is something profoundly wrong with their cosmology—that it is in need of a radical reformation of core convictions to learn how to live with reverence for nonhuman and non-Christian life-forms. Perhaps that is why the Christian priest and eco-theologian Thomas Berry said, in all seriousness, that it would be wise for Christians to forget Jesus and shelve their Bibles for a while so that they can reconnect to the earth, the primary revelation of the Creator.[29] Maybe then they will stop crucifying the planet and the Creator who is in "all things." The world is deep in the throes of an ecological crisis based in Western

---

27. Ibid., 24.
28. Unfortunately, in their desire to project destructive practices upon Indigenous populations, a string of scholars (most notably Shepard Krech III in *The Ecological Indian: Myth and History*) have attempted to portray Indigenous peoples as genocidal killers on par with Europeans. Their theory of the Pleistocene overkill is one such example. Fortunately, others have debunked their work, demonstrating the absurdity of such hypotheses. See, for example, Vine Deloria Jr., *Red Earth White Lies: Native Americans and the Myth of Scientific Fact* (New York: Scribner, 1995) and Derrick Jensen, *Endgame: Volume II, Resistance* (New York: Seven Stories Press, 2006), 540–43.
29. Ilia Delio, Keith Warner, and Pamela Wood, *Care for Creation: A Franciscan Spirituality of the Earth* (Cincinnati: St. Anthony Press, 2008), 10.

economies of hyper-exploitation that Christianity fuels with its anthropocentric blessing. We will not survive unless Christians change their beliefs and practices.

The temptation for some readers of this chapter will be to dismiss my perspective as that of an "angry Indian." Even the most well-intentioned, liberal Christians often cannot deal with criticism and instead seek to silence or eliminate those who challenge their perspectives. This is why "good Indians" are heard so much more often by white people. But of course I am angry! I, and my Indigenous sisters and brothers, have good reason for it. Chew on the overwhelming colonial narrative and facts—not just the minor exceptions to this narrative, which many of us will want to cling to. Now consider the lived realities of Indigenous peoples today. There is no comparison between Native and non-Native/white experience(s). We have been radically dispossessed of land, life, and well-being—hence the high suicide, addiction, and violent-crime rates, the loss of language, the loss of our children, the loss of sacred traditions and ceremonies (our "scriptures"), and so much more. If you and your people had experienced such massive waves of violence, generation after generation, how would you feel? If the United States and Canada were colonized and occupied by another people of another faith, and pretty much everything was taken from you (and it was okay, because God and/or their church said it was), how would you respond? Would you rage against the machine? Would you be happy if such a people told you to get over it? Would you sit quietly by while they spent most of their time washing their hands and denying that their ancestors had done wrong or that they currently benefit from what had taken place?

Even Jesus, a dyed-in-the-wool pacifist, got angry once in a while, as he tried to overturn the religio-political system of his day (Mark 11:5-9). Rather than being defensive, Christian settlers need to do the hard work of decolonizing their lives, their faith(s), their churches, their countries, and join in a not-so-passive struggle to liberate our common land-base. And they need to do it now.

"Instead of Ruling"—Prayers

i.

Creator of the universe, we who have claimed to be your people in our words have betrayed you in our actions. We who have presumed to teach and convert others—we ourselves need to be reconverted and reinstructed. Our Jewish neighbors remember what our Christian forbears have done to them. Our Muslim neighbors remember. Our Indigenous neighbors—in North America, South America, from the Arctic Circle to the South Pacific—they remember. The descendants of the colonized and enslaved remember. Millions of people suffered and died because people of our faith tradition have turned from your ways and followed a broad and easy road instead—a road of injustice, apathy, arrogance, greed, racism, religious supremacy, and harm. We do not wish to go forward on this path. We want to stop, rethink, let our identity as colonizers and oppressors go, and let a new, future identity as good neighbors and peacemakers come. Help us, Teacher and Guide. Empower us, Fire and Wind of the Spirit. Lead us, Model and Mentor.

ii.

You are the God who hears the cries of those we and our ancestors have oppressed. When we launched inquisitions and persecuted heretics, we hunted and persecuted you. When we marginalized religious minorities, we marginalized you. When we divided from others we deemed less orthodox than ourselves, when we taught our children to distrust or avoid those different from us, when we tried to convert and assimilate what we didn't respect or understand, you suffered at our hands in the pain of the other. We have sinned against you—because we have sinned against others, not treating them as we would have been treated.

iii

Creator of the earth, artist of all creatures, friend of the birds of the air and flowers of the field, your creative Spirit can be felt breathing throughout creation—and also in the stories of the Bible.

Truly the Bible can be a library to make us wise. But we have been fools and turned it into a license to destroy. We extracted verses from Genesis to Revelation to justify exploiting and destroying what the Bible as a whole told us you created and treasured. We deforested valleys, plundered mountains, plowed prairies, and leached and eroded soils. If it couldn't be mined, plowed, cut, sold, or otherwise monetized, we considered it wasteland. We drove species to extinction—carelessly, greedily, ignorantly, knowingly. Egocentric individuals created an egocentric civilization, which in turn formed egocentric individuals, and we are those individuals, part of that dark and destructive civilization. How can we apologize for what we have defaced, degraded, despoiled, and destroyed? We do not merely ask for forgiveness: we ask for you to transform our hearts so that in the future we honor our fellow creatures—our sisters and brothers the eagles and deer, the ravens and bullsnakes, the hemlocks and clovers, the salmon, whales, and crayfish. We want to join you in your love and appreciation for what you have made, and from this point forward, we want to read the Bible wisely, not as a license to destroy but as a commission to preserve, respect, save, and love.

iv.

Instead of ruling over creation as despots and tyrants, we want to care for creation as gardeners and protectors. Instead of subduing the earth, we want to serve it, to heal it, to restore it, and to support its unfolding beauty and diversity. We do not know what that potential is, so we must approach your creation with respect and humility—students, not teachers—for your world is full of your wisdom that we have been too proud to learn. We repent for our human supremacist thinking. We resign as creation's tyrants, exploiters, rulers, and subduers. We seek to be readmitted to creation as fellow creatures. Teach us, Creator Spirit, we pray. Help us, for we will not thrive apart from reinhabiting the humble yet wonderful role you intend for us in your beautiful, magnificent world.

v.

What a tragedy, Living God, Creator of Life. We presume to call ourselves pro-life, yet we are merchants of death—death by greed, death by fear, death by war, death by overconsumption, death by hoarding, death by bombing, death by aggression, death by self-inflected afflictions and addictions. We presume to call ourselves pro-choice—but we choose against health, against restraint, against sharing, against foresight, against respect, against sustainability, against preservation. We deceive ourselves, God of truth. Help us to see who we truly are, and help us to become who we can, in your grace, become.

vi.

God, how often have you spoken truth only for us to twist your truth and fashion it into a weapon? Jesus told us that he was the way, meaning that he—the embodiment of love without intimidation, of nonviolence without timidity, of courage without threat—truly led to you, and that nobody could come to you by way of intimidating others, threatening others, or harming others. We misinterpreted his words and weaponized them. He sent us into the world to teach what he had taught—love, compassion, mutuality, reconciliation, benevolence, and concern for the common good. We twisted that commission and turned it into a mandate to conquer, control, subjugate, dominate, assimilate, exclude, convert, and ruin. We traveled over land and sea to make converts, and too often, remade them in our own distorted image. Our self-righteousness, spiritual arrogance, and sense of privilege and supremacy have had the direst of consequences, and before we can proceed, we must humbly sit in silence, seeking to learn from our past and present so that our future can be different and better.

vii.

God who loves all children everywhere as your own—who loves them with the fierce and tender love of a mother and father, in recent years we have been scandalized to hear about the sexual abuse of children by religious leaders, and disgusted to hear that those abuses were covered up. Yet what of the abuse of Indigenous children in mission schools over recent centuries, which we continue to cover up and deny? And what of the abuse of Muslim children who are bombed with weapons our tax dollars build and drop, or the children of migrant workers whose parents pick the vegetables we eat, or the abuse of children from same-gender parents or undocumented parents whose lives are harmed by our discrimination? Your Son Jesus taught us that it would be better to be thrown into the sea with a millstone around our neck than to harm a child, so we call to you: fill us with compassion for children and help us face our failures, past and present, for the sake of all children in the way of your Son.

viii.

Lord, we have lost our way. When we look into the eyes of others, we see mirrored back an image of ourselves that is humbling indeed. They are telling us that we have nothing, absolutely nothing, to teach anyone else, because we have become monstrous to them. We have a long record of doing harm to others and to this beautiful, fragile planet—all the while presuming our moral superiority. We are beginning to realize that before we can dare to teach or preach again in good faith, we must first listen and learn from those we have harmed. Then, humbled by our history, we must listen and learn again from you. We must never again preach Christianity or promote Christianity. Instead, we must seek to see, learn, and live your ways, which can never be owned or contained by any human label or organization. Help us learn with others, so that together with them, we may all move closer to your dream for us so that what has been wounded can be healed and what has been so wrong can be made good and right again.

—*Brian McLaren*

Sick Christianity, Cloroxed Christ

My birthplace is on the border between Mexico and the United States. Indigenous blood runs through my veins, but so does Arabian. I am a child of two very different worldviews that have clashed from the time Europeans set foot on our continent. I am Mestizo, Ameri-Indian.

I am also a Christian, torn one way by the damning history of the church in these lands, and torn the other by the glimpses of a beautiful Kin'dom that I experience now and again. My mind can't let go of images I have seen in David Stannard's book, *American Holocaust*: images of Indigenous people being strung up on racks in groups of thirteen—twelve representing the disciples and one representing Christ—because they refused to convert to Christianity. And yet, I have perceived other realities—of a God of utter compassion who longs for creation to be reconciled; that we are all interconnected, many parts of one larger "creation body"; that all are sacred and necessary. But these life-giving truths still seem to elude the larger church, riddled as it is with racism and human supremacist ways.

I find so much more within Indigenous cultures that is concurrent with "original" Christianity than the mainstream Christian culture of the United States. I think the main reason for that has to do with the fact that this supposed "Christian Nation" has been built on the heinous sins of mass theft and genocide, something that we still refuse to acknowledge and deal with in any real sense. As philosopher Angelo Corlett says, "Given its history of unrectified oppression [i.e., the failure to pay massive reparations to Indigenous peoples and African Americans], the United States qualifies as one of the most evil countries the world has ever known."[1]

Christianity is always clothed within culture, and here in America, the governing culture is shockingly violent and coercive. It's a culture that continues to secure its wealth and well-being

---

1. Angelo J. Corlett, *Heirs of Oppression: Racism and Reparations* (Lanham, MD: Rowman and Littlefield, 2010), 294.

through dispossession, fraud, and thievery, and as such, it produces a distorted and "sick" Christianity. As theologian Walter Wink argues, "When an entire network of Powers becomes integrated around idolatrous values, we get what can be called the Domination System."[2]

But it's not just American Christianity that's sick. It's the American Jesus, too. Consider the words of the Lakota medicine man, John Lame Deer, spoken in the 1960s:

> You've made a blondie out of Jesus. I don't care for those blond, blue-eyed pictures of a sanitized, cloroxed, ajaxed Christ . . . Jesus was a Jew. He wasn't a yellow-haired Anglo. I'm sure he had black hair like an Indian. The white ranchers around here wouldn't have let him step out with their daughters. . . . His religion came out of the desert in which he lived, out of his kind of mountains, his kind of animals, his kind of plants. You've tried to make him into an Anglo-Saxon Fuller Brush salesman, a long haired Billy Graham in a fancy night shirt, and that's why he doesn't work for you anymore. He was a good medicine man, I guess.[3]

The cloroxed Christ is all around me here in the United States. But the Christ I was drawn to and the Christianity I pursue are radically different ones; they're found on the margins and in the ghettos of the dominant culture. It's a faith that is seeking to listen and learn from all creation, privileging those who are silenced; a faith that rejects hetero-patriachary and white normativity; a faith that speaks of unconditional love for each other and for the earth; a faith that calls for the sacrifice of our own nonviolent lives in the service of friends and "enemies"; a faith that can enable one to forgive even the gravest of sins (think of the Amish Nickel Mines school shooting on October 3, 2006).

I struggle with the fact that I call myself a Christian. I always will. But my hope and prayer is that my life will continue to grow into that life-giving way that Jesus—a marginalized, brown-skinned Palestinian Jew—actually embodied, a way that the church has grasped on occasion. As part of that journey, I

---

2. Walter Wink, *The Powers That Be* (New York: Random House, 1999), 27.
3. John Fire Lame Deer and Richard Erdoes, *Lame Deer: Seeker of Visions: The Life of a Sioux Medicine Man* (New York: Simon and Schuster, 1972), 162–63.

need voices like Peter Cole's—uncomfortable voices that narrate the "sick Christianity" that oppresses so many, and that I must continually reject. The Israelites had outsider prophets who railed against their corporate religion, which had sacrificed the Creator to pursue Babylonian dreams. Most ignored them. I pray we don't. I don't want the church-of-the-domination-system to be the final word and understanding of Christianity.

—Iris de León-Hartshorn
(Mestizo)

14

Coyote and Raven Visit the Underworld
Religion, Myth, Story[1]

By Peter Cole (Stl'atl'imx)

Coyote and raven are walking through the woods up home harvesting fungus and mushrooms and admiring the autumn colors when they come upon a small clearing

well would you look at that coyote   richie richardson the ground squirrel on his way home with some goodies   let's follow and intervene

so as quietly as they can (in their socks birkenstocks and beads) they skulk from tree to tree   shrub to shrub   watching richie with his acorns and other groceries tucked into his cheeks and shopping bags   some balancing on his head   c and r are always

---

1. Three notes to the reader: First, the footnotes in this chapter are not Peter Cole's, but those of the editor. Second, as you will discover, Cole's style of writing does not conform to mainstream, Western standards. That is very intentional. Cole seeks to resist dominant forms of language and foreign ways of knowing, the kinds of hierarchical and elitist structures that were drilled into him—and hundreds of thousands of other Indigenous youths—at residential school. But it is not merely an act of resistance. Cole writes without "imported colonialist paraphernalia" as a means to recover the wisdom of Aboriginal oral traditions. And so this trickstered style—a form that looks chaotic to Western eyes at first glance—actually embodies an Indigenous way of cultural renewal, a way of radical freedom, respect, and noninterference. In Cole's words:

looking for ways to trick richie out of his comestibles and just as
they are about to go into their   "oh hi" routine richie pops down
a hole in the ground   and that was that

oh pooh   says   raven   *xa7mil'c*[2] just when we were getting to the
rising action

but all is not lost   says coyote *kalan7wi*[3] let's take a listen and use
our ecoliteracy skills

put your head down coyote and do an aural reconnoitre   I'll keep
guard

why do I always end up doing the dirty work

your hearing is more acute

---

controlling the cascadings   the rhizomatic dancing of words
regimenting them into genres orthographies schemata formulae
is more than coyote and raven are wont to do or could even
imagine

the words come in precipitations   transpirations evaporations
sussurations
rhythms   stresses   tones   elisions   pauses   silences   beats
stutterings
not to have their meaning dancing cavorting controlled harnessed tethered
by a priori molds casts channels recipes paths pre-scriptions
post scripts

the words are not (only) symbols   symbolic   representational
metaphorical
the narratives of our own lives are more than the descriptions of
them
coyote and raven are scribes scripted   enscribed   conscripted
scribbled
they are   the written   even as their pens loop and arc

Finally, Cole encourages the reader to read his text aloud, using ears and mouth
with eyes so that the story can come to us more easily and more meaningfully.
2. *Xa7mil'c* (revised Ucwalmicwts language) is a trickster term meaning
"anticlimactic."
3. *Kalan7wi* (Ucwalmicwts language) is a cautioning term like "beware!"

you mean my listening is   I pay more attention

as creatures of the forest we have to look out for one another and model reciprocity   and we should be three   one to listen one to surveil   the third as backup   lookout

ama7 sqit[4]   cedar my beautiful sister will you keep guard with me

the cedar swishes sways and scents assent

coyote puts her head near the hole   a few mushrooms please raven I'll need some sustenance to power my auricle

you silly   says raven you should get melina tom to inspect them first to make sure there aren't any unwanted psychoactive indole alkaloids

I've been eating fungus for millennia and can see that these mushrooms are in a teacherly mode

but are you in a learnerly mode   says raven well okay   I might as well join you

chomp chomp what do you hear down there asks raven resting against coyote

chomp chomp steps   there's a party going on   move closer do you hear it

oops   I think I'm going doooown

yikes we're both   shrinking   honey I shrunk the. . .

. . . plunk

. . . keplunk

---

4. *Ama7 sqit* (Ucwalmicwts language) is a salutation.

well alice here we are   I guess we won't be emceeing the
powwow at *sachteen*[5] tonight

come on coyote let's check out this party we weren't invited to
my tummy is grumbly and my ego is bruised

will you look at me he says feeling his new parts I'm a bunny
coyote   a bit late for hallowe'en but just in time for easter

so alice and rabbit follow the party sounds and thanks to their
fungal forest friends' in(ter)vention coyote has shapeshifted into
coyoterabbit and raven has become ravenalice   coyoterabbit
has long floppy ears a twitchy nose and a wiggly tail while
ravenalice has long ginger braids and a pinafore   striped blue
on white though this is not a political statement   they have also
tranformed gender roles

the sounds of partying get closer as they descend deeper into the
earthen burrow which with their increasingly diminished stature
seems cavernous far off singing can be heard . . . *one pill makes*
you larger and one pill makes you small and the ones that mother
gives you . . .[6]

so this is where my old friend grace disappeared to   says
ravenalice   she liked putting fairy tales and children's stories to
music

swish swoosh   klippety klip step step

in the faint light we see three far off figures advancing   who seem
to know the trail   no skip in their step   a sombre trio for sure

do you like this transformation coyoterabbit

---

5. Sachteen is an Indigenous Stl'atl'imx community southeast of Whistler,
British Columbia.
6. Grace Slick, "White Rabbit," recorded 1965, http://www.lyrics007.com/
Grace%20Slick%20Lyrics/White%20Rabbit%20Lyrics.html (accessed 14 January
2013).

I prefer to be in charge of shapeshifting   not on the receiving end
of tricksterism

says ravenalice the mushrooms and fungus are teacherplants we
must respect and honour them as shamans   with no residual nasty
thoughts about getting even

they go   deeper into the earth   it's getting colder frosty   steel
cold   then suddenly it begins to warm   billowy breezes blow

the three figures are now close   a curly haired man in a puce
chiton tunic   a lyre over one shoulder walking trancelike   a swivel
rearview mirror attached to his head   a woman twenty paces
behind wears a beige tunic with a forest green *apoptygma*   a taupe
himation trailing behind from a *koplos*   she takes a cloth to wipe
her brow   walking beside her is a man in a beige linen suit   a *qr
code* stamped onto his wrist   writing notes

ravenalice takes out her iphone flips to the qr code app and scans
the man's code   —hm maurice blanchot 1907 to 2003   french
anti-realist symbolist   he researched orpheus[7] for sixty years
refused to let anyone photograph him   never spoke publicly

sounds like a fanatic says coyote I like him already[8]

as coyote and raven walk with heads turned watching the trio
in the murky dark they simultaneously step onto a slippery clay
slope and whoosh they're whirling down
down
down
around and around and over and up and
down
and around and plunkety
plunk

---

7. In ancient Greek myth, Orpheus was a poet, prophet, and musician who had
the ability to charm all things—even the rocks—with his music.
8. Douglas Johnson, "Maurice Blanchot: Enigmatic French writer committed to
the virtues of silence and abstraction," 1 March 2003.

they're delivered sprawling into the middle of a party   but nobody
notices because everybody arrives the same way

quite a site   teeming masses of four leggeds   bird people insect
people spider people creepy crawlies   windup toys automatons
two leggeds shades and ghouls dancing twittering drinking
laughing   reminds me of the bar scene in bladerunner

checking his weather app   coyoterabbit says   whew   88 degrees
celsius hey look over there ravenalice   those party people on the
other side of the river look fierce but interesting   some have
horns some even have hooves   let's check it out this is too slow
for my taste   everyone is so polite sober and middle of the road
I'm in the passing lane

they walk through the crowd to the ferry

got any change asks ravenalice   brushing dust from her marigold
vegan cowboy boots

no but there's a change machine

who says you can't take it with you ravenalice chuckles taking her
visa out of her pocket and putting it into the machine

whizz tlok zp clunk

three coins for you three for me   when you meet the ferryman
give one to him and put the others over your eyes to acclimatize[9]

how do you know it'll be a him

this is patriarchy central   trust me

coyoterabbit mutters   this purgatory is a bit dull

---

9. In Greek mythology, Charon was the boatman who would ferry the dead
across the river Styx, but at a price. The Greeks would place coins (an *obulus* or
a *danake*) in the mouth or over the eyes of the dead to pay Charon's fee.

it's actually heaven   see the gps coordinates and 'no trespassing'
sign   says ravenalice

this is heaven but no-one has wings harps or halos   and they
don't seem very happy

you tuck   your wings in when you're not doing courier work   a
towering blond stevedore built like an inverted pyramid says from
out of nowhere   tuck them in or you get featherchafe   as for
the harps they're *outré* and the halos can only be signed out for
special occasions   payday is friday   we'll be grumbly until then

it's good to meet a local   I was wondering where the indigenous
people might be

says the massive stranger all the christians are with their
denominational vision and stuck with it until they can move on
  the rest reside in whatever hereafter they believed in   it's based
on expectation   lowest common denominator

are we dead   is that what this is about   I don't feel clammy cold
or pallid

of course we're not dead says ravenalice we're doing data
collection

reminds me of digging escape tunnels at residential school says
coyoterabbit   I was claustrophobic   but would do anything to get
away from that ethnic cleansing camp

you did say it was hell   but that said I'm not that impressed
with heaven I wouldn't give it three stars   michelin wouldn't
touch it

you have to remember says the towering one   this is the
manifestation of a single collective vision fixed by the clichés of an
inflexible set of patriarchal belief systems

off they go across the river   the water is boiling

steaming gurgling   swooshing and swirling everywhere in it
are crocodilians leaping lizards dinosaurians of terrible aspect
canadian mining company executives missionaries lawyers
anthropologists linguists provincial and federal indian affairs
policy makers including premiers prime ministers writhing and
gnashing and wailing in the black broiling dantean morass

I'm glad we're across the river says ravenalice   oh oh there's
a fifty ton canine with a hundred biting heads[10] and it's not on
a leash   it's coming our way   something tells me this isn't a
dream   within a dream

pretend you're imagining it says coyoterabbit   unimagine it

I didn't imagine it in the first place when is the next ferry   I'll try
to imagine it

ravenalice you have to train yourself to not see what your
imagination wants you to see   remember it's what we did at
residential school to make the torture bearable

so what do we do   asks ravenalice anxiously with the imaginary
d-9 k-9 charging us because unimagining it isn't working   and I
had to check my shapeshifting kit at the door

imagine a truckload of kibbles laced with morphine that'll   keep
himherit busy

and sure enough cerberus is suddenly lying down   and within
minutes every head is snoring

come on let's do a walkabout

they take the main path and in a few steps   reach massive gates
1000 feet high made of searing white flames

---

10. In Greek and Roman mythology, the multiheaded dog Cerberus guards
the gates of the Underworld, preventing those who have crossed the river Styx
from escaping.

coyoterabbit   pulls out a canadian tire store fire and brimstone
extinguisher from his imagination   and smothers the flames   the
gates turn to ash   he presses a universal remote and they disintegrate
      a wind from nowhere blows the ash away   the resulting black
cloud hanging across the river

ravenalice looks surprised   I didn't even know you had pockets

I'm all pockets   says coyoterabbit conceptual pockets spacetime
pockets falsewitness pockets   anyway the extinguisher like the
fiery gates was illusionary

whew is it hot here

coyoterabbit wipes his brow and looks at his thermometer app
it's 95 degrees celsius   I'm steeped   pass the lemon

a smooth tenor voiceover   speaks   it's just weather   ignore
it   temperature is meaningless here   the laws of physics
chemistry   biology and mathematics do not apply   rationalism is
not mainstream   it doesn't even have creek   status

hey coyoterabbit says ravenalice look who's here   mefisto[11] and
johann faust[12]   *wie gehts mein herr*[13]   you look just like the 16th
century woodcuts I've seen of you

ja sicher[14] I posed for the artist *immer und ewig* says *herr
faust(us)*[15]   one doesn't age here *siehst du*[16] for one thing   there is
no time   and the heat   keeps your pores open

---

11. Mephistopheles is the demonic figure that appears in Christopher Marlowe's
sixteenth-century play *Doctor Faustus* (New York: Penguin, 1969).
12. Johann Faust was a historical person—alchemist, astrologer, and magician,
the lead figure in *Das Faustbuch*, a chapbook from earlier manuscript ver-
sions published in 1587 by Johann Spies of Frankfurt. The doctor makes a pact
with the devil in which he exchanges his soul for a life of pleasures. See http://
en.wikipedia.org/wiki/Faustbuch.
13. *Wie gehts mein herr* (German) means "How goes it, my lord?"
14. *Ja sicher* (German) means "Yes, certainly."
15. *Immer und ewig* says *herr doktor faust(us)* (German) means "Forever and
ever, says Dr. Faustus."
16. *Siehst du* (German) means "You see."

time doesn't exist on the trapline either says coyoterabbit it was
imported   we didn't even have a word for time

mefisto is on his cellphone   looking the other way   listen bro/
sis he says   you have to come now   the natives are restless
we need your mediation skills they want lower taxes collective
bargaining and academic freedom

what natives are restless asks ravenalice

it's just an expression says faust   they're actually immigrant
refugee settlers from heaven the boat people   tunnelers
hanggliders windsurfers stowaways from paradise   every day
millions more arrive   put these on you'll need them

herr doktor passes c and r two pair of very thick wraparound
aviation shades

are these for uv   infrared   or are we welding something

they're for when mefisto turns around and for when his guest
arrives   one of his half brothers who is actually a brother-sister a
transformer will be teleporting any   moment now

suddenly mefisto turns around and even with the goggles on his
image sears into c and r's retinas then straight into their visual
cortexes   and out the other side

don't take the shades off yet   his guest is due

and sure enough *poof*

in a flash a shining white figure pops into view with long flowing
hair and a radiant smile   complete with perfect seven-seven
occlusion   great oral hygiene or awesome veneers the smile and
halo blind us   we're thinking it's a nuclear explosion   when the
retinal image fades s/he reminds me of the ladyboys of thailand
refined elegant graceful suave

coyoterabbit ravenalice says mefisto I am mefisto lord of
darkness meet yay-zeus[17] prince of light the anointed one and
please no gender markers case indicators or honorifics mefi
mefisto will do and yay or y-z

coyoterabbit gives him a high five elbow jive double hand slap
bump

it's been a while yay last time I saw you was at trickster school in
haida gwaii you're looking good   so you have a new name and
digs you always did like hot weather

with unfeigned surprise and a levantine accent difficult to nail
down the bright and shining one responds   my old and dear
friend coyote we must catch up how are they treating you my
what long ears and short nose and tail you have   you must avoid
estrogen mimicking molecules gmo wheat and dairy laced with
growth hormones

it's the mushrooms they affect the voyeur as well as the voyant
trust me we're all in the same declension

of course   the fungus   the teacher plants that sprout after
the rain welcome to my winter and weekend residence   your
ginger braided friend looks much like my old friend raven   the
last time I saw you we were snowshoeing on the lillooet glacier
some 200 centuries ago with the wooly pachyderms please let's
mingle and meet the gang we've quite an assortment

I'm impressed   waterfront property says ravenalice   you scored
well

everyone insisted so I accommodated   I try to make it
comfortable but it's getting crowded with settler refugees from

---

17. Yay-zeus is Cole's Jesus figure, a trickster of indeterminate gender, who
stands over against the dominant Christian tradition and praxis of the church.

heaven trampling the perennials   the inherent indigenous spirits
are getting crowded out but the council of freedom-seeking
settlers says they have a right to settle because the land is not
fenced or land-mined they say we're not making full use of it
so are proclaiming manifest destiny   and you know how long
restorative justice circles sometimes take   everybody wants a say

same old bull eh says mefisto   the bull of 1155 *laudabiliter* giving
ireland to the english king 1184 *ad abolendam* a bull condemning
heresy   1233 *vox in rama* condemning satanic meetings black
cats geese and thin pale men   watch out clint   lee van cleef[18]
and sherlock

not to forget says ravenalice the bull of 1252 *ad exstirpanda*
allowing torture on suspected heretics burning them alive 1302
unam sanctam   there is no salvation outside the church

coyoterabbit smiles quizzically with a bull bull here and a bull
bull there . . . parthenogenesis can breed discontent and feelings of
disconnection

next the papal bull 1442 *dundum ad nostram audientiam*
allowing ghettos for jews to separate them from christians 1452
dum diversas allowing perpetual slavery of pagans 1455 *romanus
pontifex*   sanctifying the seizure of newly 'discovered' lands and
encouraging the enslavement of native peoples

confirmed in 1456 says mefisto   by *inter caetera* in 1478 by *exigit
sincerae devotionis* which allowed ferdinand and isabella to create
the spanish inquisition nasty business then there was another
inter caetera in 1493 giving the americas to spain and portugal
followed five weeks later by *piis fidelium* giving the green light to
send missionaries to the 'indies'

---

18. Clint Eastwood and Lee Van Cleef are Hollywood actors who appeared
mostly in western (cowboy/Indian) movies.

worst of all says yay-zeus   during pope clement vii's reign
the bull *intra arcana* was passed allowing for violent
evangelization   though the next pope paul iii in 1537
issued the bull *sublimus dei* forbidding the enslavement of the
indigenous peoples of the americas   whom he declares to be
rational and possessing souls   it didn't change any on the
ground realities but added words words (holy) words

says mefisto   the settler-refugees from heaven are citing the papal
bulls to gain entrance to hell the chickens are coming home to
roost but the rooster has flown the coop

says ravenalice to yay-zeus I'm surprised to find you over here
I thought you'd be over there with the angels apostles prophets
holy sisters and popes

most of the angels have migrated here says yay   as for apostles
and disciples there's peter paul and mary mark matt   cool hand
luke big bad john   st george ringo paul and the others they have a
soccer team and big band   last I heard the popes cardinals *et alii*
were on an inter-galactic evangelizing tour and their starfleet was
drawn into the massive black hole *terra nullius mcdxcii [1492]*

ravenalice looks over at the apostles and disciples playing soccer
and notices the ball is made of white fire   the ball must scorch
their bare feet

you get used to it   when the pain is constant it's tolerable   and
can be quite pleasant   it's the intermittent pain   like toothaches
that are a challenge

coyoterabbit inquires   you get toothaches here

of course   says yay look at the variety of sweets available and in
this hot weather the bacteria and viruses multiply   I don't know
how many root canals I've had

you have viruses and bacteria

indeed where do you expect them to go when they pass on says
mefisto they're not in body form here but in spirit but as you
know spirit has agency

I thought you were perfect and unblemished says ravenalice that
was drilled into us in residential school

the viruses and bacteria are also perfect including grammatically
the blemishes are part of their perfection after all are human beings
not the hosts of nuclear and mitochondrial dna and rna these
are the domesticating viral agents that created 'higher' life forms
and inhabit every cell we are their metropolises their galaxies
their suburbs their strip malls

says ravenalice who are those men over there and why do they
look so miserable

they're participants of the first council of nicaea says mefisto
they taught themselves to think only in orbits and cannot make
transorbital interorbital connectivities they only believe in
rationality and logic they'll argue *ad infinitum* though that too
is a rationalist concept

ah the council of nicaea says coyoterabbit ad 325 organized by
emperor constantine it was spring salmon season I couldn't
make it to the conference

it was a gathering of men says yay who wanted to create another
androcentric hegemony based on unique binaries triplicities
quartos quincunxial quintessences of sexagenarian septuagint
hermeneutics octavos by novitiate decadents

mefisto turns to ravenalice you attended the council didn't you
in other form

yes I was with the persian delegation the council was a hodgepodge
of canons and bulls people arguing about resurrection father-son-
holyghost trinitarian stuff mary's immaculate conception being

born without original (or aboriginal) sin   baptism by heretical
christians   so many saints and wannabe hagiomorphs
everywhichwhere that I had to carry a cedar-fungus-sage-sweetgrass
bundle to ward off bad medicine

were any grassroots invited to the council   says coyoterabbit

only elite hollyrollers says the shining one   men men and
more men   women were present but not part of the official
conversation   they swept cooked cleaned washed   tidied up
minded the children   got firewood   the council was not for
them or the slaves and servants   it was for the burgeoning male
catholic hegemony who didn't want women to be literate in case
they got uppity   one uppity on us

you should also know that this gathering was not homogeneous
in terms of belief   there were egyptian *isis*ites with their own
conception of the trinity   there were those advocating for
the *theotokos*   which led to mariology   there were even
henotheistic[19] romans and some mithraists[20] present carrying with
them their mystical symbolism and sacraments[21]

everyone called everyone a heretic or crazy   like kindergarten or
faculty meetings

this absorption of so-called heretical elements to create a
normalized christian hegemony says coyoterabbit   is not well
publicized to the average churchgoer   how can something be

---

19. Henotheism is the belief that more than one god exists, and, more often
than not, that "my god" is the most powerful one (at least over the territory "I"
inhabit). Most contemporary scholars believe that the Bible contains traditions
that convey an Israelite belief in henotheism.

20. Mithraism was a mystery religion practiced in the Roman Empire
between the first and fourth centuries CE. It was suppressed by Christianity.
Archaeologists have even found Mithraic religious objects buried beneath early
church sanctuaries.

21. F. Mershman, "Advent," in *The Catholic Encyclopedia* (New York: Robert
Appleton Company, 1907), http://www.newadvent.org/cathen/01165a.htm
(accessed 14 January 2013).

heretical if a canon has not yet been "normalized"   heresy is about
challenging the status quo

says shining yay   the church was savvy   enough to know that in
order to survive it needed to absorb the local beliefs and practices
of powerful pagan forces and center itself in the city of rome   the
seat whence christians were martyred in the belly of the beast

says ravenalice so too for pagans   how can a group represent
paganness if orthodoxy had not yet been constructed (or as
some say downloaded) how did such a heterodox group create
orthodoxy   in which facets of a consensual holiness were
privileged

yay-zeus laughs   if holy means religious and religious means
hegemony and hegemony means male power   then you can
retroactively call them all holy   thereby validating the past
progressive from a future perfect location   holy in words
however is not always coincident with holy in action   as for
orthodoxy   it was the purpose of the council to manufacture and
enact the notions of orthodoxy and canon out of competing and
highly combustible/combative elements and it believed that it had
to be strict in enforcing its laws otherwise no one would take it
seriously

suddenly fireballs shoot across the sky in great numbers   at
hypersonic speed

don't worry says mefisto it's not an asteroid shower or alien flyby
 it's part of the meteorological phenomena some say it's the souls
of the damned being transported en masse to hell   many of
these "holy" men wanted my incarnation to be divine in order to
empower themselves   I was to become one with yahweh and his
ghost   with the demiurge[22] hovering like a thought balloon

---

22. The demiurge was a god, but not "the one" god—a subordinate deity who
was responsible for fashioning matter, which was eternal and not created. The
demiurge was a popular concept among a variety of Platonists and Gnostics.

reminds me of hamlet   says coyoterabbit father   step father
son and ghost   and medusa with the missing vowels of the
tetragrammaton tattooed to her forehead

mm says y-z   we became at the same time one and three   singular
and plural not unlike a pi meson during its strangeness period of
fewer than 6.02×10^{-23} seconds or a charmed quark   but nicaea
had no max planck[23] or chief dan george[24] to interpret and
re-refract the bent light of eternal presumption and predestination

getting back to what you said about progressive and future perfect
tenses says ravenalice some christians see themselves in the
process of being saved   others see themselves as having been
saved so a new believer becomes sanctified   redeemed justified
born again   that is the power of positivist essentialist doctrine

right says yay-zeus   the "faithful" need to believe in something
immutable so the bishops created a closed-minded hegemony
which as I see it leads to papal bulls justifying the kidnapping of
indigenous children from their families and turning them into
christians or killing them or working them to death all done
in my name and my father's and step father's and their earthly
representatives   about some of whom the less said the better

what's the idea behind   the threesome becoming a onesome asks
ravenalice I assume it's not just more words about more words or
the benefits of a forked stick

the men needed to solidify power over the lives of everything   they
needed to find a way of incorporating diverse religious beliefs into a
single orthodox text   hence this 3 in 1 plus 1 prestidigitation   it
kept the theologians confused fuzzy logic ruled

---

23. Max Planck (1858–1947) was a German physicist who originated quantum
theory.
24. Chief Dan George (1899–1981) was a leader of the Tseil-Waututh Nation,
a Coast Salish community located in present-day Vancouver, British Columbia.
He was also a logger, author, poet, actor, and activist.

one upping double talk to triplicate   says coyoterabbit

says yay if you want solid ideomaniacal converts you need a hook
in this case   a captivating series of stories procedures doctrines
wardrobes properties and rituals that are simultaneously clear
muddy unequivocal ambiguous and mystical leaving you satisfied
confused and ambivalent   in times of insurrection against
systemic oppression and tyranny   you want a strong god on
your side   one who is powerful and mystical   one you cannot
understand through words alone but need intercessionary agents
ceremony   ritual

in this case ravenalice says three male gods not counting the
demi-urge none of whom was born of woman because that would
have given a female the power of birthing god who couldn't be
co-eternal or even collateral   with the others because the mother
would have come first   not the primal male force   unless genesis
operates differently *in excelsis*

getting back to immigration and transportation   says coyoterabbit
a bridge would be a good engineering project   though I don't know
how deep the river is   it could be built on pontoons   are
there tides and currents   violent weather seismic activity

if you can imagine it or dream it we've got it says mefisto   or can
import it

a bridge from heaven to hell built of brimstone would be good says
coyoterabbit   or maybe pearls   are there enough freemasons to
do the job

they were in the starfleet with the popes   says mefisto
pause   the stygian[25] elements would make short work of any
transpontificators if they didn't eat the bridge first

---

25. "Stygian" is a reference to the river Styx, which, according to Greek
mythology, formed the boundary between the Earth and the Underworld.

all anyone has to do is imagine a bridge or ferry fleet interjects
yay-zeus and it materializes   but no-one wants to take
responsibility for the consequences

turning to ravenalice her/his saffron halo rotating like a ninja disc
yay says I have a question for you

fire away

in your experience on earth when and how do people stop being
indigenous and once you unbecome it can you reacquire it

ravenalice winks   considering palestine's recent overwhelming
acceptance as a nation as stated by its peers I wonder if you have a
particular analogy in mind

yay-zeus smiles true the indigenous canaanites were not invited
to co-author the pentateuch nor even coresearch it

now concerning my own indigeneity my ancestors returned to
the british columbia interior 12,000 years ago says ravenalice
when the glaciers had begun to recede   we were indigenous to
the territory but not wanting to be *sub glaciarium* we moved into
adjacent unglaciated territories   though we often spent time
amongst the glaciers

are you saying says mefisto that indigeneity can migrate or
transform when faced with say genocide or climate change
and repropagate itself after long absence   can one become
indigenous to another's territory   how is indigeneity measured
and mapped   located

for me says yay indigeneity is a way of honouring the sovereignty
and self-determination of a territory as a living self-sustaining
inter-relational agential process   I used to be on the other side
of the river but it felt sterile limiting and uninspiring   as though
constructed from top-down principles that did not celebrate
diversity I needed to be closer to temptation and to people who

liked to put their hands into the earth and feel the emotions and
sensations of our bodies   some people are terrified of the
livingness of the earth

ravenalice ruffles her feathers inquisitively and asks   yay you were
an angel originally weren't you   since you don't have the concept
of time here how do you move through development   and why do
you still have nouns   for verbs to push around

what you hear us saying might not be what we are saying   our
languages do not privilege certain kinds of knowing or feeling over
others   nor do we treat language as only about representation
on earth you might become habituated to expecting to hear certain
things and turn your hearing off for much of your conversations
and much of your thinking   because clichés complete them
just as no-one worries about a few inconsistencies in the wet
concrete   because we know the finishers will pay loving attention
to the details   we identify with the connectivities the surface
characteristics of occulted roots and rhizomes   yes we all begin
as messengers on wing patrol   I learned the business from the
ground up   rather than the sky down   I can fly but I often
prefer to burrow   hop   swim or slither

who's left asks coyoterabbit   behind the pearly gates   it sounds
like 21st century detroit

in the first place   there are no pearls left   says yay-zeus since the
capitalists were traded there   I never spend summer there any
more   I need to spend it as a body-spirit   not just in spirit
no-one freely chooses heaven anymore   now you need a visa to
leave

looking at the shining one with a sidelong glance ravenalice
says there's something familiar about you   are you richie the
groundsquirrel   I know you're a very capable shapeshifter
did you entice us here   make a trail of sparkles from the cocktail
party   are you the indoles and ketones the enzymatic pathway
disrupters   the serotonin and   synaptic transmitters

laughter like the ringing of bells fills the air   do you expect me
to say that I am that I am   you know better coyoterabbit than
to ask closed questions of deceased politicians   we don't do
multiple choice

ravenalice sees a group of people gathered at a massive stunningly
beautiful games table buzzing sounds and flashing lights   don't
believe we've met   ravenalice

charmed says a man with an aristocratic demeanor who calls
himself dorian gray[26]   sorry I'm a character and can only speak
the words written for and about me other/wise I ad lib   I am
bound to act in character like many earth people who assign
themselves roles

welcome to the club   I'm judas call me jude deputy mayor in
charge of security

christopher marlowe call me kit   I work with mr iscariot
eavestroughing weather stripping   hot tar roofing cedar shakes
and shingles   insulation ventilation as occasion warrants

says coyoterabbit I didn't know it rained or otherwise
precipitated is there even weather here

it does says another man but not water things are perpetually
falling sometimes they even go up you see we have levity as
well as gravity   you wouldn't believe the weather by the way
I'm adrian leverkühn[27]   pardon me I'm in recovery from
textual containment and musical fetish and like dorian I'm always
in character   trying to break out

---

26. In 1890, Oscar Wilde wrote *The Picture of Dorian Gray*, the story of a man
who sells his soul for a hedonistic life of beauty and personal fulfillment.
27. Adrian Leverkühn is the fictitious composer in Thomas Mann's version of
the Doctor Faustus story.

hello   laura riding jackson[28]   pleased to meet you   I specialize
in rationalism and anti-poetry

what an interesting looking game board   goodness me says
ravenalice

how do you do I'm joseph knecht[29]   *magister ludi*   it's your turn
my friend

but I don't know the rules says ravenalice   suddenly hovering three
feet above the patio

ha remarks coyoterabbit   that never stopped you before   you
always made rules up   changing them to suit your cards

mr coyoterabbit   says adrian please choose a place around the
board table

where are the dice the spinner the tumble balls coyoterabbit asks

no dice   no spinner no balls says knecht it's not a game of chance
nor even control   nor is it a competition not even a game really
it's convolution and convolition   the universe changes as we play
we are at the epicenter which is everywhere everywhence

so in this glass bead game   says ravenalice how does one take
one's turn   I'm supposing there is a predetermined goal

---

28. Laura "Riding" Jackson (1901–91) was an American poet, essayist, and
short-story writer. She believed that language was the elementary wisdom of
humanity, though for a period of twenty years she renounced poetry.
29. Joseph Knecht is the lead character in Hermann Hesse's *The Glass Bead
Game: Magister Ludi* (1943; reprint, New York: Vintage, 2000). Knecht is part
of an intellectual elite who spend much of their time playing the mysterious
glass bead game. Though he becomes master of the game, he eventually discerns that he cannot continue to occupy himself with purely intellectual pur-
suits, divorced from the real problems in the world that surrounds him. Knecht
quits the bead game, but dies not long after.

no goal no rules says mefisto not even turns   it's more like a
sharing circle

suddenly everything on the board begins to move in slow motion
   then fast forward the lights flicker the wind rises falls   the
trees sway the focus changes and again the stars whirl about
people's appearances change massively then return   petrified
   the milky way is absorbed into a tiny point then expands   the
whole geography turns buttery with multiple tremors then utter
monochrome   silence and stillness   an eerie feeling of anomie

says mefisto you choose a position to stand in and are
repositioned   player and played   I always found causality
boring and predictable and reason a bit of a stretch   glutenous

the shining one like a slow motion comet strides gracefully across
the piazza now gliding fifty feet above the flagstones   suddenly
s/he occupies the whole northwest quadrant of the gameboard
like the pilot of a starship   the board is maybe 150 feet across
as his bare feet fit into the templates on the patio the board lights
in myriad colors blinking rotating mist smoke and tracers create
a luminous cloud forest over the dancing glass beads discordant
music harmonious interludes atonic tympani offbeat
percussion the entire board whirls around wildly shaking tilting
individual sections move independently there is a little clink and
all is profoundly silent as though the gameboard were absorbing all
ambient sounds

what was that asks coyoterabbit   it was amazing

the whirling says knecht was the sprouting of a pine seed in
the peace country which had a massive effect on a spiral galaxy
a hundred thousand parsecs[30] distant   the tiny clink was the
milky way switching poles   for you see sprouting is more than

---

30. A parsec is a unit of length used in astronomy, equal to about 30.9 trillion
kilometers or 3.26 light years.

a biological description of a gymnosperm awakening   each
exertion of lifeforce has universal repercussions with every part of
creation   and beyond

no-one understands what the game means says the shining one
     the idea of meaning and understanding are based on human
rationalist symbol systems   there is no way of talking about
them except obliquely   reason has no place here   only poetry
and silence   chanting singing humming   and scat

mefisto adds many of us spend a lot of time at the board as the
board with the board in silence because there is nothing to say
about anything   or nothing

yay-zeus   teleports back to their talking circle

coyotealice asks him/her   yay you don't seem to have any special
stature here   you're just one of the gang

consensus brings us together in dynamic unity says the shining one

for the very young   mefisto notes there are no words   just
sensational gestural inter-relationalities   magic is normalized for
language   and neither gets in the way of the other

says ravenalice   many early protochristians believed that evil had
no independent existence but was a lack of the goodness and mercy
of divine being   but if that's the case why did so many christian
denominations try to beat the evil out of indigenous children or
create papal bulls that legalized hemispherical theft and genocide

yay-zeus breathes deeply   the writs of the bishops   priests and
their agents were not of divine origin   I/we am/are not their
words despite our collective divinity

heaven and hell are our constructions mefisto adds softly
constructions created by our part of the collective imagination the
consensual visioning

suddenly a scintillating twinkly swirling mist descends as we
each lose our individual essence becoming the massive flickering
whirling vibrating misting glass bead game and we are played
upon by 250 gamesters assembled on the perimeter of our shared
machina body   our agency is connected with theirs   we are
unnumbered spiral galaxies whirling into a point   expanding
contracting   dancing whirling madly alive in scent taste
texture   ecstatic spaces of silence   this is the place all spirits are
connected to

whoooah thinks *ravenalicecoyoterabbityayzeusmefisto* we are
now a machine plugged together into one another   part of a
greater self-other me-it-us trans-relationality involving yahweh
demiurge   tetragrammaton and the holy ghost as a churning
reverberating essence   the threshhold of ecstasy draws me in
holds me

then   just like that   coyote and raven are unhooked from
lifeafterdeath support

time's up says yay-zeus   his own person again   you have been
part of the game for a myriad myriad millennia you must return
now back to the work   of life

it felt like barely an instant says raven   now himself again and near
the hole

it was says the voice of mefisto   but a lot can be squeezed into it

says yay-zeus   heed the teacher plants   honour the shamans
the other than human

. . . always says coyote   *nia:wen*[31]

. . . and our original instructions says raven   *kukwstum'c*[32]

---

31. *Nia:wen* (Mohawk language) means "thank you."
32. *Kukwstum'c* (Ucwalmicwts language) means "thank you."

Small Hope amidst Empire

> It seems a good book—but strange that the white people are
> not better, after having had it so long.
> —*Chief Drowning Bear on the Bible
> and white Christianity (1836)*[1]

When the First Nations of the Americas came face to face
with Western culture, it was a collision of two very different
worldviews. For most Indigenous peoples, the worldview was
one of interconnectedness—all things dependent on one another,
all things connected to the spiritual powers, and thus all things
sacred and to be treated with respect. In contrast, the Western
worldview, influenced by mercantilist capitalism, Renaissance
theologies, and eventually by Newtonian science and the
philosophy of Locke, trended toward radical individualism and a
separation of humanity from "all things" (at least, all things "wild"
and "uncivilized").

And so the earth became an object to be controlled, rather
than a living organism connected to community and one's animal
self. The sadistic words of Francis Bacon (1561–1626) illustrate
such views perfectly: "My only earthly wish is . . . to stretch the
deplorably narrow limits of man's dominion over the universe to
their promised bounds . . . [nature will be] bound into service,
hounded in her wanderings, and put on the rack and tortured for
her secrets."[2]

Science, economics, and theology profoundly shaped the
Western worldview, but there was more to it than that. Perhaps
the biggest influence was the ethos of empire, a devastating
spirit of imperialism to which the church succumbed in the
fourth century, as the Roman Empire embraced Christianity
and Christianity embraced the Roman Empire. This marriage,
induced by Constantine the Great, would forever alter the Jesus

---

1. As quoted in Ronald Wright, *Stolen Continents: Five Hundred Years of
Conquest and Resistance in the Americas* (Boston: Houghton Mifflin Harcourt,
2005), 306.
2. As quoted in Derrick Jensen, *A Language Older Than Words* (White River,
VT: Chelsea Green, 2004), 19.

faith. Most at the time thought it was a good thing, providing the "missionary thrust" needed to spread the gospel to heathen lands. Many still think so. Others, like me, believe that it wholly compromised Christianity. The church was a subversive movement that had resisted Caesar's ways, but now it was in bed with Caesar.[3] The church had exchanged its grassroots, nonviolent power of liberation with the down 'n' out for the seemingly more effective and successful power of the state. And thus, like Marlowe's Doctor Faustus, the church sold its soul to the devil. "When a particular Power becomes idolatrous," says Walter Wink, "when it pursues a vocation other than the one for which God created it and makes its own interest the highest good—then that Power becomes demonic."[4]

The early church was about community, discipleship, and a deep love/following of God. The church did not condone violence, but preached against it, and refused to participate in the Roman army (at the cost of many lives). It was a movement animated by a bloodied, crucified resister-savior, a community rooted in a sacrificial allegiance to the "least of these." And they believed that God's passion was the noncoercive reconciliation of all creation here in this world. In one of my favorite books, *Saving Paradise: How Christianity Traded Love of This World for Crucifixion and Empire*, Rita Nakashima Brock and Susan Palmer write, "in the early church, paradise first and foremost was this world, permeated and blessed by the Spirit of God. It was on earth."[5]

A few years ago, I had opportunity to visit Rome, and one of the most significant things I learned was that there are very few symbols of the cross in the catacombs. Most of the pictures surrounding the burial sites of these first Christians are symbols of life—creaturely life. There are vines and grapes, whales and fish, sheep and shepherds, doves, and even a few peacocks. What this says to me is that the early church was focused not on the

3. Jack Nelson-Pallmeyer, *Jesus Against Christianity: Reclaiming the Missing Jesus* (New York: Continuum, 2001).
4. Walter Wink, *The Powers That Be* (New York: Random House, 1999), 29.
5. Rita Nakashima Brock and Susan Palmer, *Saving Paradise: How Christianity Traded Love of This World for Crucifixion and Empire* (Boston: Beacon Press, 2008), xv.

hereafter—at least, not a "heavenly" rescue from earth—but on the re-genesis of this present world. They believed that the Creator was holding and sustaining all things in and through that One whom the Powers tried to crush, that he/she was bringing all the parts back together in wholeness. It's the notion of interconnectedness.

Prior to Rome, I was in Syria, and while there I was able to see an early Christian baptismal font. The font was beautiful, covered by a canopy that had been painted with the cosmos, the stars, the moon and sun. The symbolism captivated me. It seemed to me that this font would have reminded those being baptized—in spirit and body—that they are to rejoice in creation. In other words, those embracing Christ and the church are not called to be "otherworldly" and "set apart" from creation, but are called to a deeper communion with this earthly paradise. Moreover, that communion would necessarily entail a commitment to suffer with and for the creation, since the baptismal waters represented the choice to "take up the cross." It's this understanding of intimate solidarity with the world and radical interdependency that should have been the touch-point between the Indigenous people of the Americas and the conquerors. But it was not. And we all know the results.

I cannot and will not embrace the death-dealing Christianity of the empire. The violence used against the Indigenous was the Pax Romana, which holds that war brings peace and might makes right. This is not the Christianity I was drawn to. But I know it was a reality. I know that it still is a reality. I know what it is capable of. And my soul cries out.

I believe God was with my Indigenous ancestors, and that God has always been with them. The reason the conquerors could not see it was because their first allegiance was to the empire and not to God (not, at least, to the God of the Gospels).

It would be too simplistic to say that Christianity hasn't changed since the days of contact/conquest. Yet it would be too naive to say that today's Christianity doesn't have much in common with that "old time religion." Broadly speaking, North American Christianity is closer to the ethos of the empire than that of the early church; our ongoing treatment of Indigenous peoples, of other-than-human life-forms, and of the earth, is proof positive.

There is hope, however, for those of us who name Christ. Throughout history, there have been minority movements within the church that have pushed against the domination system and tried to recover the early traditions of healing liberation. They have been salt of the earth, a light on a lampstand, and a city on a hill. They have been glimpses of what God has intended for his/her creation all along. I think of St. Francis, the early Anabaptists, John Woolman and the radical Quakers, Martin Luther King and the black church, Oscar Romero and the base ecclesial communities, the Catholic Workers and the Ploughshares Movement, Wendell Berry and the emergent "earth first" Christian circles.

I could go on. But I know that my list would still be small and partial in the dark shadow cast by history. And this shows that Peter Cole is right. Christianity, particularly in its relationship to the Indigenous, has been a toxic religion, and there's no way we can defend the results (deny though we try). It brings tremendous sorrow to me. My hope, faltering as it is at times, is that the glimpses of true Christianity can be a testimony to the Creator's love and compassion for all (even a "weak" testimony, like the cross). And my prayer is that those of us who follow Jesus will resist the urge to shirk or silence this shocking history. We must grab hold of it, and allow these still-bleeding scars to wound us. Though we despise this brutal inheritance, it can lead us to radical humility, it can call us back to our original instructions. It might even save the church and prevent us from future harm.

—*Iris de León-Hartshorn*
(Mestizo)

PART 4

WHERE TO FROM HERE?

SIX NATIONS

AND THE 2006 LAND RECLAMATION...

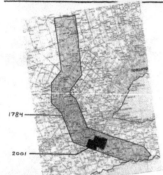

IN 1784, SOME 950,000 ACRES OF LAND, OBTAINED FROM THE MISSISSAUGAS, WAS PROVIDED TO THE 6 NATIONS FOR THEIR ROLE AS A BRITISH ALLY DURING THE 'AMERICAN REVOLUTION. THIS WAS THE 'HALDIMAND TRACT' IN SOUTHERN ONTARIO.

OVER THE LAST TWO CENTURIES, THROUGH SALES AND GOVERNMENT THEFT, ALL THAT IS LEFT TODAY IS SOME 46,500 ACRES (5%).

SIX NATIONS IS THE BIGGEST BAND IN CANADA, WITH OVER 23,000 MEMBERS. SIX NATIONS IS ALSO ONE NAME FOR THE HAUDENOSAUNEE (PEOPLE OF THE LONGHOUSE).

THEY WERE ORIGINALLY 5 NATIONS: THE MOHAWKS, ONEIDAS, CAYUGAS, SENECAS, AND ONONDAGAS. AFTER THE TUSCARORA JOINED IN 1722, THEY WERE KNOWN AS THE SIX NATIONS.

THE FIRST TREATY THE HAUDENOSAUNEE MADE WITH EUROPEANS WAS IN 1613, WITH THE DUTCH. THE TWO ROW WAMPUM BELT SYMBOLIZED THIS AND WAS THE BASIS FOR ALL FUTURE TREATIES.

THE TWO ROW WAMPUM REPRESENTED TWO PEOPLES, SIDE BY SIDE AS EQUALS. NO ONE WAS TO INTERFERE IN THE AFFAIRS OF THE OTHER.

—*Gord Hill (Kwakwaka'wakw)*

262

15

REFLECTIONS OF A CHRISTIAN SETTLER IN THE HALDIMAND TRACT

By W. Derek Suderman

Our family recently bought a house in Waterloo, Ontario, that lies less than six miles from the Grand River and thus within disputed territory in one of the best documented land claims in Canada. Although we weren't aware of this issue when we purchased our first house in the area, this time we did so quite consciously.

This has prompted some soul-searching. Do I identify myself as a "settler"? What is my responsibility in such a role? And, more pressingly, what difference does—or *should*—it make that I am committed to live out the gospel of Jesus Christ? In these few pages, I will reflect personally on the complexity of this issue and venture some modest, initial suggestions for living purposefully and peacefully as a Christian settler on this land. But first, some background.

In 1784, recognizing their role as allies to the crown during the American Revolutionary War, a coalition of six Indigenous nations from upper New York was promised a tract of land "Six Miles deep from each side of the [Grand] River beginning at Lake Erie and extending in that proportion to the Head of said River, which Them and Their Posterity are to enjoy forever."[1] Soon after

---

1. The treaty text and a description of what happened are available at *Six Nations*, http://www.sixnations.ca/SNGLobalSolutions-Web.pdf (accessed 1 January 2013).

this treaty, which preceded the formation of Canada by nearly a century, plots of land were sold and settled with little trace of the money supposedly held "in trust." In 1805, a group of Mennonites from Pennsylvania purchased sixty thousand acres of this land, the Block 2 territory on which my house, my college, and my church sit.[2] Decades after early inquiries into the matter, cases remain before the courts for an accounting of what happened, recognition of the land claim, and some form of compensation.

My own family history illustrates the dynamic of being both displaced from a homeland and settling recently "acquired" territory. In 1786, Catherine the Great was in search of people to settle the western frontier of Tsarist Russia (today Ukraine), and invited Mennonites, among others, to emigrate from Prussia. Her promises of land, freedom to worship, and exemption from military service "for all time" were welcomed by hard-pressed Mennonites as a positive development and even an answer to prayer. Catherine's motives were undoubtedly more strategic. By agreeing to the relative autonomy of these immigrant groups, she was able to solidify her hold on a region that had recently been annexed from the Crimea in 1783.[3] In addition, Catherine could make lands recently cleared of Indigenous Kalmyks, Cossaks, and Nogai tribes agriculturally productive through what she referred to as settler "talent, craft and hard work."[4] Catherine hoped either to assimilate the remaining Native peoples through agriculture or to displace them from Russia permanently. The Indigenous resisted this program and the settlers in various ways, but often to no avail. My ancestors were among these settlers, who are now commonly referred to as "Russian Mennonites."

A century later, a similar pattern occurred halfway around the world. In Canada, the British crown "opened" the frontier

---

2. E. Reginald Good, "Lost Inheritance: Alienation of Six Nations' Lands in Upper Canada, 1784–1805," *Journal of Mennonite Studies* 19 (2001), 92–102.

3. Christian Neff and Richard D. Thiessen, "Catherine II, Empress of Russia (1729–1796)," *Global Anabaptist Mennonite Encyclopedia Online*, May 2007, http://www.gameo.org/encyclopedia/contents/C45763.html (accessed 6 June 2012).

4. Willard Sunderland, *Taming the Wild Field: Colonization and Empire on the Russian Steppe* (New York: Cornell University Press), 93.

westward, and offered land for European settlement by the Red and Assiniboine rivers, key territory/homelands to both the First Nations and Métis populations. Mennonite immigrants and refugees embraced this opportunity and settled in these contested lands, obtaining large "reserves" from the government. In doing so, they also (often unwittingly) furthered the disenfranchisement of Native peoples. While difficult, I believe it is essential for those of us who are descendants of

Joseph Brant, Iroquois leader who pressed Frederick Haldimand for a grant of land on the Grand River (portrait, ca. 1786)

these settlers to recognize and reevaluate our role and even complicity in dislocating others in the course of our migration story.

My father's grandfather came to Manitoba, attracted by the promise of land and pushed by poverty. My mother's parents came decades later as infant refugees, fleeing the chaos of roaming armies and bandits during the Bolshevik Revolution following World War I. For my family, western Canada provided a place of refuge for a displaced people. Looking back, I can imagine them saying with the psalmist:

> Do not let my treacherous enemies rejoice over me,
>   or those who hate me without cause wink the eye.
> For they do not speak peace,
>   but they conceive deceitful words against those who are
>   quiet in the land. (Psalms 35:19-20)

Another group of Mennonites, who had previously migrated from Europe to Pennsylvania in pursuit of religious freedom, eventually settled in Waterloo County. For these "Swiss Mennonites," my wife's ancestors among them, the last phrase of verse 20 became something of a motto or badge of identity. To be Mennonite was to be the "quiet in the land" (*Stillen im Lande*) who kept their heads down, worked hard, and sought to be left alone to live in peace and tranquility within their communities.

My nuclear family emerges from these two streams of Mennonite immigrants. Looking back, the histories of Mennonites and Indigenous peoples in both Waterloo County and southern Manitoba have been intertwined and complex, with remarkable similarities and substantial differences. All of these groups have been uprooted and displaced, often resulting from some form of breached agreement. All have developed a deep sense of connection to the land. There is even a shared history of government-sponsored settlement; where the newly founded Canadian government sponsored Mennonite settlement in Manitoba during the 1870s, Sir Frederick Haldimand, on behalf of the British crown, resettled Six Nations along the bank of the Grand in the 1780s.

Differences have also been significant. Where the treaty with Six Nations recognized their military prowess and allegiance, Mennonite faith has prompted migration so as *not* to be involved in the military. Where a link to the land was forged in one case through hunting, fishing, and ancient ways of life, in the other this grew out of a long-standing farming tradition that *tamed* the land to make it *productive*.

Along the Grand River, both Six Nations and Mennonite communities have been deeply rooted in the land for more than two centuries. And today, waves of immigrants continue to arrive in the area, so that there is a large and complex population, reflecting many religious, cultural, ethnic, and national backgrounds who call this area home. While many factors have been at play in bringing about these migrations—social, economic, religious, ecological, and global political factors—the loss and promise of land is the foundational experience.

Here also lies a substantial link to the biblical witness, since land provides the backbone of the biblical narrative: the creation of land, promise of land, pursuit and gaining of land, loss of land, hope for and return to the land, and finally living under occupation in the land. This motif is so central that the Hebrew term for "land" (*'erets*) appears on average every ten verses in the Hebrew Bible.[5] So, when we Christians think that land doesn't really matter, that reflects not a Biblical posture but more often our privileged status, which allows us to take land for granted.

Moreover, this concern for the land is not simply an "Old" Testament priority. At the very beginning of his ministry, Luke describes Jesus entering his home synagogue in Nazareth and reading the following words from the Isaiah scroll:

> The Spirit of the Lord is upon me, because
> > he has anointed me
> > > to *bring good news* to the poor.
> > He has sent me
> > > to proclaim *release* [*aphesin*] to the captives
> > > > and recovery of sight to the blind,
> > > to let the oppressed *go free* [*aphesei*],
> > > > to proclaim the year of the Lord's favor.
> > > > > (Luke 4:18-19)

After reading these words from the scroll, Jesus declares the passage fulfilled in their hearing and sits down. As the rest of Luke reflects, this passage both summarizes and sets the course of Jesus' ministry—and does so by instituting a profound socioeconomic reordering. While in our day "evangelize" (the Greek term for "bring good news" or "gospel") is often understood in a spiritual sense, here it refers to very concrete steps to alleviate the plight of the dispossessed: releasing captives, healing blindness, and freeing the oppressed. In fact, the terminology reflects the very words previously used to institute the Jubilee:

> And you shall hallow the fiftieth year and you shall proclaim *liberty* [*aphesin*] throughout the land to all its inhabitants. It shall be a *jubilee* [*apheseos*] for you: you shall return, every one of you, to your property and every one of you to your family. (Leviticus 25:10)[6]

---

5. The term appears 2,505 times in 23,213 verses (just under 10.8 percent), with Deuteronomy and Jeremiah leading the way with one in six of the verses (over 17 percent) using this word.

6. Although slightly different in form, these terms for Jubilee come from the same Greek root *aphesis*, which could also be translated as "release," "liberation," "deliverance," and "pardon."

Jesus builds upon Isaiah's gospel message of hope for an imminent return from exile and access to land in a concrete, tangible way. But Jesus does not only pick up the theme of land, he begins his ministry aligning himself with the most radical view of land in all of Scripture—Jubilee.

The concept of Jubilee is truly revolutionary. Within the Bible, it functions as a socioeconomic "reset" button that returns land to its original owners every fifty years, so that, whatever inequities have built up in the meantime, the people return to a "level playing field" (Leviticus 25:8-28). Jubilee builds on the basic conviction that people do not ultimately "own" land; the Creator does. Thus, land is not something to be owned and sold so much as a divine lease to be cherished and tended: "The land shall not be sold in perpetuity, for *the land is mine*; with me you are but aliens and tenants" (Leviticus 25:23). While this idea does not rest easily with Western capitalism, it resonates strongly with traditional views of land I have heard from Indigenous teachers, including Adrian Jacobs (Cayuga), a former Six Nations pastor.

Although Jesus' audience initially resonates with this message, the scene changes dramatically once he applies this gospel of hope and liberation beyond the expected bounds of the community. What initially prompted cries of affirmation as the crowd identified *themselves* as the beneficiaries of this transformative agenda soon become shouts of anger, as Jesus extends his message to foreigners beyond their group.

The complexity here is both striking and profound. Although Jubilee talks about bringing people back to their land, this concept is also based upon tribal and family allotments to the people of Israel made possible by driving others off of it.[7] While declaring

---

7. Jubilee reflects an understanding of the land as a divine gift given to the people of Israel; however, the Bible consistently recognizes that this group did not originate in this territory, but names its previous inhabitants as "Canaanites" (Genesis 12:6), "Canaanites and Perizzites" (Genesis 13:7), "Hittites, Girgashites, Amorites, Canaanites, Perizzites, Hivites, and Jebusites" (Deuteronomy 7:1), and so on. Whether the land was "conquered" quickly, as Joshua would suggest, or gradually settled, as Judges implies, the ones who stand to benefit from the Jubilee in Leviticus are not "indigenous" to this territory. Although too often neglected, this insistence on the land as a gift—and thus something that can be revoked, rather than given as a divine right—qualifies the language of "taking

the fulfillment of the Isaiah passage in his ministry, Jesus throws a wrench into the concept of Jubilee by broadening his message beyond Israel to include foreigners, as well. Small wonder his listeners were concerned.

In our day complexities also arise. Six Nations has long struggled to have their treaty recognized, and I believe they are right to demand an account of how the land was sold, where the money went, and so on. Interestingly, as I understand it, this treaty claim does not derive from being Indigenous to the area, but rather to compensate for land lost during the American Revolutionary War. This raises the issue of whether there were other groups that preceded the Six Nations along the Grand River, or whether this was "empty land" prior to their arrival. If the former, should *they* also have a claim to the land?

For their part, Mennonites believe they purchased land in the Haldimand Tract in good faith, and they sought to develop and care for it the best they knew how. So how do shady dealings and financial mismanagement or corruption before and after affect this long-standing history? What is the status of the many others who have arrived in the area and sought to make a home for themselves in the decades and centuries since?

While the issues are complex, recognizing complexity does not let me off the hook. If Jubilee provides a foundational plank for Jesus' "political platform," surely it should concern contemporary Christians, too?[8] So, I face an uncomfortable question: How do I follow the one whose gospel proclaimed a Jubilee orientation and embodied a way of being that challenged the empire of his day? What does this imply for a community committed to following in Jesus' path?

For one thing, it is crucial that we open our eyes and ears to other perspectives on the history of this land than we commonly encounter. The intersection between my personal history and

---

possession" and "occupying" the land, and thus challenges attempts to use this language to support contemporary occupations.

8. Yoder illustrates the political nature of this orientation and helpfully argues against the tendency to "spiritualize" this passage. John Howard Yoder, *The Politics of Jesus: Vicit Agnus Noster* (Grand Rapids, MI: Eerdmans; Carlisle, U.K.: Paternoster Press, 1994) 21–53.

contemporary issues became particularly poignant for me when I stumbled upon the historical background of Stony Mountain Penitentiary. Opened in 1877, a few years after my ancestors settled about 130 kilometers away, this prison was built outside Winnipeg, Manitoba, on a site where soldiers had been stationed to quell the Riel rebellion/resistance.[9] As such, the prison signaled a shift from military suppression to law-enforced pacification. From the beginning, this penitentiary was used to house dissidents, with three of its first inmates being Indigenous leaders: Big Bear, One Arrow, and Poundmaker. The connection is hard to miss. The government that allowed my ancestors to settle the prairies had done so by pushing others off the land, building an impressive stone prison in part to house Native leaders standing in the way.[10] Greater awareness of the context of the founding of this institution, as well as the devastating legacy of the residential schools, has transformed the way I think about the extremely high Aboriginal prison population I witnessed in Manitoba.[11] "Proclaiming liberty to the captives" reads very differently for me, now, both in light of these systemic issues, as well as through having interacted with people "behind bars."

Indeed, Indigenous peoples are not the only ones who should be concerned with the legacy of colonialism. The limited range of perspectives that "make sense" and histories that are told in our society represent a profound colonization of the mind that stunts our imagination. I myself am particularly struck by how this has affected our interpretation of the Bible. As the current volume demonstrates, Indigenous views hold the potential to enrich the Christian tradition invaluably and to challenge this colonization of our own imaginations.

---

9. Métis leader and founder of Manitoba Louis Riel led two resistance efforts against the Canadian government for a variety of grievances, including the dispossession of lands.

10. Giesbrecht demonstrates that Mennonites in the "East Reserve" of Manitoba received preferential treatment, including being allowed to settle land claimed by the Métis people who preceded them. Donovan Giesbrecht, "Metis, Mennonites and the 'Unsettled Prairie,' 1874–1896," *Journal of Mennonite Studies*, 19 (2001), 103–11.

11. While I was working with the John Howard Society of Manitoba in the mid-1990s, the Aboriginal population in the province was less than 10 percent; in this federal prison it was more than 50 percent.

While it is tempting always to cast oneself as the hero of the story, encountering Indigenous perspectives challenges our tendency to monopolize the role of the speaker in history and within the Christian tradition. Returning to Psalm 35, this passage is striking in light of my ancestors' experience. However, it can also powerfully illuminate the voice of Six Nations. From its first verse, the psalm uses the language of legal wrangling to call upon God in the context of a contentious court case:

> Contend, O LORD, with those who contend with me;
> fight against those who fight against me!

By asking God to identify himself as the psalmist's "salvation" (v. 3), the speaker does not simply seek a heavenly reward, but wants God to intervene in this very concrete, earthly context.[12] The psalmist continues to use court language, worrying about "malicious witnesses" (v. 11), calling on God to come to his defense, support his cause, and vindicate him (vv. 23-24). This appeal is rooted in a conviction about the character of God as one who will act on behalf of the downtrodden:

> You deliver the weak from those too strong for them,
> the weak and needy from those who despoil them. (v. 10)

When I consciously move out of the role of the speaker and "hear" this psalm in light of the Six Nations community's situation, the words jump off the page.

Psalm 35 repeatedly expresses frustration, the extent of which I can only imagine my Indigenous neighbors must feel in response to the protracted Haldimand treaty court case. The legal language of the psalm, the sense that the cards are stacked against the speaker, and the frustration with a dysfunctional judicial process all seem to resonate with this contemporary setting. The psalmist's appeal to God to respond to the self-serving greed of his opponents, as well as the concern with being "swallowed up," evoke contemporary concerns of assimilation, isolation, and ongoing marginalization. Strikingly, though, the psalm does not finish with an appeal to God, but rather with an appeal *to the listening human community.*

---

12. Where the English term *salvation* lends itself to a spiritualization of this passage, the Hebrew term *yeshua* (also the basis for the name Jesus) may be translated as "victory" or "liberation."

This is key, and something many Bible readers miss. We often assume the psalms are prayers and, therefore, speech to God. Yet time and time again the psalms turn to address a *social* audience. Where we might expect vertical appeals to God, the psalmist also repeatedly turns horizontally to call on the broader hearing community to respond to the speaker's pleas. Psalm 35 is no exception, ending with the following:

> *Let all those who rejoice at my calamity* be put to shame and
> confusion;
>> *let those who exalt themselves against me* be clothed
>> with shame and dishonor.
> *Let those who desire my vindication* shout for joy and be glad,
>> and say evermore, "Great is the LORD, who delights in
>> the welfare of his servant."
> Then my tongue shall tell of your righteousness
>> and of your praise all day long. (vv. 26-28)

Relinquishing the "voice" of this psalm and hearing it instead through that of the Six Nations community, I am confronted by this strong challenge: am I one who "exalts himself" and "rejoices at the calamity" of this group, or do I "desire its vindication"? And, since listening, discerning, and responding to such a lament represents a crucial task for the contemporary Christian community, how might we respond?

An initial response lies simply in seeking out and attending to the voice of this people. The Six Nations community is speaking, but has largely been silenced, muted, and pushed to the periphery, falling out of media headlines until a dramatic roadblock or stand-off. Where Waterloo County Mennonites once saw themselves as the "quiet in the land," Six Nations have become so by imposition rather than by decision. Simply paying attention and building greater awareness in our own communities is one important response. What might be possible if mine were the last generation that could plead ignorance on such issues?

Another possibility lies in joining our voices with theirs in calling greater attention to this issue and advocating for a Six Nations perspective to be heard. As the Psalms reflect time and again, social isolation multiplies pain and suffering, and I imagine this community may feel both isolated and alone. As this community seeks to be heard, I hope that Mennonites and other faith communities will dare to become the *not so* "quiet in the land" and stand in solidarity with them as a listening community. As heirs to the initial settlers in Waterloo County, it could be highly symbolic for us to strongly support Six Nations' call for a fair hearing.

Another significant possibility could be to foster greater connection between our communities. Dialogue and listening can be invaluably enhanced by eating and playing together, by experiencing each other's cultures and traditions, and by sharing our various histories. While not automatic, greater solidarity and understanding can be fed by such contacts. I hope for increased interaction with people from Six Nations in the coming years, interaction that cultivates greater understanding, enlivens our imagination, and leads to new ways of living in solidarity.

Finally, as a Christian of European descent I believe we must also reevaluate and critique our own traditions. Indigenous peoples have good reason to be suspicious of Christian communities, given the legacy of residential schools and other ways in which we have been co-opted as instruments of colonialism. As churches, we need to become more aware of our own complicity, as well as to recognize aspects of our tradition that have been used to justify and support such practices. Members of Christian churches need to be willing to question and challenge our own tradition, as well as to propose alternative understandings of it. Here too, Jesus' entry into the synagogue provides a striking example, since his ministry starts with a critique of his own people and tradition—which is itself based *within* this tradition.[13] I seek to do the same.

---

13. This reinterpreting aspect of Jesus' ministry reflects an ongoing motif in the Bible generally. For instance, the story of Ruth provides a strong challenge to the exclusion of Moabites from the people of Israel (Deuteronomy 23:3), building on both the description of "gleaning" in Leviticus 19:9-10 and her role as an ancestor to David (and subsequently Jesus). Similarly, Isaiah 56 opens the door not only to foreigners but also to eunuchs to join the people through observing the Sabbath (vv. 3-8), against precedents in the law (Deuteronomy 23:1). In both instances, this shift represents a reinterpretation of law in light of the legal tradition itself, and reflects an abiding concern with justice. And once again, these are not merely "spiritual teachings," but calls for a very real transformation in the social realm, as Isaiah 58 makes clear: "Is not this the fast I choose: to loose the bonds of injustice, to undo the thongs of the yoke, to let the oppressed go free, and to break every yoke?" (v. 6).

If I am honest, I can empathize with Jesus' audience that day in Nazareth. A Jubilee message is more easily heard by someone who has been oppressed or is currently landless. While this may describe some of my ancestors, it does not reflect my own experience. For me, as one who has purchased land and benefitted from the system as it has evolved, it is difficult to hear Jesus' message. On the other hand, if Christian faith were not demanding, would it be as precious or inspiring? Would the kingdom of God still be a pearl of great value?

I pray that I may be open to the possibilities, partnerships, and opportunities that a Jubilee perspective prompts, and that I will find others who wish to walk this path as well. And I hope for a day when my Indigenous neighbors and I will be able to say together the words of the psalmist:

> *How very good and pleasant it is*
> *when kindred live together in unity!* (Psalm 133:1)

—*Gord Hill (Kwakwaka'wakw)*

Hope Springs Eternal

Creation glimmered all around, a glory to behold
A history of magnificent stories many more yet to unfold
Our myths and legends pay witness to the four-legged ones,
the winged-ones, the rock people and trees
All alive within the Sacred Hoop bearing witness to
Our Father Loving, Manitou, Father of Thunders, the Great Mystery

Each day we awoke to the sacredness of life
Till one day the two-legged ones rolled up on strangely crafted wood
Death would come to the Circle, to life as we once understood
They spoke of their Jesus, His Cross and the Great I Am
Being good hosts we welcomed them to share our land

Were they not also children of a loving and caring God?
We treated them as such welcoming them into our lives and heart
The painful lesson came abruptly as sickness hit hard
Sores erupted on our faces, our breasts, our bellies and hands
People were covered with agonizing sores from head to toe
As the illness spread, we realized we had a new foe
So dreadful was it that no one could walk or move and even lift
their head
The sick were so utterly helpless that they could only lie upon
their bed

Today the plagues have come and gone
A distant memory of horrors past
Creation glimmers less brightly, but in our hearts we still hope
As we continue to pray and fast

Some have welcomed Jesus; but our numbers are few
Host people find it difficult to sit in the white man's pew
As Christians we walk that sacred Red Road
As we find God in the wind and trees and the sacred earth
We again are reminded of our worth

Always there beside us from the beginning to now
Hope springs eternal as each day we bow
Like sheaves of wheat blowing softly in the wind
We bow before Jesus our Savior our King

—Anita Keith (Mohawk)

16

BROKEN COVENANTS AND RESTORATION:
A PERSONAL JOURNEY

By Steve Berry

All cultures first imparted their wisdom and understanding through stories, first told face to face at communal gatherings, often around simple campfires. Passed on from generation to generation, this oral tradition was a primary way of communication for preliterate people. The written word later helped preserve the stories, values, and beliefs of the community, sometimes liberating the imagination, but sometimes stifling it.[1] Whether oral or written, memory continues to be the vital link to the creative process of storytelling.

---

1. David Abram eloquently explains the stifling power of the written word on oral stories from an animist perspective: "Once the stories are written down, the visible text becomes the primary mnemonic activator of spoken stories—the inked traces left by the pen as it traverses the page replacing the earthly tracks left by the animals, and by one's animal ancestors, as they moved across the land. The places themselves are no longer necessary to the remembrance of the stories, and often come to seem wholly incidental to the tales, the arbitrary backdrops for human events that might just as well have happened elsewhere. The transhuman, ecological determinants of the originally oral stories are no longer emphasized, and often lose their oral, performative character, forfeit as well their intimate links to the more-than-human earth. . . . The human senses, intercepted by the written word, are no longer gripped and fascinated by the expressive shapes and sounds of particular places. The spirits fall silent." *The Spell of the Sensuous: Perception and Language in a More-than-Human-World* (New York: Vintage, 1997), 183–84.

Consider the Hebrew Torah, a complex written tradition refined from spoken words and recorded (scholars surmise) following the Jews' exile in Babylon (597–538 BCE). While in captivity, Jews remembered the past and then looked forward, contextualizing their lived story within the framework of the creative activity of Yahweh. Despite suffering exile and imperial domination, many believed their God had been faithful, and that it was the *people* who had broken their Covenant. Jewish scribes compiled stories in order to speak this "good news" back to their people, and even to the nations.

The garden of Eden tale (Genesis 1–3), believed to have been written during that Babylonian captivity, captures the essence of this idea. The flood narrative (Genesis 6–9) goes even further, viewing the destruction of the earth as the direct consequence of negative human desires, which bred waywardness and violence. These are hard stories. Yet by reimagining their ancestral heritage from Abram's family onwards, hope for the future was opened in the midst of a stark, contemporary reality of great loss.

The pain of their existence is captured in the following lament:

> By the rivers of Babylon—
> there we sat down and there we wept
> when we remembered Zion.
> On the willows there we hung our harps.
> For there our captors asked us for songs,
> and our tormentors asked for mirth,
> saying, "Sing us one of the songs of Zion!"
> How could we sing the Lord's song in a foreign land?
> . . . O daughter Babylon, you devastator!
> Happy shall they be who pay you back
> what you have done to us! (Psalm 137:1-4, 8)

Such biblical verse may help us imagine how the original inhabitants of the Americas must have felt after white settler occupation. Through centuries of conquest and colonization, a majority of Indigenous peoples were uprooted and suffered catastrophic losses. To many, it seemed that everything they believed in and stood for was lost. Most questioned the foreign invaders, but some questioned themselves, and even their religions (or life-ways), which were so closely connected to their homelands and to the natural world. Where was Manitou? Wakan Tanka? Yoru? Where was the Great Mystery? Did Creator care what happened to them? Comparisons between the Hebrew people's dispossession and the past/present story of Turtle Island's Indigenous people are striking.

In the following, I will explore aspects of the relationship between settler and Indigenous communities by remembering significant moments in my family story. I will also examine the meaning and significance of "covenant," and conclude with words from a respected medicine man that have encouraged me to embrace the subversive memories of Christ in an age which looks distressingly "Babylonian."

Not on the *Mayflower*: my family's story

My mother and father were born in the United States as second-generation citizens; their grandparents or one of their parents migrated from Europe at the end of the nineteenth century. My mother's family originated in Wales and arrived in Boston via Canada. My father's people came to Boston from Switzerland. I was born in Boston.

Early on, I knew that I was growing up in "Indian" Territory, like everybody else in the Americas. The Indigenous people who lived in the central plateau of Massachusetts were the Nipmucs. They spoke a Massachusetts dialect, and were members of a loosely constructed, inland Eastern Algonquin confederation of nations. The place where I lived was called Quabog, which means "before the pond." This was a fitting name because the Nipmuc (which means "Fresh Water People") had many villages in the area, stretching southward toward the sea, yet not beside it. They preferred living inland, where there was less competition and rivalry for coastal resources. Unlike the Wampanoag, Pequot, Mohegan, Niantic, and Narragansett—who had all sought to defend their control of shell-fishing beds—the Nipmucs were content with freshwater fishing along the interior waterways, ponds, and lakes. The inland hunting had been better as well, with an abundance of all types of eastern woodland game. In time, agriculture had become a key part of the Nipmucs' economy, as they planted and depended upon "the three sisters": maize, beans, and squash.

Algonquin (Nipmuc) Indian council gathers in Providence, Rhode Island, ca. 1835.

Quabog was once an independent village, but had joined together in an alliance with other villages when need arose. This was the case in 1660, when white settlers came and built their plantation right in Quabog, eventually disrupting the lives of the host peoples. When settlers first came, they were careful to acquire lands by formal purchase, yet as their numbers grew, the Nipmucs' land-base eroded, as squatters claimed land as their own. To make matters worse, the settlers claimed the best farmland. In this way, the places that had provided the primary Nipmuc food sources were lost, and they had difficulty acquiring enough comestibles to sustain themselves. By 1675, most of the Nipmucs had joined Metacomet (King Philip) of the Wampanoag, the grandson of the great *sachem* Massasoit, in what became the First Indian War against the settlers. After this war, Nipmucs who had not been killed or sold into slavery fled to Canada, or to the Mohican and other tribes further west along the Hudson River.

This battlefield was the place where I grew up. In this fertile land, I breathed the air and felt the sun on my face as I walked across the field, marveled at the beautiful earth, planted my first garden, pulled weeds, and got into manure fights. It was the place of my first school and adventures with friends, where I built snow forts and tree houses. I walked the paths through those woods, went on hunting parties with the men to shoot pheasant and partridge, fished for native trout, ran through streams, found turtle eggs, encountered skunks, and discovered baby cottontail rabbits. It was my garden of Eden, my place of wonderful dreams.

In my adventures I sometimes came upon arrowheads. These were unsettling experiences, because during my childhood I was taught only the story of the white town called West Brookfield. Omitted from that history were the pre-settler days; my elders and teachers never told me about the Nipmucs. The only traces of their story were found in the unforgettable markers placed throughout the town:

> Brookfield: Settled in 1660 By Men From Ipswich
> On Indian Lands Called Quabaug.
> Attacked by Indians In 1675.
> One Garrison House Defended to the Last.
> Reoccupied Twelve Years Later.

and

> Here Stood the First and Second Meetinghouses
> First Burned By Indians, August 4, 1675.

and

> The Well at which Maj. Wilson was Shot 1675.

and

> Here Stood Fort Gilbert
> Built about 1688 to protect the Second Settlement
> of Brookfield called Quabog From Indian Raids.

Another monument, on the southwest corner of the Old Indian Cemetery on Cottage Street where I lived, lists six names, under which is this inscription: "Killed by Indians, July 20, 1710." It was called the Old Indian Cemetery not because Indigenous people were buried there, but because settlers killed by "Indians" were interred on that site. There were no markers or monuments in West Brookfield honoring the dead, dispossessed, and forsaken Nipmucs. There were no Nipmuc laments like Psalm 137 recorded in our official stories to unsettle us "Babylonian" settlers.

West Brookfield, my happy home, had been Quabog, the peaceable and happy home of the Nipmucs. Once I learned that, I could never forget it. It was disturbing to know that another people had been driven from its home for white settlement to occur. When our family left West Brookfield, I carried with me something of the spirit of that Nipmuc place. Places are certainly made more sacred when we who inhabit them come to know their stories, and allow them to scar, bless, and transform us.

God's cathedral

My first discovery of God came through community and family. The second came through nature. The opening stanza of my grandfather's favorite hymn expresses well how I've experienced God through creation:

O Lord my God, when I in awesome wonder,
consider all the worlds thy hands have made,
I see the stars, I hear the rolling thunder,
Thy power throughout the universe displayed.
Then sings my soul, my savior God the Thee,
how great Thou art, how great Thou art!

With the small inheritance that he received after my grandfather Andreas died in Switzerland, my father purchased property in northern Vermont near the Canadian border. The place was called Eden, and I spent my childhood summers in this extremely rural locale. I loved it—so much less domesticated and populated than Massachusetts. Between West Brookfield and Eden, I had an incredibly rich experience of nature. By the time I was a teen, I could identify trees by their needles, bark, and leaves. I learned how to differentiate birds by their calls and songs. I could distinguish animals by the signs they left; I knew their tracks and recognized their diets from their droppings. I learned where the trout liked to hide in the brooks under alder brush overhangs, and made rafts from dead hemlock trees I cut down. I whittled staffs and walking sticks.

When I got married, I lived in Vermont full time. My next-door neighbor was a powerful tree-stump of a man named Tom, of the Abenaki First Nation. Tom owned Bluetick and Redbone coonhounds, with whom he hunted bear for food and sustenance. One winter day, he killed a huge black bear and hung it in a tree just a few hundred feet from our front door, curing the animal before he skinned it. The frozen bear was quite a spectacle, especially when icicles hung from his gaping mouth. Some of our European relatives were visiting us at the time; they took plenty of pictures, never having seen anything like this.

Throughout the summer, Tom often took his dogs out at night to get them conditioned for hunting season. Once he invited me to tag along. We walked deep into the forest, aided only by moonlight. The dogs ran on ahead, and soon picked up the scent of an animal. They howled and bayed the whole way, and finally stopped at the base of a huge pine. Tom, who was a lineman for the Vermont Electric Co-op, promptly put on his climbing belt, fastened pole spurs to his boots, turned on the miner's light that was affixed to his helmet, and scurried up the tree at a furious pace. He was about sixty feet up when he yelled, "Got it!" Then: "He went higher!" Finally, at the summit of the great pine, Tom firmly grabbed the tail of the cornered, thirty-five-pound raccoon and flung him from the treetop, calling, "Here he comes!"

The raccoon crashed through layer upon layer of cushioning branches. I quickly moved away from the trunk. No sooner had the raccoon landed with a thud at the bottom of the tree than the dogs were on top of him. I watched the raccoon fight for his life. Then, faster than he had gone up the tree, Tom was back on the ground, pulling the dogs off the animal to give it space. Amazingly, the stunned raccoon recovered in a matter of seconds, and as Tom held back the dogs, it lumbered off into the woods. Examining his hounds, Tom commented, "Tough critters, those raccoons. Imagine! He falls the equivalent of nine stories, hits the ground, has four hounds on him, and manages to cut up Buster and Bonehead pretty good. And just like that, he gets up and walks off into the forest. Something to admire about that gutsy guy! Let's go home. I need to bandage the dogs." I thought Tom was going to kill the animal; instead, he applauded it.

Tom and I had other outings in the woods, including plenty of trout fishing. I always learned something from him. On one such outing, I asked if he would be interested in attending church worship with me. "Sorry, Steve," came Tom's reply. "I'll pay my respects at funerals. I'll take in a wedding here and there. But my church is nature. That's where I take communion." I didn't press the issue; indeed, I understood Tom's perspective. As attested by Carl Gustav Boberg's 1885 poem "How Great Thou Art" (upon which the hymn is based), one can truly experience the beauty, power, and mystique of the Creator in nature. God's home *is* sacramental. What saddens me is that, for Tom, and for many others I know just like him, the connection between nature and the church is missing, maybe even at odds.

The church, for various theological, sociopolitical, and economic reasons, is largely divorced from the rest of creation, and it shows. The vast majority of us Christians are missing out on the communion that people like Tom experience. How can we change this? How can we recover the good news that the transcendent God has to be worshiped with a deep reverence in and through the earth and her life-forms? How can we realize, in our bones and souls, that we cannot love God well unless we know, respect, and love the bears, raccoons, trees, and trout in our respective "Edens"?

Learning covenant theology from Arnold Dreyer

In the 1970s, Eastern philosophy was the rage. I took some classes in Zen, which I found enlightening. But I was drawn more into nature, into serving the needs of people living on the margins in northern Vermont, and into deeper exploration of my own faith tradition, rooted in the Jesus way. Unfortunately, when I went to seminary at Yale in 1976, there were no classes that interrelated the natural sciences with theology. Nor, unsurprisingly, were there any classes on Native American spirituality and philosophy.[2]

During these years I wrote a play with my father, Ed, a Congregational pastor. It was a story about the Pilgrims, the *Mayflower* landing, the first tragic winter when most of the

---

2. Native American philosophy is a discipline largely unknown in Western circles. Alongside the works of Vine Deloria Jr., two texts that the reader might find helpful are Dennis H. McPherson and J. Douglass Rabb, *Indian from the Inside: Native American Philosophy and Cultural Renewal* (Jefferson, NC: McFarland, 2011), and Viola Faye Cordova, *How It Is: The Native American Philosophy of V.F. Cordova*, ed. Kathleen Dean Moore (Tucson: University of Arizona Press, 2007).

nonconformist separatists died, and how in the spring they were befriended by Squanto, a Patuxet, who taught them how to survive. Squanto, who had been captured by the English and sold into slavery in Spain, had made his way to London, and then back to the New England coast. Upon his return he found that his people had been wiped out by what was likely a smallpox epidemic spread by settlers. Instead of harboring resentment, he helped those who had unwittingly decimated his people. This Pilgrim and Wampanoag story taught me that relationship and interdependency is the key to human survival. The crisis facing the Pilgrims was solved thanks to the goodness of the host people. The sharing and cooperative spirit embodied in this story could have and should have been the prototype of the famous Puritan vision of "a city set on a hill"; tragically, it was not.[3]

In 1979 I graduated, was ordained, and called to pastor the Pilgrim Congregational Church in St. Louis, the first church west of the Mississippi River to intentionally welcome African Americans into their community. In that congregation was Arnold Dreyer, a brilliant man self-taught in theology and the natural and behavioral sciences. One of the most important things I learned from him concerned the meaning of "covenant." Though a central Biblical concept, covenant was largely tangential to the curriculum seminarians were required to take at that time. Though Scripture references "covenant" over 290 times, it had been an afterthought in my theological training.

Arnold helped make up that deficit. He explained that *brit* (the Hebrew word for covenant) lost much in its translation into English. It was not a "formal contract" but an abiding relationship; the covenant established between the Creator and all of creation was a bond of care and mutuality. What was really unique about Arnold's interpretation was his cosmological understanding: the

---

3. In 1630, the Puritan leader John Winthrop wrote a sermon entitled "A Model of Christian Charity" in which he encouraged the future settlers of New England to be God's city on a hill, before a watching world. Ironically, Winthrop formulated this idea while aboard the ship *Arbella*, before he had even seen the colony! This noble trope was later used in the formation of the consequential (and deeply problematic) nineteenth-century American ideologies of exceptionalism and Manifest Destiny.

covenant-making God is the Whole, and everything else is a part of the Whole. The covenant, he explained, establishes the connection that God has with the created order and every part in and of it.

For years we discussed this covenant relationship through Scripture and science, and I came to understand that everything, absolutely everything, is connected and interdependent. The God of the Bible is in all and through all. Moreover, as theologian Raimundo Pannikkar suggests, God's life-giving transcendence and immanence are inseparable one from another, like a proverbial Möbius strip.

Exploring the various ways that this interpretation made theological sense, Arnold and I rejected pantheism (everything is god) as being off the mark, but found much to commend in the panentheistic outlook (God within all things). We did not speak much about Indigenous worldviews and spirituality, but we knew just enough about Native American traditions and ceremony to conclude that their view was closer to a true biblical covenantal theology than that of most American Christians. A covenantal theology forbids the mistreatment of the earth and "all our relations"; if we are all parts of the Whole, then what we do to the earth, to Indigenous people, to the waters and the trees, we do to each other and to God. Such a worldview—embraced by some within the deep ecology movement—cuts against the grain of a culture ensnared in the violence of consumer capitalism.

In the early 1970s, the great Lakota thinker Vine Deloria Jr. argued in *God Is Red* that there appeared to be little that Indigenous religion shares with Christianity other than a belief in the activity of a creator. Regrettably, Deloria's critique remains valid because we Christians haven't followed the essential beliefs of covenant inter-relatedness found throughout our Scriptures. Randy Woodley, a Keetowah Christian and scholar, maintains that the ancient Hebrew understanding of *shalom* is very close to the Native American religious understandings of balance and interdependency. In his *Shalom and the Community of Creation: An Indigenous Vision*, Woodley describes what he believes is a largely pan-Indigenous worldview that he calls the "Harmony Way" (see also Woodley's chapter in this volume). This is precisely the covenant theology that Arnold and I discussed. It is a theological worldview that, if we have eyes to see, can be supported not only by the Bible, but by quantum mechanics and evolutionary biology.[4]

I have sought to honor Arnold Dreyer's insights by weaving this theology of non-separatedness into the classes I teach and the social action initiatives in which I am involved. Today, this theological view is gaining acceptance in the Church, particularly through the writings of my good friend, the recently deceased scholar Walter Wink.[5]

The wisdom of Two Trees

During these formative years my wife and I had three sons. We tried to pass on to them stories of how the Indigenous peoples of America had been betrayed and were still suffering, but also stories of Indigenous strength and resurgence. In 1988, after the completion of a mission trip to help build a home in Ashville, North Carolina, my family and I drove over to nearby Cherokee, then on to Old Fort. I had heard about Chief Two Trees, a medicine man and prophet, and thought it would be good for all of us to meet him. If he was open to it, I wanted to engage him in some dialogue, exploring connections between Christianity and Indigenous traditions.

We turned off the two-lane highway and headed up a side lane to the place where Two Trees lived. He came out on his porch, greeted us, and immediately recognized a physical ailment in my eldest son. On the spot, Two Trees made a diagnosis, suggested some natural remedies, and prayed for his healing. Then he turned his attention to me, inquiring what kind of man I was. I shared that I was a pastor and teacher who was interested in learning more about Indigenous spiritual paths. He was happy to converse.

During our visit, Two Trees related his belief that Jesus was a shaman of sorts, and that he had come from God and walked with his people. He told us that the Lord's Prayer and the twenty-third Psalm both contained "power words," and that Jesus' name was the key "power name" (see Philippians 2:9-11). He went on to describe

---

4. For a fascinating exploration of the relationships between these different ways of knowing, see Diarmuid O'Murchu, *In the Beginning Was the Spirit: Science, Religion, and Indigenous Spirituality* (New York: Orbis, 2012).

5. See Walter Wink, *The Powers That Be: Theology For a New Millenium* (New York: Random House, 2010).

how the world was in deep need of healing, but that this could only come by exposing the sickness, and then taking concerted, direct action, all of which needed to be spiritually discerned through prayer. He offered us a litany of warnings about our current "civilization": our overreliance on pharmaceuticals; the inherent danger of genetic engineering; the lustful pursuit of youth; the appropriation of aborted fetus cells for use by cosmetic companies; and much more. Two Trees predicted that corporations would seek control of the food and water supply, and then soberly told me that nature had been so disrupted and devastated that only a monumental and urgent effort would restore any semblance of harmony. As Two Trees finished, he made things personal, asking me to do all in my power to share what he said with people that I met along the way, and challenging me to stand up against exploitation, doing justice for all creation, both human and nonhuman.

Two Trees and Arnold Dreyer confronted my sensibilities and compelled me to take action as a Christian. I realized that *not* to address their concerns would only continue the long cycle of Christian covenant-breaking. It is hard not to agree with Waziyatawin (see her chapter in this volume) that a major reason the Western world finds itself in a grave ecological and ethnocidal predicament is that a majority of Christians live out a white-supremacist way of life fundamentally disrespectful to all things Indigenous (or, in my words, that we Christians do not live out the call of Jesus to embody lives of risky truth and compassionate justice). Indeed, our Church institutions are often reluctant even to speak that call for fear of reprisal (from within and without). We tend to be admirers of Jesus, but find following him too demanding, costly, and cruciform.

In the past, wars have been waged between races, tribes, cultures, and religions, and creation has groaned. Now our industrial economy is waging a war against the entire earth. A new imperialism is being advanced, as corporate dictatorship over natural resources pushes creation to the brink of disaster. Environmental philosopher and activist Derrick Jensen writes:

> We all know the numbers, or we should. Two hundred species per day driven extinct, 90 percent of the large fish in the ocean extirpated, more than 98 percent of native forests destroyed, 99 percent of prairies, and on and on. Every biological indicator

> is going in the wrong direction. Native communities—human
> and nonhuman—are under assault. . . . The planet is being
> murdered.[6]

The situation is grave. And many of those who are at the vanguard of this march toward oblivion consider themselves Christians. We must confess that they are delusional. To be sure, we are all enmeshed in this rapacious system, as "Indra's net," the Buddhist concept, makes plain. But we are not all equally responsible.[7] As followers of Jesus, we must try to do all we can to subvert this corporate, industrial culture, to join hands with Indigenous people as well as non-Indigenous (and non-Christian) allies who are struggling for respect and well-being.

We are truly in this together—connected, inseparable, interdependent, and covenanted with all things and the God who is in all. By joining hands with other communities of conscience we can mount a meaningful effort to restore the balance and harmony for which the vast majority yearns. We must act now. The sanest of seers and scientists are weeping by those "Babylonian rivers," loudly lamenting not only what we have lost, but what we will lose if we don't collectively make massive change. And soon.

---

6. Derrick Jensen, "Loaded Words: Writing as a Combat Discipline," *Orion*, March/April 2012.

7. Are the Indigenous, the poor, and the "two-thirds world" as responsible as the First World? And are First World citizens as responsible as giant corporations run by a small cadre of elites that consumes an inordinate amount of resources? By levelling culpability, we not only load ourselves with guilt that isn't ours, we are led to erroneous, individualized convictions like simple living and green consuming. These are not key pathways of action for the current crisis. By recognizing the larger culprits and their responsibility, we can focus on the bigger system: industrial civilization.

My Scars Are Yours

My scars are yours . . . do you not see?
It was my land first, the place I ran free
It was once my garden of Eden
Mother Earth's bosom gushing forth life
The loss of my land cuts my heart like a knife

I ran in those valleys
Breathed the air where I once roamed
Felt the sun upon my face
As I walked through the fields of gold
No more to call it home

There I marveled too at Mother Earth
At her medicines you now call weeds
This was the place of my first school
Where I learned of nature
And had adventures as I ran free

I too walked the paths winding through the abundant woods
Went on hunting parties, set trap lines for food
This was my place as well of wonderful dreams
I ran daily through the forests and the streams
Marveling at all I came across and the wonders I would see

Adventures I had often, encountered many a threat
Once I found a lost wolf cub and kept it for a pet
At times the threats came from another tribe
Breaching our defense; but none was so devastating
As the settler when he arrived

There are no markers or monuments now to honour our dead
There are no Indian mothers to lament the men their lives they shed
My peaceable and happy home is now forever gone
It is terribly disturbing to me that he preached Christ crucified
As he took away my life, my dream, my place, my home

Yes, all lands are sacred and even more holy
When we who inhabit it come to know its stories
You and I, Indian and settler alike, share the scars;
The struggles and each bear witness to the others victories
    and glories
But the transformation we each will undergo
Will depend on the mercy of Christ, and if we can agree to
    be friend
and no longer foe

—*Anita Keith (Mohawk)*

The Land Is Devastated

I live on Tolowa land, that is, land stolen from the Tolowa Indians. Prior to the arrival of Europeans, the Tolowa lived here for at least 12,500 years, if you believe the myths of science. If you believe the myths of the Tolowa, they lived here since the beginning of time. In either case, in human terms they lived here forever. This means that, by definition, they were living here, in this place, sustainably.

When the first Europeans arrived, the place was a paradise. Salmon ran so thick that people were afraid to put their boats in the water for fear they would capsize. There were so many fish that you could hear them for miles before you could see them. There were so many fish that entire rivers would be black and roiling with their bodies. Rivers. Not streams. Rivers. Sitting by a river you might see grizzly bears every fifteen minutes. The redwood forests were so thick that the first Europeans who came by land could only travel a couple of miles per day.

This is where the Tolowa lived. This is where they lived forever.

The massacres and the land thefts began soon after the Europeans arrived. Yontocket. Achulet. Howonquet. Again and again. Of course.

Throw a dart at a map of the United States and you will strike the site of a massacre. And of course, if you throw a dart at a map of the United States, you will strike stolen land.

And of course, if you throw a dart at a map of the United States you will strike devastated land. The Shawnee Tecumseh's brother Chiksika once said, "The white man seeks to conquer nature, to bend it to his will and to use it wastefully until it is all gone and then he simply moves on, leaving the waste behind him and looking for new places to take. The whole white race is a monster who is always hungry and what he eats is land."

The grizzly bears are gone. Salmon are hanging on, as are lampreys and others. Forests are remnants. Frogs and newts and salamanders are going. Even the insects have been hammered. The Tolowa lived here for more than twelve thousand years. The place was a paradise.

The dominant culture arrived less than two hundred years ago. The place is devastated.

The Tolowa are not the only people whose land has been stolen by the dominant culture. The California grizzly bears are not the only nonhuman people who have been exterminated by the dominant culture.

With the entire world being murdered, you might think we'd ask: what is wrong with the dominant culture? Why do they act so monstrously? Why are they always hungry? Why do they eat the land, and those who live on it? What can we do to stop them?

—*Derrick Jensen*

17

JUST CREATION:
ENHANCING LIFE IN A WORLD OF RELATIVES

By Daniel R. Wildcat (Muscogee)

You see, I am alive, I am alive
I stand in good relation to the earth
I stand in good relation to the gods
I stand in good relation to all that is beautiful
I stand in good relation to the daughter of Tsen-tainte
You see, I am alive, I am alive
                                        —*N. Scott Momaday*[1]

All of creation is a gift, a miracle, a mystery we can only partly know. And as we grow, so does it: the mystery, the beauty that surrounds us, and sometimes a keen awareness of the ugliness and destruction that humanity produces. Attentiveness to our relatives, our relationships, and our responsibilities is what's missing today. In such a situation, a discussion of creation justice will seem esoteric to many and self-indulgent at best. Reasons for such reactions are at the heart of why this conversation is now more necessary than ever before.

For the sake of clarity, I will briefly identify four features of Indigenous spiritual traditions or "worldviews," which produce conceptions of justice desperately needed in this human-centered Age of the Anthropocene and its current global life crisis. These

---

1. Excerpt from "The Delight Song of Tsoai-Talee," in *In the Presence of the Sun: Stories and Poems, 1961–1991* (Albuquerque: University of New Mexico Press, 2009), 16.

different areas of thought involve the nature of reality, the community, our ethical/moral environment, and Vine Deloria Jr.'s 3P formula of diversity: power plus place equals personality.

These conceptual issues are interrelated and deeply connected to Indigenous views of creation, life, and ultimately justice—a justice understood in Indigenous traditions more as a life-way, embodying honesty and respect, than as an identifiable set of beliefs, values, or doctrines.

The nature of reality

Reality is always a metaphysical quicksand. So, why go there? Because literally and figuratively speaking, we are already there. Without going into Socratic irony, very few people worry about the nature of reality, even when they should. Perhaps the most interesting distinction between Western and Indigenous ontologies is the way in which the Western tradition, following Aristotle, believes that we cannot know something until we have properly categorized it. In other words, we have to find the right definition or category where something we know or do fits into the overall scheme of things to understand it. In contrast, Indigenous understandings of reality, as embodied in language and worldviews, constitute what might be called unbounded ontological systems. Simply put, what is real is understood experientially as full of mystery and the miraculous. What constitutes "fact" is easily grasped in the strictest empirical sense, yet reality is also acknowledged to include dreams, visions, and even feelings, which may be the most troublesome dimension for the modern realist in objectivist traditions.

Indigenous traditions are exceptionally open minded with respect to the abovementioned dimension(s) of reality and, consequently, what we accept as ways of knowing (epistemology). This explains why there are no traditions of proselytizing within Indigenous "religions." Why would anyone argue with another over their relationship to the Creator or creation? Creation is large, complex, and diverse enough that it seems for many Indigenous peoples perfectly reasonable that people coming from another place on this blue-green planet might have a different understanding of their relationship to the Creator and the world we inhabit. Unlike those who came to our homelands with very narrow and bounded notions of both reality and knowing, Indigenous nations had an unbounded notion of reality that tells us much about the creation in which humankind participates: we are only one among many actors in an "enchanted" world. And that brings me to the second factor that distinguishes Indigenous spirituality from settler religious traditions.

The community—more than human

Our worldviews recognize many other-than-human persons as participants in our activities. Community is more than human. The beauty of this feature of Indigenous worldviews is that, while plant and animal persons share fundamental features of consciousness, volition, and power (i.e., they are sentient beings), they are also not exactly like us. Salmon, bear, eagle, and bison experience and know things that we as humans do not. And within our communities you can find—if you are open to it—many human relatives who have acquired knowledge from these other-than-human relatives with whom we share our homelands.[2]

Ethical and moral environment

Third, and following directly from the point above, the ethical and moral sphere of life for many Indigenous peoples is not restricted to humankind, but is coextensive with the ecosystems and natural environments we call home. While Western thought has embraced the importance of acknowledging human society as *the* site of moral development and generation of ethical systems, a surprising number of Indigenous communities continue to understand ecosystems and all of their living members as the appropriate sphere for morality and the generation of ethics. This is hardly naïve romanticism; we should leave that description to those of our kind who insist on

---

2. On interspecies communication, Deloria writes: "it seems as if the other creatures are waiting for humans to make an overture to the higher spirits, and once the quest for a relationship is set in motion, they join in, bringing their knowledge to add to our understanding and enabling us to receive special roles in life and powers to fulfil the roles. Often, it appears that certain birds or animals [or plants] have been watching particular individuals, and, detecting an attitude of respect, they then initiated communications with them, either by dreams or during a vision experience." *The World We Used to Live In: Remembering the Powers of the Medicine Men* (San Francisco: Fulcrum, 2006), 107.

acting as if justice is ultimately about "just us" (humankind). I prefer to acknowledge the good life and its active expression of holistic justice as found in most First Nations spiritual and ethical traditions. This is Indigenous realism.

The 3 Ps and the nature-culture nexus

Fourth, if there is one common feature among the diverse spiritual ways of living of Indigenous peoples in the Americas, it is that we have unique and powerful relationships with those landscapes/ seascapes where our creation as Peoples occurred, where our relationship with the Creator(s) began. No fundamental insight runs deeper than the recognition that our distinct tribal identities as Peoples emerged out of the landscapes and seascapes where our cultural traditions were born. In short, our spiritual ways of life were given to us in creation.

Our life-ways, both spiritual and material, vary widely—as they should—for our original instructions were not about humankind or nature in the abstract. Instead, they were of *powers* that resided in specific *places*, and how with attentiveness to those powers we might develop as peoples (and individual persons) with distinctive *personalities*. This is Deloria's 3P formula, and in the following quotations, he seeks to help us grasp what this means and how it differs from mainstream western modes of knowing:

> . . . power and place are dominant concepts [in Indigenous worldviews]—power being the living energy that inhabits and/ or composes the universe, and place being the relationship of things to each other. . . . Power and place produce personality. This equation simply means that the universe is alive, but it also contains within it the very important suggestion that the universe is personal, and, therefore, must be approached in a personal manner. And this insight holds true because Indians are interested in the particular, which of necessity must be personal and incapable of expansion and projection to hold true universally.[3]

---

3. Vine Deloria Jr. and Daniel Wildcat, *Power and Place: Indian Education in America* (Golden, CO: American Indian Graduate Center and Fulcrum Resources, 2001), 23.

The acknowledgement that power and place produce personality means not only that the natural world is personal but that
its perceived relationships are always ethical. For that reason,
Indian accumulation of information is directly opposed to the
Western scientific method of investigation, because it is primarily observation [privileging lived experience]. Indians look
for messages in nature, but they do not force nature to perform
functions that it does not naturally do.[4]

Deloria's 3P formula helps us to understand the incredible diversity among Indigenous peoples, and why the Indigenous are, broadly
speaking, comfortable with such diversity. It is a result of what I call
the nature-culture nexus: the unique interaction between a people
and a place—the relationships that unfold between relatives human
and other-than-human in personal, particular locales. The result
of these ideas is that justice can only be conceived as a life-way,
a practical, everyday life-way that could never embrace detached,
disembodied Enlightenment science or ascetic religious traditions,
for our lives are enriched in the living creation. And yet, this living creation, as Deloria suggested in the title of his last book, *The
World We Used to Live In*, is one that is considerably disenchanted.
Has "the world we used to live in" gone away? Was it never there?
Or have we merely stopped paying attention? I hope the situation
is the latter, for if so, we can recover attentiveness to the world of
which we are a small and significant part, intentionally recollect-
ing the vital insights we have lost. Maybe then humanity's behavior
will improve and the injustice we perpetuate as a way of life will be
lessened.

As we look at the state of the planet—what many Indigenous
peoples throughout the Americas have thoughtfully called Mother
Earth since before contact[5]—few topics are as pressing as the need
to begin a dialogue between religious traditions about what each
teaches regarding the "nature of creation," or, more accurately, "the
creation of nature." Such a dialogue will involve difficult discussions,
for creation, whether conceptualized broadly or narrowly, tells us

---

4. Ibid., 27.
5. See Ward Churchill's discussion regarding the origins of "Mother Earth" spirituality in *Fantasies of the Master Race: Literature, Cinema, and the Colonization
of American Indians* (San Francisco: City Lights Books, 1998): 105–17.

Chief Red Jacket (Sagoyewatha), ca. 1750–1830

much that we have forgotten about our selves and our relatives. A discussion of creation in the context of justice is doubly difficult, for very few people on the planet who live in the midst of industrial and postindustrial societies give creation much thought. If people still have an idea of a creator, the idea they have is largely derived from the classroom/sanctuary—through formal religious teaching or pedagogy—rather than from experience. So let's "keep it real!" as one of my students used to say, and carry this discussion with honesty, caution, and humility.

An invitation to radical humility and openness

It is worth remembering Seneca Chief Red Jacket's famous response to missionaries who wanted to enter Haudenosaunee lands to proselytize:

Brother, continue to listen. . . . You say that you are right, and we are lost; how do we know this to be true? We understand that your religion is written in a book; if it was intended for us as well as you, why has not the Great Spirit given it to us, and not only to us, but why did he not give to our forefathers the knowledge of that book, with the means of understanding it rightly? We only know what you tell us about it. How shall we know when to believe, being so often deceived by the white people?

Brother, you say there is but one way to worship and serve the Great Spirit; if there is but one religion, why do you white people differ so much about it? Why not all agree, as you can all read the book?[6]

Before Red Jacket ultimately told the missionaries to go home, he told them, "We never quarrel about religion." We should follow Red Jacket's advice. That does not mean we refuse to examine religious traditions and their many teachings regarding the birth of the cosmos, our Mother Earth, and our place within it. Not at all. We should welcome discussions of differences, especially as they relate to understanding the human-induced crises the planet now faces, for diversity and active complexity are important features of Mother Earth.

In a story widely repeated among First Nations, an Indigenous elder is called to testify in an important land case. He is asked to share his deep knowledge and understanding of the importance of the land that has sustained him. Through a translator, the elder, a traditional hunter, is asked to swear on the Bible to tell the truth. Upon hearing the interpreter's translation, and after a pregnant pause, the elder responded: "I cannot tell 'the truth.' I can only tell you what I know."

This story may illustrate better than a deep philosophical analysis the complex worldview and extremely open attitude toward knowledge, which many Indigenous peoples struggle to maintain in a world where recent arrivals to their ancient homelands continually seek to impress upon them that "We know better." Missionaries, teachers, businessmen, and governments repeatedly tell us First

---

6. As quoted in Granville Ganter, ed., *The Collected Speeches of Sagoyewatha, or Red Jacket* (Syracuse, NY: Syracuse University Press, 2006), 141–42.

Peoples, "We know the truth." An Indigenous response to such a declaration could be, "But do you know how to live well?"

The strength of Indigenous "religious" traditions is found in a reality where what Indigenous peoples practice, and what some (mostly outsiders) label religion, is understood by the People themselves as a way of life. The theologian Tink Tinker, a member of the Osage Nation, explains:

> Most adherents to traditional American Indian ways characteristically deny that their people ever engaged in any religion at all . . . but prefer to talk about a spiritual way of life—a way of living. Rather, these spokespeople insist, their whole culture and social structure was and still is infused with a spirituality that cannot be separated from the rest of the community's life at any point.[7]

The distinction between having a "religion" and having a "life-way" is pivotal in understanding a fundamental difference between how North American Indigenous life-ways and many traditional Christian theological examinations approach questions regarding creation and justice. One begins with the gift of life—"You see, I am alive, I am alive"—and the other begins with the exegesis of sacred texts and philosophical analyses of denominational theology and traditions. The latter is more historically oriented than present-experiential.

In his classic work, *God Is Red*, my mentor Vine Deloria Jr. observed, "It is the nonphilosophical quality of tribal religions that makes them important for this day and age." No Indigenous theologies exist in our tribal traditions, at least in a manner recognized as such by Western traditions of theological study. And thank god for that! We have no Indigenous American holy scriptures, no written texts, to argue over or on which endless exegesis can be performed. Indigenous peoples have something more palpable to draw upon for their experiential understanding of creation and justice—the world, the very creation we inhabit right here, right now. It is a living relation to the land—the rest of the creaturely, spirits-infused world—that is of paramount significance.

---

7. George E. Tinker, "Religion," in *Encyclopedia of North American Indians*, ed. Frederick E. Hoxie (New York: Houghton Mifflin, 1996), 438–39.

Where do we begin?

When most people think of creation they contemplate something that happened a long time ago. Yet for most Indigenous peoples around the world, creation is primarily the reality that surrounds us daily. Creation—this land, air, water, and all of the other-than-human persons (relatives) with whom we share this planet—is an ongoing reality. This is why I once heard an elder refer to the land, air, and water as the natural "law" for humankind and the biological life of Mother Earth. If humankind violates or disrespects any of the three, we will receive a harsh sentence, potentially a death sentence.

What happened a long time ago, creation in that "beginning" sense, is also here, but it is something that we would never debate. On this point, Indigenous People seem to follow the Seneca leader Red Jacket's declaration, "we never argue about religion," for peoples all around the world have their own stories, accounts, and traditions surrounding a Creator and their creation. Unfortunately, some people on the planet believe they have *the* creation story—the one, true account and that everyone else on the planet should give up their narratives to embrace it. What happens when one group of people from one part of the planet go forth all across the planet, convinced they have *the* truth is painfully clear in the five-hundred-year history of European colonialism. This history of domination illustrates a profound problem that Western civilization and many branches of Christianity now face. Or perhaps we should say "the" problem?

Not long ago, Dr. Henrietta Mann, a Southern Cheyenne elder, told my students at Haskell Indian Nations University, "We are born spiritual beings struggling to become human beings." This is where we begin any discussion of creation. We acknowledge the powerful spiritual dimension of our life and the life of the cosmos.

Yupiaq scholar Angayuqaq (Oscar Kawagley) named and called on that power when he began his presentation at the first American Indian and Alaska Native Climate Change Working Group meeting with the following words: "The Spiritual Person of the universe, God if you will, grant us wisdom as we talk about issues that are so very important to us and Mother Earth." Such invocations and prayers are commonplace in Indian country—indeed, are proper protocol. Of course, this may make some in modern Western institutions (legal, political, economical, and governmental) uneasy and exasperated. Yet we First Peoples cannot help but do so, for we come from traditions where spirit is life.

This prayerful life-posture might be considered a common denominator for Christian and Indigenous spiritual traditions, yet the difference in respective practices is telling. Christians often ask for something in their prayers: salvation, health, forgiveness, and so on. Think of the prayer that Jesus taught his disciples: give us daily bread, forgive us our debts, lead us away from temptation. In contrast, Indigenous traditions of prayer are overwhelmingly focused on giving thanks. Certainly, both Christian and Indigenous traditions contain petition and praise/gratitude. The point is that even when asking for something Indigenous peoples request attentiveness to the gifts they have received and for the welfare of their communities, including (importantly) the other-than-human relatives (all the four-leggeds, winged ones, plants, rocks, and so on) they consider part of their community. This is, from my vantage point, a significant lacuna in all but marginal Christian traditions.

How we understand creation

Within the world's religions, considerable diversity exists in the stories of Earth's creation. Indigenous peoples, in their panoply of creation traditions, bear witness to realities in which we now live, but also include our recollections about that particular place in the cosmos from which we came—the sun, the stars, the corn, the mountains, the waters, the lands. There are as many stories of emergence as there are nations and peoples.

We have been here a long, long time. First Nations stories of creation are full of relatives (or helpers) who lived and moved much before us; the land, air, the wind (that first breath of life), water, plants, animals, rocks. Who we are, as Abenaki, Choctaw, Dine, Euchee, Kiowa, Potawatomie, Ute, Yupik, is found in these stories of emergence. As Deloria stated, "Christianity has traditionally appeared to place its major emphasis on creation as a specific event while the Indian tribal religions could be said to consider creation as an ecosystem present in a definable place." Our Indigenous histories are stories of power and place and personalities—no one story reducible to the other—but like our Mother Earth, as diverse as her ecosystems, landscapes, and seascapes.

The oldest stories tell us about our relationships to our many other-than-human relatives. They tell us what it means to be Indigenous to a place. We truly consider these larger families 'kin.' This is where the Lakota saying *mitakuye oyasin* (to/for all our relations) comes from—a saying that many other, especially urban, Indigenous peoples, have adopted. Dennis Martinez, of the Indigenous Peoples Restoration Network, aptly describes this as our kin-centric worldview(s)—our complex relational and ultimately ecological situation within creation. At an American Indian celebration of the twenty-fifth anniversary celebration of Earth Day, back in 1997, Oren Lyons made a speech that demonstrates this worldview, and that should be a part of every ecological and religious studies program on the planet. Mr. Lyons told a crowd that in the languages of his people, the Haudenosaunee, there is no word for resources. He further explained that what scientists and policy-makers call resources, we call relatives. Warning us of the dangerous implications of the words we use, he reminded us that all nonhuman life-forms are our relatives, and that they must never be treated like resources.

To be sure, not all agree. Humanity understands creation many ways. The scientist looks for physical evidence. The artist listens to her muse, who whispers songs of origins. Followers of the major world religions for the most part pray, meditate, and study sacred texts in attempts to understand creation and its Creator. Methods of inquiry and understanding vary widely, as do their answers, revelations, and interpretations. Yet here's the key: we move much closer to a faithful appreciation of creation when we leave behind misleading dialogues and questions that devolve into *the* question of who is right, or what is *the* Truth.

The conversations we must avoid are those that preclude the recognition that, in the face of the complex and diverse living eco-systems, landscapes, and seascapes that constitute the biosphere, the unique and manifold ways that peoples of this planet understand and relate to creation and Creator(s) should be anticipated. It is wholly natural and good. Misleading dialogues seem always to devolve into monologues—believers of a tradition listening and talking to themselves as opposed to engaging in difficult conversations, truly seeking to understand the cultural and biological/ecological heterogeneity of this creation.

Many Indigenous thinkers—like Deloria, Thomas, Tall Bull, Rising Son, Momaday, Mohawk, Mann, Lyons, Basso, to name but a few—recognize that "wisdom sits in places."[8] My research on creation and justice has led me, like so many before, to realize that my primary sources for research reside in the world I live in—a physical-spiritual reality where so many of the vexing dualisms and dichotomies of Western thinking simply dissolve. Like the elders in our traditions, I prefer knowledge resulting from complex, continuous experience as opposed to controlled experiment or theoretical abstraction.

This experiential way of research and interpretation might seem simple, but it is difficult, for the other-than-human features of our everyday environments, the other-than human relatives with whom we share this planet, are currently eclipsed by our human creations and are, in what can only be described as a worst-case scenario, increasingly destroyed by our mindless, spiritless, human-made creations. Primary-source research confirms what Indigenous elders and scholars have repeatedly observed: humanity is not paying attention, and as a result, we are murdering the creation of which we are a part.

Homeland maturity

There are no experts on the Indigenous peoples of North America because the cultural diversity of our peoples is so broad. This diversity is due to the fact that our histories, cultures, the deepest features of our ceremonial lives, and more emerged from our peoples' symbiotic relationship with the manifold landscapes and seascapes of this beautiful Earth Mother. The Indigenous knowledges that grew out of these symbiotic relationships are hardly esoteric, and certainly not romantic or unrealistic. Indigenous knowledges are fundamentally practical knowledges, which, as I have written elsewhere, have "emerged through hundreds and often thousands of years of interaction with ecosystems and larger environments—a *nature-culture nexus* (NCN)—embodied in tribal life-ways residing

---

8. See, for example, Keith H. Basso, *Wisdom Sits in Places: Landscape and Language Among the Western Apache* (Albuquerque: University of New Mexico Press, 1996).

within a spiritual cosmos."[9] I call these knowledges realistic because they produced sustainable, life-enhancing social institutions and material cultures because of their integral, balanced relationship between nature and culture—the NCN. From an ancient awareness of this NCN, widely shared insights emerged in Indigenous knowledges of creation, knowledges that embody spiritual significance and power for those who are paying attention.

But note this: Indigenous knowledges (IKs) of creation and justice are not passively found in "nature." They are found in the experiential exploration of our human place, our relations/relationships within the natural world. IKs are embedded in our languages, customs, ceremonies, and habits. IKs are generated through the establishment of respectful relations in activities of providing food, shelter, clothing, and livelihood for our families, communities, and nations.

"Okay," some are thinking, "thanks for the intro lecture to Cultural Anthropology 101." However, my point is that First Peoples' knowledges are as much about the spiritual dimensions of a people's life as about their social organization and division of labor (narrowly defined). What I have called Indigenous realism proposes that these IKs cannot be understood as merely human constructions. Rather, they must be understood as collaborations with the other-than-human persons, larger ecological communities, and natural environments of the places we call home.

The increasing impoverishment of life on earth is predominantly a cultural product. And after a five-centuries-old global imposition of Eurocentric and Western institutions, it seems to me that the world would benefit from a serious examination and discussion of Indigenous ideas. It is ironic that American Indian life-ways and worldviews, exceptional for their practicality, are inevitably cast by modern societies as full of myth and romanticized recollections. Yet so-called civilized societies, with their powerful rationality and technologies, betray an adherence to a body of myths and romanticism that eclipses anything imagined in tribal worldviews and life-ways.

Primary among the myths to which modern humankind adheres faithfully is the deep-seated notion that humans constitute

9. Daniel R. Wildcat, *Red Alert: Saving the Planet with Indigenous Knowledge* (San Francisco: Fulcrum, 2009), 74.

the center of creation, around which the rest of the world rightly revolves: a position held self-evident by our (apparent) control and manipulation of the natural world. If romanticism denotes impracticality and unrealistic fantasy, can there be a more romantic myth than the idea that human beings can continually rise above the powers of nature through our rationalities and application of technology—a myth that has brought Mother Earth a litany of woes, a myth that is literally burning the planet? Yet mainstream society keeps on with it, routinely touting the idea that there will be some manufactured tech solutions, some "alternative green-energy ways," that will save us from our current problems. Contrast this anthropocentric, romantic, and ultimately arrogant myth to the ecologically humble cultures of tribal peoples whose spiritual life-ways have emerged from a respectful dialogue with unique environments that have sustained them for thousands of years.

Right now, the planet requires that privileged, dominant nations listen to what Indigenous peoples are saying, step outside the insulated ignorance within which they live, and pay attention to what our Mother is trying to tell us. As grandiose as that claim may sound, it would be dangerous to discount it as hyperbole. We live in an age of unparalleled destruction of peoples (unique cultures) and places (ecosystems and environments) on every continent of this planet.

Indigenous peoples—those who take their instructions for living from a Creator through the sacred powers of this creation, the environment, ecosystems, and climates—possess knowledges urgently needed today. But it has been and will continue to be difficult work to get people to explore, learn, and apply such knowledges willingly, when most of the Western world is radically divorced from life lived in creation. The first step, then, is to stop, unplug, and get reacquainted with the world we used to live in. Get outside the humanly engineered boxes of insulated ignorance, where increasing numbers of us live and work today, and discover—amid all the concrete and ugliness—that beauty surrounds us.[10] Discover that, behind

---

10. To celebrate the beauty of the world does not mean we close our eyes to the harshness that surrounds us. But as we seek to protect ourselves from those harsh realities, we must not seek, as most North Americans have, to remove and insulate ourselves as much as possible from "nature." As David Abram says,

the economics of commodity production and the management of resources, relatives still stand—powerful relatives who will teach and speak us into better ways (like the good news that justice is not some inalienable right, but a set of unalienable responsibilities humanity must exercise in relation to the rest of creation). I like how Kiowa-Cherokee author Scott Momaday puts it: "You say that I use the land, and I reply, yes, it is true; but it is not the first truth. The first truth is that I *love* the land; I see that it is beautiful; I delight in it; I am alive in it."[11] Let's get outside, get to know the land, look for beauty, and fall in love. And let us do it together.

We must continue the conversation, visit with each other more, and do it in deeper fashion—settler and Indigenous communities honestly speaking from the heart with, to, and for one another. Let's see if we can discuss the idea of progress and its impacts. Let's envision tangible steps that we can take to move away from systems of fear and destruction. In my work, I have to attend endless "homeland security" meetings on food, water, and health. I'm tired of it. I suspect all of our security concerns will be addressed if we enact spiritual ways of living that promote systems of life-enhancement, not just enhancement of our human lives, but life-enhancement in a world full of relatives. This won't be easy, for large-scale greed and ugliness surrounds us, threatening to overwhelm. Yet if we seek the beauty of the Earth and of one another, courageously matching gentle and open living to our high-sounding rhetoric, we can promote justice in this creation, discover radical gratitude, and embody the disciplines of homeland maturity.

"The shuddering beauty of this biosphere is bristling with thorns: generosity and abundance often seem scant ingredients compared with the prevalence of predation, sudden pain, and racking loss. . . . We simply can't get [nature] under control. . . . There are things out and about that can eat us, and ultimately will. Small wonder, then, that we prefer to abstract ourselves whenever we can, imagining ourselves into theoretical spaces less fraught with insecurity, conjuring dimensions more amenable to calculation and control. . . . Thus do we shelter ourselves from the harrowing vulnerability of bodied existence. But by the same gesture we also insulate ourselves from the deepest wellsprings of joy." As quoted in *Becoming Animal: An Earthly Cosmology* (New York: Vintage, 2010), 6–7.

11. Momaday, "A First American Views His Land," in *At Home on the Earth: Becoming Native to Our Place—A Multicultural Anthology*, ed. David Landis Barnhill (Los Angeles: University of California Press, 1999), 28.

Action Precedes Dialogue

When you think of Iraq, is the first thing you think of cedar forests so thick that the sunlight never touches the ground? That's what it was like prior to the beginnings of this culture. The first written myth of the dominant culture is of Gilgamesh murdering the forest's defender and then murdering the forests: deforesting the plains and hillsides of what is now Iraq.

The Arabian Peninsula was oak savannah.

The Near East was heavily forested.

Greece was heavily forested.

The forests of North Africa fell to make the Phoenician and Egyptian navies.

There were whales in the Mediterranean.

There were so many whales in the North Atlantic that they were a hazard to shipping, so many whales their breath looked like fog.

It was said that a squirrel could have leapt tree to tree from the Atlantic to the Mississippi without ever touching the ground.

The Great Plains were home to the greatest herds of ruminants the world has ever seen.

All gone.

Two hundred species were driven extinct today by the dominant culture. They were my brothers and sisters. And it is not only nonhumans: Indigenous languages are being exterminated at an even faster relative rate than are nonhuman species. The genocide is ongoing. In fact it is accelerating.

Stolid scientists are saying that within fifty years the oceans could be devoid of fish. Already oysters and other shellfish are experiencing "reproductive failure"—which is science-speak for the fact that their babies are dying, each and every one.

The destruction is accelerating.

The response by the dominant culture to the melting of the Arctic ice cap has not been one of horror. It has not been one of deep shame. It has not been an absolute determination to do what is right—to rectify the horrors that it has created and is creating. It has been lust. Lust for the "resources" that it can exploit. The response has been, is, and will continue to be monstrous and insane. The response has been, is, and will continue to be what it has been.

I completely agree that the world needs a radical dialogue between Indigenous peoples and settler society. Every cell in my body wants for there to be a constructive dialogue between Indigenous peoples and settler society, a dialogue that begins with profound apologies by the settler society (individually and collectively), and moves from there to an immediate return of stolen land, and to a voluntary dismantling of every bit of the dominant culture, from its physical infrastructure to its religion to its very epistemology.

But every cell in my body knows that isn't going to happen. Every cell in my body knows that dialogue only works when both sides share the same values. The wonderful Okanagan writer and activist Jeannette Armstrong once described to me the En'owkin process: the extraordinary conflict resolution method used by her people, where each side is encouraged to give their most opposite perspective to the other so that they can all gain understanding. But, and this is crucial, she said this process only works when all sides are interested in conflict resolution: it will not work when someone else wants your land.

Every cell in my body knows that the dominant culture will not stop on its own. It will not stop because it is the right thing to do.

It will not stop because it suddenly realizes it has been wrong. It will not stop because enough people explain that you cannot consume a planet and live on it too. You could not have stopped Ted Bundy by speaking to him nicely. You stop Ted Bundy by stopping him. Dialogue won't stop any sociopath or abuser from acting sociopathically or abusively. Sociopaths or abusers will use dialogue to further their sociopathic or abusive behavior.

The dominant culture will stop when it is stopped. Physically. When it no longer has the capacity to wage war on Indigenous humans and Indigenous nonhumans.

Here is the prayer that is my life, that is every moment of my waking and sleeping hours: that we, those of us who recognize the insatiability of the monster which is the dominant culture, deprive the rich of their ability to steal from the poor, and that we deprive the powerful of their ability to murder what (and who) is left of the planet.

When we have stopped them—as decisively and finally and ineradicably as they have murdered the passenger pigeons and the Eskimo curlews and the sea mink and the great auks and the Carolina parakeets and more and more each day—then will be the time we can all enter into productive dialog as to how we should live our lives.

—Derrick Jensen

Crying Indians, Stolen Lands

Creator God,
give us grace to live in balance within your creation,
thereby helping us to let loose the chokehold we have over the earth.
Show us the way back to your Eden,
grant us courage to make this journey together;
through Jesus Christ, who lives and reigns with you and the Holy Spirit,
one God, now and forever.
Amen.

Many jokes abound between Native tribes that are shot back and forth like cannon fire. For an outsider, they can sound downright mean, insulting, and politically incorrect. Where I'm from, they are shared with great amusement and love, and flow chiefly between two of the seven bands of the Lakota—the Sicanju and the Oglala—who live side by side on the Rosebud and Pine Ridge reservations.

On Friday, June 4, 1999, a once-in-a-lifetime F1-F2 tornado touched down and tore through the Oglala community, injuring many and killing one. Buildings were damaged and destroyed, leaving numerous people homeless. A few days later, the president and his entourage were flying from the east to check out the devastation. Looking out the window, the president gave voice to what he was seeing:

"Oh my! Look at all the debris and trash strewn all over the beautiful prairie. That must have been some tornado. And look at all those wrecked cars around the homes. We must do something!" he exclaimed.

One of his aides responded, "Uh, Mr. President . . . we're not over the Pine Ridge Reservation, yet. We are still flying over Rosebud."

This is one of those jokes that has some truth to it, and unfortunately it's used against the Lakota by the settler citizens of South Dakota.

When I was in my late twenties, an Episcopal priest said to me point-blank that he thought that it was wrong for people to claim that Natives are great environmentalists when our small rez communities are filled with trash and junkers. I was offended, and I recall wondering aloud, "What's the difference between burying your garbage in landfills and letting it sit out in the open air? If it's biodegradable, it will eventually be overtaken by the elements. Besides," I said, "the old cars are used for spare parts. If one looks closely at the wrecks, they're usually the same or similar model of car." I also reminded him that trash collection on the Reservation is a constant problem. Some months it runs smoothly. Other times, not at all. It's probably not the same in white towns and cities.

I didn't convince him.

Native Americans are stereotyped again and again. On the one hand, we're "dirty Indians"—a people who don't care, as we "ought to," about our homes and property. We just let it all go to rot. And that's why some white folks joke with each other, "Sorry, I'm going Indian on you," when their homes and lawns aren't as clean as they'd like. On the other hand, Native Americans are often stereotyped in the totally opposite direction, as outstanding environmentalists. It's an image that's been around since the beginning, but was given prominence during the seventies with the Keep America Beautiful campaign, and the now-infamous commercial of the "Crying Indian." Never mind the fact that this Crying Indian "chief," Iron Eyes Cody, wasn't even an Indian— that doesn't matter. The myth of the Indian as the preeminent environmentalist is incredibly powerful, still used today by many white interest groups (and some Native ones, too).

Dirty Indians. Eco-Indians. Two very different, conflicting stereotypes. What are we to make of it all?

—*Robert Two Bulls*
(Oglala Lakota Oyate)

Dangerous "Goods":
Seven Reasons Creation Care Movements Must Advocate Reparations

By Jennifer Harvey

It's difficult to acknowledge and wrestle with the fact that our most earnest attempt to do good, even when it seems to be clear and urgent, is always already distorted and damaged in fundamental ways. It's like a goldfish trying to see the bowl in which it swims. For those of us who are part of settler-colonial communities, there is nothing easy about questions that emerge out of atrocities so longstanding and deep that they seem to have no answers, questions that are so inherently shaped by legacies of harm that they may not even be the right ones. Such matters evoke unacknowledged layers of pain and guilt, so that we are tempted to avoid them altogether, reject them as too difficult, and simply move forward with our eyes and ears closed in order to proceed with the clear and urgent good we believe we must do.

But we must wrestle with these matters. It is in a spirit of honoring such pain that I argue here that settler-colonial Christian movements for environmental justice need to explicitly and unabashedly support Indigenous struggles for sovereignty and land rights *in a posture of reparations*. If we do not, we will advocate "goods" that are in reality dangerous, and which perpetuate the very structures of oppression.

Abstract goods are always dangerous

In the wake of widespread recognition of our global environmental crises, Christian communities have taken steps to articulate a theological vision of care for creation. As early as the 1990s, the World Council of Churches initiated a conciliar process called "Justice, Peace, and the Integrity of Creation," which attempted to speak to growing ecological concerns. EarthCare is another example; this Christian environmental organization has compiled an impressive list of statements and resolutions issued by nearly every mainline Protestant denomination, the United States Conference of Catholic Bishops, and even Evangelical communities.[1]

These initiatives share a commitment to undermining interpretations of God's dominion command (Genesis 1:28) as a license to dominate and exploit. "Stewardship" is reconceived as the special human responsibility to preserve and restore the earth. Many church statements also emphasize the need for Christians to recognize that humanity and nature are interdependent, indeed that we humans are formed of earth itself.

There are important critiques of the ways Christians have and continue to articulate this new vision for their relationship to earth.[2] Still, a vigorous focus on the well-being of the earth must be viewed as "good"—a positive and necessary move in the right direction. We need to recognize the devastation that human communities are wreaking on the globe and to seek radical changes in our behaviors, social structures, and ways of thinking that have enabled such behaviors. However, if advocacy for creation care is taken out of its larger historical context and pursued as an abstract "good" without explicitly linking it to Indigenous land rights and reparations, it becomes dangerous.

---

1. See EarthCare, 1 November 2008, http://www.earthcareonline.org/creation_ care_websites.pdf (accessed 8 January 2013).
2. Tink Tinker, for example, has argued that the WCC's initiative frames creation as an "add-on to concerns for justice and peace," rather than as a theological starting point. This framework remains rooted in Euro-American theological and philosophical thought patterns that essentially separate humanity from creation. Even insisting creation is "beloved of God," as the WCC document does, leaves such thought patterns intact, he argues, and will prove inadequate for transforming this crisis. *American Indian Liberation: A Theology of Sovereignty* (New York: Orbis, 2008), 37, 61.

Several years ago I was part of an email exchange between Tink Tinker (Osage activist and professor at Iliff School of Theology) and a white U.S. colleague. It concerned the 2008 formal apology by the prime minister of Australia, with the unanimous support of parliament, to Aboriginal peoples for the "indignity and degradation" they had endured. The apology lamented the egregious and systematic oppression Australian government policy had visited upon a "proud people and a proud culture." Like the United States and Canada, Australia's settler-colonial history is constituted by massive dispossession of Indigenous peoples' lands, as well as genocidal "assimilationist" policies, such as the forced removal of Indigenous children from their families into abusive boarding schools (particularly singled out in the apology).[3] My white colleague was pleased by this apology, as was I when I initially read this news in his email.

Tinker immediately pointed out, however, that Indigenous peoples should reject any apology that comes without transfers of land.[4] He argued that this apology was worse than meaningless, for while it posed as a moral recalibration, it did not alter the material realities of Aboriginal communities. Nor did it shift existing power relations between settler and Aboriginal peoples. Tinker critiqued the deeply flawed assumption that admitting responsibility without concretely redressing and repairing the actual damage was a "good" at all.

Over time, I came to agree with Tinker's reasoning. Moral activity that is decoupled from the explicit context that necessitates such activity is a dangerous "good." Thus, when it comes to Christian creation care movements, there must be an engagement with Indigenous sovereignty and land-rights struggles in a posture of reparation. In this essay, I'll offer up seven specific reasons as to why this is so.

---

3. See "Apology to Aborigines," BBC News, 12 February 2008, http://news.bbc .co.uk/2/hi/asia-pacific/7242057.stm (accessed 1 January 2013).

4. The reasons my colleague and I so unreflectively assumed this apology to be "good" surely had something to do our own settler-colonial identities, including our assumption that a settler-colonial nation can engage in repentant activity without fundamentally questioning the basis on which it exists in the first place—an important subject for another essay.

Seven reasons for creation care as reparations work

First, the specific lands on which we live when we advocate for care of the earth are not ours. It is that simple, and that complex. The United States and Canada were constituted and consolidated on lands of peoples who never ceded them. It is difficult for those of us who take the existence of our nation-states for granted to conceptualize the profound implications of this political, moral, and legal fact of history. The details differ depending on the region and the era, but from the earliest years of contact between Indigenous and European peoples, the imperial process of forming modern nation-states has been thoroughly documented by historians. European exploration (undertaken more often in pursuit of wealth than religious freedom, despite our mythologies) began with relatively amicable relations with Indigenous peoples, but as Europeans determined their need for greater tracts of land and more permanent settlements, they moved increasingly toward genocidal warfare (or the threat of such, through shows of military superiority).[5] Europeans regularly manufactured justifications for going to war to secure the takeover of lands, and overtly interpreted their successes as signs of God's intent for their possession.[6]

---

5. Taiaiake Alfred writes that most charters during European settlement stipulated separate political and territorial independence for Indigenous peoples. See "Sovereignty," in *A Companion to American Indian History*, eds. Philip J. Deloria and Neal Salisbury (Malden, MA: Blackwell, 2002), 460–74. But Francis Jennings provides a thorough and detailed account of the numerous manufactured and increasingly expansive wars pursued by Europeans as they became more rapacious. Europeans intentionally provoked Indigenous nations in the hopes that they would respond violently, thus justifying settler appeals to their home countries for military support. David Stannard gives a chilling account of European warfare that ideologically justified massacres, including the killing of women and children while they slept. See *American Holocaust: The Conquest of the New World* (New York: Oxford, 1993), 110. I offer a more extensive overview of the work of these and other scholars in my *Whiteness and Morality* (New York: Palgrave MacMillan, 2007): 51–94.

6. Numerous primary sources find European colonial Christians claiming that their "discovery" of Indigenous riches was itself a sign of God's intent for Europeans to possess the land. The Rev. Samuel Purchas, an early settler in Jamestown, went so far as to claim that it would be opposition to God *not* to take and develop the land; otherwise God would not have shown it to the English. See Gary B. Nash and Richard Weiss, eds., *The Great Fear: Race in the Mind of America* (New York: Holt, Rinehart and Winston, Inc., 1970), 3–4.

The numerous treaties made between Europeans (and later the U.S. and Canadian governments) and Native peoples were often signed only after Native numbers and political power had been decimated by a variety of colonial mechanisms. Most treaties were signed under coercive conditions and illegal practices, yet even these were subsequently violated over and over again by settlers. For example, after agreement had been reached that determined certain lands would be left "in perpetuity" for Native peoples, the discovery of desirable resources made treaty violation irresistible to settlers (the ongoing struggle of the Lakota Sioux over their rights to the Black Hills is a well-known case in point). Sometimes the "desirable resource" was simply the land itself, and the U.S. government typically looked the other way as settlers encroached on treaty territories, justified by the ideology of Manifest Destiny. If such treaty violations provoked Native resistance, the colonial military could "justifiably" intervene, and the cycle of imperial violence continued. This process enabled the formation and support of a nation-state that was constituted without the consent of the original possessors of the land.

This admittedly generalized summary of the European/Native encounter suffices to show the imperial nature of the establishment of the United States and Canada. There is no evidence that Native peoples consented at any point to permanent settler occupation of their land. Thus, when the U.S. Supreme Court, was asked to adjudicate a variety of land disputes between Natives and settlers in the 1820s (*Cherokee Nation versus Georgia* being the best known), it had no other recourse but to return to the Discovery Doctrine, which asserted that legal title to any land belongs to the government that "discovered" and "explored" it, if the original possessors were not subjects of a European Christian monarch. It further claimed that, at the "moment of discovery," Indigenous peoples had no property rights.

Most environmentally minded Christians today would undoubtedly repudiate such logic, and several church bodies have recently rejected the Doctrine of Discovery (including the World Council of Churches, the Episcopal Church, the Anglican Church of Canada, and the United Church of Canada). To advocate care for the environment and "stewardship" of the land, then, should

mean returning land to those to whom it belongs. Indeed, the slo-
gan "think/act locally" ought to focus our attention to the specific
context of our current, respective land issues. Conversely, if we try
to "honor creation" *without* responding explicitly to the history of
our contemporary land occupation, to which we have no coherent
legal, political, or moral claim, we do so as imperialists. Creation
care for settler Christians must mean robust support and advocacy
for Indigenous land-rights struggles.

Second, the belief systems that led settler peoples to wreak
havoc on the environment were and are the same ones that enabled
the displacement of Native peoples. While Puritan lawyer John
Winthrop was still on the boat from England, he drafted the legal
justification for dispossession, writing that Native peoples might
have a natural right to the land, but they did not have a *civic* right
to it, because they had not "subdued," "possessed," or "improved" it.[7]
With the same sleight of hand, Winthrop established the basis for
European colonial relations with Native peoples. To treat the land
as commodity required viewing the people of that land similarly;
ecocide and genocide go hand in hand.[8]

White Americans and Canadians in creation care movements
must recognize the death-dealing power of these concepts. When
the breast milk of nursing women among the Mohawk Nation is
found to contain 200 percent more PCBs because they have eaten
fish from the industrially polluted St. Lawrence River, we see the
relationship between ecocide and genocide.[9] When up to seventy-
five thousand cases of thyroid cancer due to radiation exposure
are documented among the Western Shoshone between 1951 and
1992, because Shoshone land has been the site of massive nuclear
weapons testing by the United States and Great Britain, we see the
relationship between ecocide and genocide.[10]

The atrocities visited upon Native lands and peoples by our
ancestors, and the devastations wrought in our time, are a seam-
less tapestry. Settler Christians, therefore, cannot fundamentally

---

7. Stannard, *American Holocaust*, 235.
8. Tinker, *American Indian Liberation*, 57.
9. Winona Laduke, *All Our Relations: Native Struggles for Land and Life*
(Cambridge: South End Press, 1999), 18–19.
10. Ibid., 98–99.

reexamine our approach to creation without also reexamining our relations to Native peoples.

A third critical reason why creation care and Indigenous reparations must go together pertains to the pervasively symbolic world we inhabit, which endlessly distorts Native peoples through white-created images and ahistorical depictions, providing support for the ongoing subjugation of Native communities. Philip J. Deloria analyzes white legacies of romanticizing and/or disparaging Native peoples within the United States; Daniel Francis does the same for Canada.[11] "Playing Indian" by dressing up "like" them is one aspect of this phenomenon, from the Boston Tea Party to the Improved Order of Red Men (which claims to be the oldest "patriotic" fraternal organization) to summer camps today. This practice can freight either romantic meanings (settlers placing ourselves in a Native lineage, embracing their wisdom, honoring their memory) or disparaging meanings (Indians caricatured as savages). White North Americans "play Indian" whenever we indulge in westerns, celebrate pioneer life, or do the "tomahawk chop" at sporting events. The symbolic functions of such rituals are either to massacre or to assimilate the savage as part of the civilizing march of settler progress. As different as the caricatures of "savage" and "sage" may seem, they do similar work: justifying settler occupation. Native peoples are seemingly always of a bygone era, either destroyed or in the process of becoming "extinct." They are never real, contemporary communities.

Settlers portrayed themselves as civilizers with a divine mandate to tame not only the unpossessed, unsubdued landscape, but also the savages who were "naturally" part of it. And while most justice-minded Christians might abhor such a symbolic world, as Deloria documents, its pervasiveness is too powerful and deadly to ignore. It is innate to how our settler identities were created, and it haunts how we relate to the land, even regarding environmental issues. It must be overtly repudiated.

More problematic is the image of the Indian "sage," which emerges often in environmental circles. It is also more complex,

---

11. See Philip J. Deloria, *Playing Indian* (New Haven and London: Yale University Press, 1998); Daniel Francis, *The Imaginary Indian: The Image of the Indian in Canadian Culture*, 2nd ed. (Vancouver: Arsenal Pulp Press, 2012).

because it is true that Native peoples lived sustainably on this continent for thousands of years. As Jace Weaver puts it, given the population of this land-base before the encounter between Indigenous and European peoples, "Native peoples could have wrought much more environmental damage than was the case"; instead, they "learned to practice reciprocity and natural conversation techniques in order to ensure ample resources for themselves and their progeny."[12] There are good reasons, therefore, that environmental movements are tempted to lift up Native communities as examples to be learned from, embodying ways of being we need to emulate.

But Weaver also carefully explores the reality that Native peoples were and are "neither saints nor sinners" when it comes to the environment. He analyzes the dangers generated by white projections of the Native person as environmental sage. Arguing that whites have always seen Native peoples "in some distorted funhouse mirror . . . seeing whatever they most desire," he insists that such romanticizing erases Native people in such a manner that they and their land continue to be exploited.[13] Weaver also points out that if settlers seek to "learn from" Native peoples as a means to improve "our" relationship to the land, we are using them for our own ends. Our romanticizing does not disrupt our imperialist assumptions, but instead reinforces our ignorance about how Indigenous land rights have been illegally eviscerated through violence and genocide.

As Kidwell, Noley, and Tinker put it: "To continue to resist just Native land claims and refuse reparations as compensation for lands illegally taken is to engage in an unhealthy and dangerous

---

12. Jace Weaver, ed., *Defending Mother Earth* (New York: Orbis, 1997), 7. Weaver's introduction is particularly useful in exploring the complex relationship of Indigenous peoples to the land and the environment. Kidwell, Noley, and Tinker's *A Native American Theology* (New York: Orbis, 2001) is another excellent resource, particularly its theological construction of Native American relations to the land as a critical category. Winona LaDuke's *All Our Relations: Native Struggles for Land and Life* (Cambridge, MA: South End Press, 1999) documents the way Native activists in various communities are resisting, not only against environmentally destructive practices that have harmed their communities, but also against colonial erosion of their original life-ways .

13. Ibid., 4. For further explication, see Philip J. Deloria and Neal Salisbury, eds., *A Companion to American Indian History* (Oxford: Blackwell Publishers, 2002).

psychological denial about the conquest of this continent and the nature of our cohabitation on it."[14] The savage/sage symbolic world is a primary mechanism enabling such denial. To actually *see* Native peoples, therefore, we must radically re-historicize the conquest and the genuine conditions of our "cohabitation," and then engage with real Native land struggles.

A fourth rationale has to do with antiracism. Communities committed to creation care are usually adamant about their commitments to interracial reconciliation, diversity, and inclusion. But hope for such reconciliation can only be nurtured through antiracist responses to the material conditions and historical legacies that have sundered our ability to be in relationship with one another—which is to say, through reparations.[15] Authentic pursuit of interracial reconciliation has to be deeply material, focused on specific forms of repair, if we hope to mend relations between Native and settler communities in the context of environmental justice movements.

A fifth reason is that for Native communities cultural and religious integrity are inseparable from sovereignty and land rights.[16] The theological vision of creation care movements often includes the claim that everything is interrelated. While such a concept is easy to proclaim in the abstract, what are its actual implications? Vine Deloria Jr. writes, "The idea that everything is related has definite space/time relevance."[17] He explains that medicine men "spoke of the places that various entities were destined to occupy," as well as "of the beginning of a world age as a time when everything was in its proper place."[18] For interrelationality to be more than an abstract platitude, it must give way to the concrete issues associated with *actual places*. In turning toward the particular, we cannot but hear the way specific locations cry out with unredressed legacies of displacement and genocide. In turn, lament about the contemporary creation crisis and our broken relations with the land should compel us to inquire about the "time when everything was in its proper place."

---

14. Kidwell et al., *A Native American Theology*, 170.
15. See my *Whiteness and Morality* (New York: Palgrave MacMillan, 2007).
16. Kidwell, 4.
17. Vine Deloria Jr., *Spirit and Reason: The Vine Deloria, Jr., Reader*, eds. Barbara Deloria, Kristen Foehner, and Sam Scinta (Golden, CO: Fulcrum, 1999), 54.
18. Ibid., 54–55.

Reason number six pertains to another deeply embedded misperception that has devastating consequences for the earth and for Indigenous peoples. At the heart of our current political economy—and of settler relations to land—lies a deep-seated assumption about the legitimacy of "private property," the use of such property for personal economic gain, and the inviolability of property rights. One of the most persistent reasons given by my white students for opposing reparations is that this would necessarily encroach on "their" property rights. Notably, the students who voice such concerns often otherwise acknowledge that justice dictates that Native and African American peoples are owed substantial material compensation for historical injustices and their continuing effects. Simply put, settler commitments to private property trump basic morality and justice.

Several interrelated issues must be highlighted here. For one, assumptions about the legitimacy of private property relate directly to the crisis of environmental degradation. The notion that parcels of earth belong to individuals undermines our ability to recognize or truly value commonality and the collective good. The idea of private property enables the belief that the one who "owns" it has the right to do with it whatever he/she wishes, even if this includes harmful activity that negatively impacts others whose lives (including non-human lives), health, and well-being are also sustained by the earth.

Another issue is the existence of an economic ideology, particularly in the United States, which understands profit and cost in harrowingly narrow terms. Carol Johnston shows how, in the development of unbridled free-market capitalist ideology, Adam Smith's basic economic question was simply how to make land more productive.[19] This question assumed that issues like long-term sustainability or the human cost of certain production techniques were irrelevant to economic questions. Smith thus opened the way for the growth

---

19. Johnston provides a comprehensive and accessible analysis of the historical development of economic theory for the non-economist, making intelligible the ways in which thinkers like Adam Smith and John Stuart Mill bequeathed to capitalism its ideological commitments to individualism, property, and profit, which have been so devastating to human communities and to the earth itself. She makes clear that such developments were *not* inevitable, and that economics can be understood differently. See *The Wealth or Health of Nations* (Cleveland: Pilgrim Press, 1998), 13ff.

of an economic system that would tolerate any number of devastating long-term outcomes (to people and to the earth) in exchange for short-term, individual gain. The individual pursuit of profit and the right to private property were, and are, fundamental building blocks for this economic ideology. So, when politicians argue today that we must continue to engage in oil drilling for the sake of economic growth—even though it is clear that the use of fossil fuels is not sustainable in the long term, not to mention threatening to Native sovereignty—we are witnessing the deadly logic of this economic ideology.

Yet another issue, here, is the fact that the pursuit of private property and individual wealth generation has determined the project of the European colonization of North America. Dispossession and genocide went hand in hand in making tracts of land available for enclosure and production in pursuit of private profit. And this also illustrates a fundamental cultural difference between Native and settler peoples, a difference so significant it was used by the latter to try to obliterate the former through forced assimilation. Under the 1887 Dawes Severalty Act, the U.S. government forcibly individualized all Native landholdings. First Nations who held land collectively prior to the Act were required to carve their landholdings into parcels, whereby individuals were allotted their own tracts of land. Not only was "leftover" land then made available for whites to purchase, but individual Native "owners" were then encouraged to sell or lease their parcels on the market. In this way, Indigenous landholdings were made available as commodities on the free market. The cumulative impact of the Act was to reduce Native landholdings from 138 million acres to only 48 million (nearly two-thirds lost) by the time it was rescinded in 1934.

While allotment was thoroughly consistent with settler understandings of economy, as discussed above, its forced creation of private property among Native peoples both furthered their dispossession and represented a cultural attack. Donald Fixico writes that it was an intentional move by Congress to destroy the communal orientation of Native societies.[20] The individualization of Native

20. Donald L. Fixico, *The Invasion of Indian Country in the Twentieth Century: American Capitalism and Tribal Natural Resources* (Niwot, CO: University Press of Colorado, 1998), 4.

landholdings was devastating: "Forced to become part of the larger colonized cultures of the mainstream, Indians were victimized in numerous ways, as with land to sell and lease, they were forced into a capitalist economic system."[21] This program was different in strategy but similar in outcome to the forced removal of Native children from their homes to boarding schools in order to make them "white." That the U.S. government would use allotment as a weapon of forced assimilation reveals the extent to which a commitment to private property is intrinsic to settler identity.

To summarize, the economic ideology and practices of private property:

- Enables the destruction of the earth;

- Has historically been used as a tool of Indigenous dispossession; and

- Was a weapon of forced assimilation that exploited fundamental differences between Native American and settler identities.

These complex matters should urge creation care movements to call into question the most basic frameworks through which we see the land and our economy, and to embrace practices of reparation.

Finally, reason number seven: issues of environmental racism, about which creation care movements are often concerned. Political exclusion and marginalization mark the experience of all communities of color in the United States and Canada. For Native peoples, however, this manifests specifically as a colonial violation and erasure of sovereignty. As Andrea Smith points out, because most energy resources are located on Indigenous lands, sovereignty violations are intrinsic to official policies of domestic energy independence, as governments exert control and decision-making power over such resources.[22] Similarly, when nuclear test sites and toxic waste dumps proliferate on Native lands, we witness not only

---

21. Donald L. Fixico, "Federal and State Policies and American Indians," in *A Companion to American Indian History*, eds. Philip J. Deloria and Neal Salisbury (Malden and Oxford: Blackwell Publishers, 2002), 384.

22. Andrea Smith, "Reparations and the Question of Land," in *Union Seminary Quarterly Review* 56:1–2 (2002), 171.

environmental racism at its worst, but an evisceration of Native sovereignty. For creation care movements to take environmental racism seriously, they must support Indigenous sovereignty.

Conclusion

I do not pretend to offer any easy answers, here, about how settler Christian environmental movements should proceed. I am aware that my argument might generate moral paralysis and despair. This is not easy work. From our current vantage point, we cannot merely think our way out of imperialism. I have tried, however, to offer a compelling case for rethinking how to do the "good" that we certainly must pursue.

And as difficult as these matters are, there are concrete examples of "trying to do good" that may animate our moral courage and vision, such as recent efforts by Mennonite and Lutheran settlers with the Young Chippewayan Cree in central Saskatchewan.[23]

In 1876, at the signing of Treaty Six, the Young Chippewayan were removed from their traditional land-base and "granted" a section of land (thirty square miles) for a reserve. Then, following the 1885 Northwest Rebellion/Resistance led by Métis leader Louis Riel, the Canadian government ratcheted up its oppression of Indigenous peoples. To make matters worse, the buffalo—the Native community's life-blood—was being exterminated by a gluttonous settler society. Facing starvation, the Young Chippewayan left their reserve and began a long search for sustenance. As they were out looking for food, the government annexed their lands without the band's consent or surrender, and gave it to Mennonite and Lutheran settlers.

In the last few years, descendents of those settlers have gathered with the Young Chippewayan at Stoney Knoll, a sacred gathering and burial place that was part of the original reserve, to acknowledge the injustice and to mutually affirm the "active and equal relationship" required by Treaty 6. Moreover, some Christian settlers have raised money to support Young Chippewayan genealogical efforts to prove they are the rightful descendents, as required by the Indian Claims Commission. It remains to be seen how the

---

23. I appreciate the insistence by the editor of this volume that my essay include concrete examples of hope.

Signing of the Stoney Knoll Memorandum of Understanding (MOU), ca. 2006.
The three persons signing the Memorandum of Understanding are Abram Funk
(Mennonite representative), Chief Ben Weenie (Young Chippewayan representative),
and Robert Schultz (Lutheran representative). The MOU has three parts: giving
thanks to the Creator; indicating respect for covenants, including treaties; and a
commitment to peace, justice, and sufficiency for all communities.

government will respond once this genealogical work is completed, and whether the resolution of such claims will meet the moral bar indicated by Tinker: land transfer. It also remains to be seen how the Mennonite and Lutheran communities in this area will respond if the government does not meet that bar. Will they seek concrete repair, or redistribute the privilege they have inherited? Yet it is significant that these three peoples have gathered on multiple occasions, and have named and acknowledged in one another's presence the real challenges this historic treaty violation poses today.[24] Here are significant minorities within settler communities looking directly at their history and its implications, rather than avoiding, denying, or ignoring it.

Another hopeful example comes from Eureka, California. In 2001, white Evangelical Christians in that community decided to ally with the Wiyot, the Indigenous people who had been struggling since the 1970s to secure the return of forty acres of their land.

---

24. Justin Krushel, "Pursuing Just Relationships in Saskatchewan," *Intotemak*, Winter 2011, http://resources.mennonitechurch.ca/FileDownload/15353/Intotemak_Winter_2011.pdf (accessed 1 January 2013).

After taking part in a reconciliation event, area churches gathered $1,000 in donations to enable the Wiyot to purchase 1.5 acres of their land. "The Wiyot claimed that this reconciliation meeting had paved the way for the City Council to return the land in 2004"—and indeed the Council returned the forty acres in May of that year.[25]

Even though this was just a small amount of land, it is striking how morally energizing such an action can be. It offers a glimpse of the "fishbowl" in which we swim, and such small acts can disrupt business-as-usual and call into question our most entrenched assumptions of what is and what might be. The Stoney Knoll work in Saskatchewan and the reparation in Eureka are miniscule in the context of the vast history of Native dispossession. Nonetheless, such acts demonstrate that concrete responses to the past, as it manifests in our present, *are possible.* They have the power to invite greater, more transformative moral courage by challenging dominant presumptions and frameworks.

The arguments made above, and the examples provided here, represent horizons toward which those of us who are part of settler justice movements must attempt to journey, as we learn to rethink our relationship to the land. The form this journey takes will necessarily vary, as diverse bodies in particular locales seek ways to support Native sovereignty struggles and land-rights movements already underway all over North America. Doing so is imperative if creation care movements hope to realize the "good." Our visions must be accountable to and engaged in conversation with those who were and are the first affected by the damages our settler ways of being have caused.

Though brokenness and harm have constituted the legacy of Native-settler relations, this does not need to be. We can change the relationship. The voices of Indigenous communities demanding that we do things in a different way have never ceased from the moment of first contact. It is thus both incumbent upon us— and *possible*—for those of us in settler communities to make an unequivocal decision to open our ears and eyes to hear and see ourselves, Native peoples, and the earth itself differently.

---

25. Andrea Smith, *Native Americans and the Christian Right: The Gendered Politics of Unlikely Alliances* (Durham: Duke University Press, 2008), 74.

Crying Indians, Stolen Lands (continued)

In the early 1870s, General Custer and friends discovered gold in the Black Hills, the traditional Lakota territory, "and before you could say 'Fort Laramie Treaty'"[1] this valuable land had been illegally seized by the federal government to open the way for fortune seekers and homesteaders. More than a hundred years later, in 1980, the Black Hills Land Claim was settled by a Supreme Court decision that awarded the Lakota Tribes $105 million for the unjust expropriation of that land. Yet the Tribes refused the money, for these hills are not resources; they are sacred, figuring prominently in many of our traditional ceremonies.

Through the ensuing years, the Lakota have fought a long, complex battle to get the land in question back. Meanwhile, the settlement money sits in a U.S. Treasury account collecting interest, and is today estimated at around $1 billion. It's a huge amount of money. And yet the Lakota have not claimed it. This refusal of the poorest of the poor to accept an enormous 'mammon' buyout runs contrary to the rules of capitalist society. It just shouldn't play out this way.

A number of court cases and bills related to this land issue have been put forth through Congress, chief among them the Bradley Bill. The gist of the Bradley Bill was to return to the Lakota some land (1.3 million acres) to right the wrongs of the past, but only the remaining federal and park lands. The bill was never passed.

Currently a battle is being fought that has to do with a certain section of the land called *Pe Sla*, or "baldy," which plays a significant role in both Lakota cosmology and our creation stories. The owners of this property had put *Pe Sla* up on the auction block in August 2012. Their great ancestor had been the original homesteader, holding title since 1876, and subsequent generations used this "open prairie" in the forest to run their cattle. The family permitted the Lakota to practice their ceremonies in this place, but now the land was to be parceled out and sold to the highest bidder.

---

1. Thomas King, *The Inconvenient Indian: A Curious Account of Native People in North America* (Toronto: Doubleday, 2012), 220.

Thankfully, the Sicanju were eventually able to negotiate with the landowners to stall the bidding, and a deal is being brokered with the Lakota.

There is a lot of emotion around this Black Hills Claim. Hearing and reading the opinions of non-Natives from the area, I sense much fear and anger. And that fear and anger is usually reinforced with one of those classic colonial stereotypes that I mentioned earlier: that if the Lakota should get the land back, they will only trash it with ramshackle homes, yards brimming with litter and crappy old cars. I can't help but laugh to myself. Compare this image with what's there now—kitschy tourist traps, billboards, mountaintops carved by men, and overdevelopment. Can it really get any worse?

A relative told me that when he was at a meeting discussing the Bradley Bill, there were a few landowners shedding tears—"crying settlers," if you will. They evidently thought that if the Black Hills were to be returned to the Lakota it would mean they would lose title to the land—which wasn't the case. I am almost positive that if, by some miracle, the Black Hills were returned to us, we would not set up house there. It would be used strictly for ceremonial purposes.

When I was a kid, my parents would load me and my siblings into the car and take long drives through this sacred land. As soon as I was able to drive, my brother and I would go up in "The Hills" and take long hikes to the sacred spaces. Even then, my young mind and heart understood and felt the spiritual significance of these places, and this without knowing the full stories of our ancestors. As a middle-aged adult, I make my visits only to find more and more development and commercialization. It's overwhelming. Maybe I'm the "crying Indian" now.

When I think back on all the historical events that have occurred between Native Americans and Euro-Americans, I come to at least one conclusion: our relations were and still are anti-gospel. Though some things have changed over the years, we really need to work at this—to restore what is broken, to make right what is wrong, and to learn to be good neighbors or "cousins" with one another. There's been too many tears and too much pain.

God our creator who is loving and always with us,
we pray for strength and humility to walk in balance within your
*   created order,*
we pray for understanding of one another
so that the wounds of this broken world may be made whole.
We pray that promises made and broken can be honored
*   and mended.*
We pray these words so that we may have healing within our
communities; and from that gift of healing, the spirit to serve you
*   in harmony and peace.*
And in the end, may we taste the sweetness of heaven come down
*   to earth,*
So that we may all find everlasting rest in your embrace.
We ask these things in your name.
Amen.

—Robert Two Bulls
(Oglala Lakota Oyate)

CONTRIBUTORS

Cheryl Bear-Barnetson is from the Nadleh Whut'en First Nation, Yinka Dene, Bear Clan. She is married to Randy, and together they have three wonderful kids: Paul, Randall, and Justice. Cheryl is a multi-award-winning singer, songwriter, and storyteller. She's also a pastor and serves on the board of the North American Indigenous Institute for Theological Studies.

Rose Marie Berger is a Catholic peace activist and poet who serves as an associate editor and poetry editor of *Sojourners* magazine. Her poems have appeared in the *Journal of South African Feminism, Beltway, The Other Side, Radix, Conspire, Radical Grace,* and the *D.C. Poets Against the War* anthology. In 2007 she coedited, with Joseph Ross, *Cut Loose the Body: An Anthology of Poems on Torture and Fernando Botero's Abu Ghraib Paintings.* In 2010 she published *Who Killed Donte Manning? The Story of an American Neighborhoood,* a spiritual biography of her inner-city Washington, D.C., neighborhood, where she still lives.

Steve Berry is a storyteller, documentarian, author, and lecturer. He earned his master's degree from Yale University, where he was a teaching assistant to author Fr. Henri Nouwen. Steve served in city ministry for a decade as senior minister of the historic First Congregational Church of Los Angeles. A recipient of the Ralph Bunche Peace Award, he finds joy in learning from and working with diverse, marginalized communities. A passionate preacher,

Steve has guest preached at Riverside Church, Duke Chapel, and the Crystal Cathedral. Lately he's been working on a book with theologian Walter Wink (recently deceased), and a series of video interviews he conducted with Rene Girard. Steve lives in Vermont with his wife, author and artist Carol A. Berry.

Di Brandt is the author of more than a dozen books of poetry, fiction, essays, and literary criticism. She has received numerous awards for her writing, including the Gerald Lampert Award for "best first book of poetry in Canada" for *questions i asked my mother*; and the Gabrielle Roy Prize for "best book of literary criticism in Canada" for *Wider Boundaries of Daring: The Modernist Impulse in Canadian Women's Poetry* (edited with Barbara Godard). Di was born in Winkler, Manitoba, and now lives and works in Brandon, Manitoba, holding the Canada Research Chair at Brandon University.

Will Braun was raised on a Mennonite farm next to the Dead Horse Creek—once known as Pinancewaywining—in Treaty 1 territory southwest of Winnipeg. He has worked on issues related to hydropower and Indigenous rights in Manitoba for the Mennonite Central Committee, Pimicikamak Cree Nation, and, currently, the Interchurch Council on Hydropower. Braun, who currently lives near Morden, Manitoba, is also a writer, part-time stay-at-home dad, and vegetable gardener.

Peter Cole is a member of the Douglas First Nation, one of the *Stl'atl'imx* communities in southwest British Columbia. He has taught at universities in Canada, the United States, and *Aotearoa*-New Zealand. Peter has published in many literary and academic journals and books, and is the author of *Coyote and Raven go Canoeing: Coming Home to the Village*, a book based on research with an international array of Indigenous peoples in the area of culturally relevant education. Written using poetic, dramatic, and storytelling voices, this work helped break new ground by making orality the foundation of its scholarship. Peter is also coeditor of *Speaking for Ourselves: Environmental Justice in Canada*. When he is not wearing an academic hat, Peter can be found canoeing or hiking.

Dave Diewert was born into a working-class family in East Vancouver, and spent much of his life on an academic path. He has taught at Regent College for twenty-two years, the first half as a full-time professor and the last eleven as a sessional lecturer. Unsatisfied with an academic career narrowly defined, impacted by human suffering due to systemic injustice, and inspired by communal struggles for freedom from oppression, he left full-time teaching and engaged in local struggles against poverty, homelessness, and other forms of structural violence. In 2007 he helped organize Streams of Justice, a faith-based social justice group in Vancouver, and currently works in solidarity with low-income resident-based groups in Vancouver's Downtown Eastside.

Laura E. Donaldson (Cherokee) is professor of English and American Indian studies at Cornell University. She has published widely on Indigenous approaches to the Bible, eighteenth- and nineteenth-century appropriations of Christianity by American Indians, feminism, and postcolonialism. When Laura isn't writing or teaching, she is gardening and spinning wool. She grows heritage vegetables year round and has a flock of Navajo Churro sheep.

Jonathan Erickson is a member of the Nak'azdli Band (Carrier-Sekani) located in Fort St. James, British Columbia. Since 1998 he has studied and practiced the First Nations art of the Northwest Coast, a journey that began with drawing, then acrylic paintings and silk screens. In 2012 Jonathan attended the Jewellery Arts Program at the Native Education College in Vancouver, B.C., where he acquired the skills needed to produce quality silverwork. Jonathan lives in Pitt Meadows, B.C., and continues to enjoy learning the histories and traditions of his people.

Neil Funk-Unrau is associate professor of conflict resolution studies at Menno Simons College in Winnipeg, Manitoba, focusing on issues of restorative justice and relations between Canada's Indigenous and settler peoples. Before beginning his full-time academic career, Neil worked for fifteen years with Native Concerns of Mennonite Central Committee Canada and Native Ministries, in what was then the Conference of Mennonites in Canada. Neil and his wife, Genny, have two daughters and are members of Charleswood Mennonite Church in Winnipeg.

Anthony J. Hall is professor of globalization studies at the University of Lethbridge in Alberta, Canada. He is author of *The American Empire and the Fourth World* and *Earth into Property: Colonization, Decolonization and Capitalism*. He has written for a range of periodicals, including the *Globe and Mail*, *Canadian Forum*, *The Phoenix*, and *Kainai News*. He is a former copresident of the Canadian Alliance in Solidarity with the Native Peoples. Professor Hall has been an expert witness in several Aboriginal rights cases in Canada and the United States, most recently in the case dubbed "The Queen and Kwitsel Tatel versus the Government of Canada."

Lawrence Hart is a member of the Cheyenne nation and a traditional peace chief. A graduate of Bethel College and Mennonite Biblical Seminary, Lawrence has combined pastoral work with an active commitment to justice and community resurgence. He was instrumental in the repatriation of many Indigenous remains, serving on the Review Committee of the Native American Graves and Repatriation Act, and is the former executive director of the Cheyenne Cultural Center in Clinton, Oklahoma. Lawrence is married to Betty, and together they have three children and five grandchildren.

Iris de León-Hartshorn (Mestizo) was born in Laredo, Texas, and raised in southern California in a very diverse environment. She is married to Leo Hartshorn, and together they have three adult children. Iris and Leo live in Portland, Oregon, with their grandson, whom they are raising. Presently, Iris works for Mennonite Church USA as director of transformative peacemaking, with a focus on immigration, antiracism, and intercultural competency. One of her favorite things to do is travel, and her two most memorable trips were to the World Christian Indigenous Gatherings in Australia (1999) and Syria (2007)—both were profound spiritual experiences.

Jennifer Harvey is associate professor of religion at Drake University in Des Moines, Iowa. She received her PhD in Christian social ethics from Union Theological Seminary in the city of New York, and is the author of *Whiteness and Morality: Pursuing Racial Justice through Reparations and Sovereignty* and coeditor of *Disrupting White Supremacy: White People on What We Need To Do*. Jennifer is also an ordained minister in the American Baptist Churches.

Steve Heinrichs [see page 360].

Tomson Highway was born in a snow bank on the Manitoba/ Nunavut border to a family of nomadic caribou hunters. Today he enjoys an international career as playwright, novelist, and pianist/ songwriter. His best-known works are the plays *The Rez Sisters* and *Dry Lips Oughta Move to Kapuskasing*, and the novel *Kiss of the Fur Queen*. Tomson divides his year equally between a cottage in northern Ontario (near Sudbury, from whence comes his partner of twenty-five years) and a seaside apartment in the south of France. He is currently at work on his second novel.

Gord Hill is a member of the Kwakwaka'wakw nation on the Pacific Northwest Coast. The author of two comics—*The 500 Years of Indigenous Resistance Comic Book* and *The Anti-Capitalist Resistance Comic Book*—Gord is also an activist, engaging in Indigenous anti-colonial and anti-capitalist resistance movements since 1990. He currently resides in East Vancouver.

Adrian Jacobs, Cayuga First Nation (Six Nations), is a single father of five and a grandfather of one. An artist, writer, Indigenous advocate, and teacher, Adrian's passions have focused on Aboriginal worldviews, cultures, and health, seeking to be a positive influence through a culturally affirming approach. Having pastored an Indigenous church for many years, he is currently keeper of the circle/principal of Sandy-Saulteaux Spiritual Centre, an Aboriginal ministry training school for the United Church of Canada, located in Beausejour, Manitoba.

Derrick Jensen is a long-time environmental activist who lives in Crescent City, California. He is the author of more than twenty books, including *Endgame, The Culture of Make Believe,* and *A Language Older Than Words.* Derrick has taught creative writing courses at Eastern Washington University and Pelican State Prison. The majority of his energies are spent trying to animate resistance against the violence of industrial civilization, a culture which is destroying the planet at an alarming pace.

Frances W. Kaye is professor of English and Native American studies at the University of Nebraska-Lincoln. She has also taught as a Fulbright scholar at the Universities of Calgary and Montreal. She lives summers in Calgary and the rest of the time in an old farmhouse near Lincoln. For the past twenty years she has been volunteering in the Nebraska state prison system, mostly with Native inmates. Several of these men are among the greatest teachers she has ever met. She also volunteers on behalf of Native children in or near child welfare systems.

Anita L. Keith, Tsi Niká:ien Tekanonniákhwa Nateriíohsera (The One That Dances The War Dance) is of Mohawk/British descent, a mother of three children and grandmother of four. An instructor in Aboriginal education at Red River College, Anita also serves as a minister in the Salmon House Diocese, Communion of Evangelical Episcopal Churches. She has served in a variety of First Nations ministries, including the North American Indigenous Institute for Theological Studies. Anita was a former powwow dancer who travelled internationally. Today, she is an avid reader and writer.

Terry Leblanc is a Mi'kmaq/Acadian, married to his partner Bev for over forty years. Together, they have twin daughters, Jennifer and Jeanine, and one son, Matt. The founding Chair and Director of the North American Institute for Indigenous Theological Studies (NAIITS), Terry also oversees iEmergence and My People International, organizations focused on building capacity with Indigenous people. In addition to thirty-five years of grassroots work in the Native North American and global Indigenous contexts, Terry has taught at various seminaries and universities, and authored numerous journal articles. In June 2010, for his work on the creation of NAIITS, Terry became the twenty-eighth recipient of the Dr. E. H. Johnson Memorial Award for Innovation in Mission.

Lee Maracle is Sto:lo First Nation, a grandmother of four, and mother of four. Born in North Vancouver, B.C., she now resides in Innisfil, Ontario. Her works include the novels *Ravensong* and *Bobbi Lee*, the poetry collection *Bentbox*, and the non-fiction work *I Am Woman*. She is also editor of a number of poetry works and has contributed to dozens of anthologies in Canada and the United States. Ms. Maracle teaches at the University of Toronto and is currently both the mentor for Aboriginal students and the traditional cultural director for the Indigenous Theatre School.

Stan McKay was born at Fisher River First Nation Reserve, a Cree community in northern Manitoba. As a youth, Stan attended the Fisher River Indian Day School and the Birtle Indian Residential School. In 1971 he graduated from the University of Winnipeg, was ordained by the United Church of Canada, and became a pastor. A former moderator of the United Church and director of the Dr. Jessie Saulteaux Centre, Stan presently focuses his energies on building cross-cultural relations, participating in dialogues that address injustices resulting from colonial history. Stan and his wife Dorothy live in Gladstone, Manitoba, and have three children and three grandchildren.

Brian McLaren lives in southwestern Florida, not far from the site of an ancient Calusa village. He was a college English teacher and a church planter and pastor, and now writes, speaks, and tries to plot goodness and kindness where he can. His books include *A New Kind of Christian*; *A Generous Orthodoxy*; and *Why Did Jesus, Moses, the Buddha, and Mohammed Cross the Road?* He blogs at brianmclaren.net, and in his free time can often be found kayaking among dolphins, sea turtles, and manatees.

Kathy Moorhead Thiessen is delighted whenever she is able to dig through finished compost. She doesn't mind the many-legged insects that squirm through the dark, rich, new earth, and loves the thought of the worms and microbes that will take up habitation in the vegetable garden. When she is not digging in the garden in Winnipeg (where she lives with Vic Thiessen), she works half the year with Christian Peacemaker Teams in Iraqi Kurdistan (northern Iraq). There she joins teammates from various countries, as well as Kurdish partners, to strive to "embrace the diversity of the human family and live justly and peaceably with all creation." The wooden compost box in Sulaimani is now home to eight months' worth of vegetative matter, as well as two lizards and a mouse.

Ched Myers is an activist theologian who has worked in social change movements for thirty-five years. With a degree in New Testament studies, he is a popular educator who animates Scripture and issues of faith-based peace and justice. Ched points to his solidarity work with Indigenous peoples in and around the Pacific Basin in the 1980s as key to his political and spiritual growth. He has authored more than a hundred articles and many books, including *Binding the Strong Man: A Political Reading of Mark's Story of Jesus* and, most recently, *Our God Is Undocumented: Biblical Faith and Immigrant Justice*. He and his partner, Elaine Enns, a restorative justice practitioner, live in the Ventura River watershed in southern California, and work with Bartimaeus Cooperative Ministries (www.bcm-net.org).

James W. Perkinson is a "recovering" white man and long-time activist and educator in inner-city Detroit, currently teaching as professor of social ethics at the Ecumenical Theological Seminary and lecturing in intercultural communication studies at the University of Oakland (Michigan). He is the author of *White Theology: Outing Supremacy in Modernity* and *Shamanism, Racism, and Hip-Hop Culture: Essays on White Supremacy and Black Subversion*, as well as a book of poetry entitled *Dreaming Moorish*. Jim has written extensively in both academic and popular journals on questions of race, class, and colonialism in connection with religion and urban culture. He is also a recognized artist on the spoken-word poetry scene in the inner city.

Marcus Rempel is a homemaker, homesteader, and homeschooler living on the banks of the Brokenhead River in Manitoba, at Ploughshares Community Farm. As a Manglican (a Mennonite who has wound up communing with Anglicans) he now lives in a church family with both an ugly colonial legacy and a strong and increasingly vocal Aboriginal wing. When the outdoor work is done and the dishes are washed, he blogs about his halting journey from a displacing faith towards an incarnational=indigenized gospel at brokenheadsojourn.blogspot.com.

Rebecca Seiling lives with her husband Derek Suderman and daughters Zoe and Eden in Waterloo, Ontario. She has worked as a teacher, writer, and editor. Her written works include *Plant a Seed of Peace, Don't Be Afraid, Let Justice Roll Down*, and curriculum for Brethren Press and MennoMedia. In addition to writing and teaching, Rebecca enjoys family hikes, photography, Bollywood dancing, connecting with people of other cultures, and spending time in the woods canoeing, camping, and dreaming.

Leanne Simpson is a writer of Mississauga Nishnaabeg ancestry. She is the editor of *Lighting the Eighth Fire: The Liberation, Protection and Resurgence of Indigenous Nations* and *This Is an Honour Song: Twenty Years Since the Blockades* (with Kiera Ladner). Leanne also authored *Dancing on Our Turtle's Back: Stories of Nishnaabeg Re-Creation, Resurgence and a New Emergence* and *The Gift Is in the Making*, a retelling of traditional stories (forthcoming in 2013). Her first collection of short stories, *Islands of Decolonial Love*, is also soon to be released.

Derek Suderman lives in Waterloo, Ontario, with his wife Rebecca Seiling and daughters, Zoe and Eden. He attends St. Jacobs Mennonite Church and enjoys traveling, meeting new people, and playing music (guitar and banjo). He has worked as a conflict resolution trainer in Colombia and as a community service worker in Manitoba penitentiaries, and is now an assistant professor of religious studies (Old Testament) at Conrad Grebel University College. Currently Derek is involved in a fledgling group seeking to promote just relationships with Six Nations neighbors.

Tink Tinker, a citizen of the Osage Nation (*wazhazhe*), is the Clifford Baldridge Professor of American Indian cultures and religious traditions at Iliff School of Theology, where he has taught for twenty-five years, bringing an Indian perspective to a predominantly Amer-European school. As an American Indian academic, Tinker is committed to a scholarly endeavor that takes seriously both the liberation of Indian peoples from their historic oppression as colonized communities and the liberation of white Americans, the historic colonizers and oppressors of Indian peoples. He continues to volunteer at Four Winds American Indian Council in Denver, an American Indian community project, where he serves as a traditional spiritual leader. Tinker has written more than fifty journal articles and chapters for edited volumes, and his most recent books include *American Indian Liberation: A Theology of Sovereignty* and *Spirit and Resistance: American Indian Liberation and Political Theology*.

Vic Thiessen loves winter and always looks forward to snow and cross-country skiing. He also enjoys hanging out with his two daughters and their husbands, as well as with his wife, Kathy, when she happens to be in the same country. Reading theology and watching films (along with talking and writing about film) are his other key interests. In his spare time, Vic works as chief administrative officer and executive minister of church engagement for Mennonite Church Canada.

Robert Two Bulls is an enrolled member of the Oglala Lakota Oyate and resides on the Pine Ridge Reservation in southwestern South Dakota. A fourth-generation Episcopalian, Robert is the youngest son of a retired Episcopal priest—the Rev. Robert Two Bulls—and is himself an ordained priest, working within Native American communities. For over twenty years, he has been married to Ritchie, a southern woman of Scot-Irish descent and a cradle Episcopalian. Together, they are the proud parents of two teenage children, Grant and Reed.

Vonåhe'e (Erica Littlewolf) is of Tsitsista, German, and Jewish descent. She grew up on the Northern Cheyenne Reservation in southeastern Montana, and currently lives in New Mexico. Vonahe'e is the director of Mennonite Central Committee's Indigenous Vision Center (Central States, USA), which seeks to identify and resource Indigenous strength and genius while staying on the path of decolonization and relationship. She is "a practicing human being" who enjoys loose-leaf tea, spending time with her nieces, and avoiding holidays.

Waziyatawin is a Dakota writer, teacher, and activist committed to the pursuit of Indigenous liberation and reclamation of homelands. Her work seeks to build a culture of resistance within Indigenous communities, to recover Indigenous ways of being, and to eradicate colonial institutions. Waziyatawin comes from the Pezihutazizi Otunwe (Yellow Medicine Village) in southwestern Minnesota. After receiving her PhD in American history from Cornell University in 2000, she taught at Arizona State University for seven years. Currently Waz holds the Indigenous Peoples Research Chair in the Indigenous Governance Program at the University of Victoria. She is the author or co/editor of five volumes, including *What Does Justice Look Like? The Struggle for Liberation in Dakota Homeland.*

Daniel R. Wildcat is a Yuchi member of the Muscogee Nation of Oklahoma. He is director of the Haskell Environmental Research Studies (HERS) Center and (acting) dean of the College of Natural and Social Sciences at Haskell Indian Nations University, in Lawrence, Kansas. Dr. Wildcat received BA and MA degrees in sociology from the University of Kansas and an interdisciplinary PhD from the University of Missouri at Kansas City. He has taught at Haskell for twenty-five years, and is the author and editor of several books, including *Power and Place: Indian Education in America* (with Vine Deloria Jr.) and *Red Alert: Saving the Planet with Indigenous Knowledge.*

Randy Woodley (Keetoowah Cherokee) serves as distinguished associate professor of faith and culture and director of intercultural and Indigenous studies at George Fox Seminary in Portland, Oregon. Dr. Woodley has authored many books, chapters, and articles, including *Living in Color: Embracing God's Passion for Ethnic Diversity* and *Shalom and the Community of Creation: An Indigenous Vision*. Over the past several decades, he and his wife Edith (Eastern Shoshone), have been involved in mentoring and supporting grassroots activism among Indigenous peoples. The Woodleys have four children and continue to lead a local Native American gathering at their home in Newberg, Oregon.

SUBJECT INDEX

SCRIPTURAL INDEX

THE EDITOR

Steve Heinrichs lives in Treaty 1 Territory, in Winnipeg, Manitoba, along with his spouse Ann and their three children, Abby, Aiden, and Isabelle. A former reservist with Christian Peacemaker Teams in Palestine, Steve pastored a Mennonite church in northern British Columbia in a predominantly white, defunct mining village neighboring a Carrier community. Currently Steve is Indigenous relations director for Mennonite Church Canada. When he's not traveling around the country, or fretting about the state of the world, he enjoys chasing his kids around the house, drinking tea, and reading books. On Sunday mornings, Steve and family walk a few blocks to join Hope Mennonite Church—a community of activists, doubters, and Jesus-followers—for worship, Word, and nursery chaos.

What next?

Many who read *Buffalo Shout, Salmon Cry* are asking, "How can I respond?"

• To continue the conversation with Steve, contact him by email at sheinrichs@mennonitechurch.ca.

• For questions and potential action responses to the chapters in *Buffalo Shout, Salmon Cry*, check out the study guide available at www.HeraldPress.com/StudyGuides.

• *Paths for Peacemaking with Host Peoples* is a booklet intended to help communities and individuals respond to these issues. You can download a free copy here: http://bit.ly/1PiJhE9.

CPSIA information can be obtained
at www.ICGtesting.com
Printed in the USA
JSHW042141050522
25586JS00005B/240

9 780836 196894